MANAGEMENT, AUTOMATION, and PEOPLE

By
RICHARD A. BEAUMONT
ROY B. HELFGOTT

Industrial Relations Monograph No. 24
INDUSTRIAL RELATIONS COUNSELORS
New York: 1964

Manufactured in the United States of America by
The Book Press, Brattleboro, Vt.

INDUSTRIAL RELATIONS COUNSELORS, INC.

Industrial Relations Counselors, Inc., is a nonprofit research and educational organization, founded in 1926. It is dedicated, by its charter, "to advance the knowledge and practice of human relationships in industry, commerce, education and government."

At the time of its formation, Industrial Relations Counselors was the only organization in the country specializing in industrial relations research and its practical application. The research activities of Industrial Relations Counselors have been facilitated over the years by its continued close relations with an ever-growing number of companies representing a cross section of industry and commerce, both here and abroad, and with governmental, professional, educational, and other groups interested in this field of research.

Industrial Relations Counselors has issued numerous studies over the years which analyze and evaluate trends, needs and opportunities, as well as current experience, in the industrial relations field. A list of these studies is available on request.

THE BOARD OF TRUSTEES

FOREWORD

At this very moment technological change is taking place within every progressive economic entity in the United States. Where this change is dramatic, it is referred to as "automation." In these situations, computers and other advanced electronic systems are installed to regulate the workaday processes. They methodize the mixing of batter and shaping of crackers and biscuits in large modern bakeries, the many involved operations within petrochemical plants, the processing of steel in highly integrated mills, and the myriad recording and accounting transactions of banks and insurance companies.

The scope of change in many plants and offices may seem insignificant by comparison to major technological innovation, but nonetheless it can represent a forward step in doing things better and faster. Modifying the shape of a food container makes it adapt more readily to handling or packaging; mounting larger tires on a piece of farm equipment enables it to roam more widely over the land devoted to cultivation; changing the size and shape of a pallet revolutionizes the loading process in a warehousing operation.

Whether extensive or limited in scope, technological change has a significant effect on the people who are immediately touched by it, regardless of their occupational level or status. As new types of processes and equipment come into use within a plant or office, new skills and responsibilities are required of all individuals. Machine operators, craftsmen, and professionals—especially those who finished their formal education some ten, twenty, or even thirty years ago—often find it difficult to comprehend new job demands. The attitudes and role of organized labor are also put to the test in adapting to the realities of a dynamic economic and industrial environment. The industrial relations philosophies of companies, and management concepts of structural organization as well, undergo modification to meet the demands of a technologically progressive system of enterprise.

These and related human relations aspects of the impact of technological change on the blue-collar workforce have been studied and are reported on in this volume. A future study will deal with technological change in the office and its effects on white-collar employees.

The present study concentrates on the effects of technological changes which have occurred within the last decade. This is a significant period because within it revolutionary forms of modern technology have materialized, with multiple effects on jobs and people. Often the observation has been made that change is itself nothing new; it is the nature of change in terms of its qualitative impact on work that has been startling in recent years.

In this volume, the authors present, in profile, the experience of a variety of companies in dealing with the problems attendant to change, as disclosed through on-the-ground observations and interviews with their managements. This firsthand review of company experience in adjusting to the actual demands of new operational processes has particular relevance today, since there are growing numbers of issues arising between management and labor over changing outmoded work rules and methods, increasing operating efficiency, and the like.

The dramatic and emotional are shorn from our discussions of actual experience in adjusting to change, even though they would make more exciting reading. Far too much has been written already about what could be, might be, or will be the effects of technological innovation; but often the prognosticators have had but surface knowledge of what has happened and what is taking place. It is safe to say that pessimism over the immediate dislocations of change will not halt technological advances, for the problems of today are clearing the way for the opportunities of tomorrow.

It is our hope that the findings of this study will be of value to management, labor, and community groups, for they recount the exigencies generally encountered by companies in coping with and adjusting to technological change. From these experiences, other companies may be alerted to, and aided in, the development of programs relevant to technological changes in their organizations.

As in all the research projects of Industrial Relations Counselors, Inc., which entail field work, the utmost in cooperation was extended by the 36 companies which permitted their operations to serve collectively as our laboratory for studying the impact of technological change. We take this opportunity again to express our appreciation for the time and effort afforded to us by the management representatives of these companies. They gave information freely and pursued in depth all questions raised, subject only to an understanding that the companies would not be identified. The authors also acknowledge with appreciation the constructive assistance of their colleagues in Industrial Relations Counselors in discussing the subject areas, with special reference to Maud B. Patten, who worked closely with the authors throughout the preparation of the study, to John Burr and Charles A. Tasso, who reviewed the manuscript, and to Theodora R. Bergen for research assistance.

A project of this scope requires, of course, substantial financial support, and we were fortunate in securing such support from two sources. First, funds were provided by some 30 forward-looking companies who contribute regularly to IRC research activities. These funds were supplemented by a matching grant from the Ford Foundation, through its "Program in Economic Development and Administration," for which Victor R. Fuchs was then Program Consultant. To these companies and this group, we owe a debt of gratitude, for it is their interest and assistance which made this study possible.

Richard A. Beaumont,
*Vice President and Director of Research
Industrial Relations Counselors, Inc.*

March 1, 1964, New York City

CONTENTS

ix

Management,
Automation,
and People

CHAPTER I

Introduction

I nterest and excitement over technological innovation in this era would abound if it were seen not as a threat but as a boon to personal well-being. However viewed, technological advances have deep significance and hold great promise for mankind. Progressive changes in technology, work methods, and forms of organization combine to enhance the efficiency of our productive enterprises, thereby satisfying the basic needs of all people and leading inevitably to the improvement of man's lot. While there is still much room for improvement on a world-wide basis—even in the more developed economies—there is also some basis for anticipating the unparalleled opportunity for greater leisure that man will some day have to further his esthetic and social interests because of technological change.

Signs of progress and the picture of a future in which men harvest the rewards of their productive efforts are beclouded, however, by the gloomy predictions of those who see advancing technology as posing serious threats to the very foundations of our society. It has been suggested that our social and cultural norms will have to be restructured in anticipation of the great new industrial revolution and the resultant social revolution which may be before us.[1] These observers of the industrial process appear to view progress as disastrous. Temporary occupational dislocations are regarded as irreparable, and the current level of unemployment, which justly or not is attributed to technological change, is expected to increase.

Technological change does have a disquieting effect. Employees resist the adoption of new production and operational methods because they fear the unfamiliar. Labor unions attempt to retard technological advances in many major industries when their members react against these advances. Our educators are in a quandary because the new educational requirements have not been defined, and our educational system is challenged by the need to reconstitute the curriculum in order to prepare the young for new and comparatively unique job opportunities. Taken together, these are but manifestations that the customary order of things has been disturbed. It has been, indeed; but the problems do not defy solution.

IMPRESSIONS IN A CHANGING SCENE

The call today is for new ideas to cope with a new force—sweeping technological change. Innovations have compelled adjustments of an immediate nature and have left in their wake some problems which will test the ingenuity of those who are obliged to deal with them. But this is nothing new in the history of civilization. Man as a thinking being is also a doer—always looking to improve. Sometimes

[1] See, for example, Paul Jacobs, *Dead Horse and the Featherbird* (Santa Barbara: Center for the Study of Democratic Institutions, The Fund for the Republic, 1962), 62 pp.; Donald N. Michael, *Cybernation: The Silent Conquest* (Santa Barbara: Center for the Study of Democratic Institutions, The Fund for the Republic, 1962), 48 pp.

he is motivated by the economics of a situation; sometimes by an innate laziness that leads him to conceive labor-saving techniques; and sometimes by a simple urge to find a better-than-usual way of doing things. Given the inventiveness inherent in man, improvement is an objective; and the inevitable is change—change in methods and organization of work, in the fashioning of the tools and equipment used in work, and even in the locale of work. Such changes, in turn, place new demands on people and institutions, for their roles must be adapted to meet these changes.

That people and their institutions are still capable of adapting to rapid change is evident. Vast changes have already occurred and are still taking place in the United States and in most of the nations of Western Europe. Within these economies the dimensions of change have been such that wholly new problems of adjustment have had to be faced. And yet, in the main, they have been resolved quietly and realistically. Consider the changes that have taken place in the United States—in terms of the drift of its population to the western states since 1940, and in terms of the changes in work induced by the rise in new investment in plant and equipment by private enterprise.

If these developments seem significant for the United States, which is a far more cohesive political, social, and economic unit than the nations of Western Europe as a group, consider the progress of those countries since the war. Certainly, prior to 1950 no one could have foreseen the rate of economic progress that has since obtained in France and Italy, nor the rebuilding and revitalization of the German economy which was so wasted by the war and the years of Nazism. But these changes have occurred and have carried with them social, occupational, and economic rearrangements of an order that many consider to be far more dramatic than any experienced in the United States in a ten-year period. For example, the Common Market in Europe was looked upon in the early 1950's as visionary, given not only the nationalistic orientation of European countries but their differences in political philosophy and cultural outlook.

Change is an inherent part of a dynamic socio-economic system. It emerges out of shifting patterns of taste, desire for new and different products, inventions and discoveries which derive from our fund of knowledge, population growth and movements, depletion of resources, development of underdeveloped areas, and revitalization of areas which have lost their economic advantage. The very essence of man's relationship to his society embodies the spark of change. And the business organization thrives on change, especially in a period of technological breakthrough and wherever there is competition within a nation or from without. This is as it is, and as people in progressive societies have always wanted it to be.

Norbert Wiener, one of the first popular prophets of the application of computers and other electronic systems to the problems of production, has viewed technological change in a broad frame of reference. He has pointed to the many developments and refinements that would follow and, in his opinion, create crises for man and his institutions.[2] But Wiener has been able, at times, to be optimistic about the ability to make the necessary adjustments to new methods of production; however, others have believed that the adjustments could not be achieved without extensive turmoil. The latter group has felt that great improvements in technology must inevitably lead to a restructuring of the culture of society, as it moves from being work-oriented to being leisure-oriented.[3]

The pessimistic writers contribute to their own dilemma when they speculate with anxiety over the impact of technological change on people. In anticipating dramatic change in industry and in promising a social and cultural upheaval, they are bound by the fetters of their current views. If there

[2] Norbert Wiener, *The Human Use of Human Beings; Cybernetics and Society* (Boston: Houghton Mifflin Company, 1954), 199 pp.

[3] See, for example, Nels Anderson, *Work and Leisure* (New York: The Free Press of Glencoe, Inc., 1961), pp. 25–49.

is change of the magnitude they anticipate, they must throw off the restrictions imposed by existing institutions. Only then can they objectively analyze the problems they foresee and thus be prepared to contribute solutions through understanding.

The optimists see in technological advances an opportunity for greater abundance.[4] They expect short-term dislocations but feel that these need not disturb the social or economic equilibrium. This group looks upon automation as the key to future accomplishment, and it relies on a variety of forces in our economic system to facilitate any transformation innovation may entail. These observers may be called the realists, for they are aware that technological change has been occurring step by step and that it will continue along somewhat evolutionary lines, well removed from revolutionary upheaval.

To a great extent, concern over the impact of advanced technology is partly the result of a natural desire to look ahead to a stable socio-economic system in which logic and order prevail. But even computer technology does not help us to comprehend all the problems and to deal with all the interests and desires of people as they may be in the future. The changes of recent years may not be as significant as those which lie before us, for perhaps where we now stand is only the threshold of the automation age. But the facts are that man has always found his strength in his ability to adjust and that he is yet in the process of adjusting to manifold changes.

Change is a many-stepped process around which an infinite number of varied but harmonic developments occur. It appears that we are always moving from a static position to a new situation. But we never appear to complete the short

---

[4] The President's Advisory Committee on Labor-Management Policy (Washington), *Benefits and Problems Incident to Automation and Other Technological Advances*, 1962, 11 pp.; John T. Dunlop, editor, *Automation and Technological Change*, Papers presented under the auspices of the American Assembly, May, 1962 (Englewood Cliffs: Prentice-Hall, Inc., 1962), 184 pp.

run; nor do we ever reach the long run, in the classic under-standing of the terms. Thus, studying change, especially in production operations, is somewhat unreal, for it is too much a part of an on-going process. The business organization is rarely static, and change is an inherent part of business itself. Technological change cannot actually be isolated from the overall business complex. Economics impinge on an enter-prise. A company, because of its performance in its product market in a past period, may or may not be able to invest in a new machine. Relocation of a factory or a manufacturing unit may become necessary because of a shift in its product market or sources of supply. Obviously, the total process of an industry or company can never be studied in such a way as to capture all phases of the dynamic process. But it is possible to examine aspects of the industrial relations impli-cations of major technological change, and that is the purpose of this study.

DESIGN OF THE STUDY

Given the wide diversity of publicized views on current technological developments, the role of the researcher who attempts to examine this on-going process of change is a diffi-cult one. If he views the developments with suspicion, in terms of their short-run impact on people and employment, he can be accused of overly particularizing or of losing sight of the necessity for economic progress. If he dwells on the advantages of change from a more long-term viewpoint, the results of his work may be too general to be of value to workers, managers, and their advisers, who are presently faced with the everyday reality of working out adjustments to spe-cific new situations.

Considering the nature of the problems presented by technological change, particularly its impingement on people, there is a temptation to conceive a grand design for a study that would surely shed light on the multiplicity of interrelated problems and ways of resolving them. Even though it is possible to design such a study, it is likely that the effort would be of questionable value. On the basis of available information concerning trends in the industrial sector and their impact on employment and the economy at large, there is little reason to be sanguine that much would be learned about the effects on people and jobs in human terms.

Alternatively, the impact of technological change could be examined by studying in depth a few selected industrial situations. A study of this kind would yield information about the adjustment of employees to technological change and the effects of change on work and work relationships in those environments. However, the small assortment of cases might only give access to study of situations that are unique rather than broadly representative. There have already been some notable single-case studies of technological change.[5] From them, it is possible to gain an understanding of the nature of the problems in a given situation and their solutions in that particular application of new technology. The shortcoming of such studies is that they leave to the theoretician and the practitioner the task of generalizing from the particular and then applying the theory to another situation in which there is a different set of facts.

Or still another course is possible—the one decided on for this study. This procedure calls for examining several operations involved in technological change, representing different situations as to the nature of change, the size of the operation, the size of employee groups, the skill patterns of employees, union representation, and type of industry. In such a study, a *range* of experience can be obtained which might suggest general problems and solutions in situations

[5] See, for example, Floyd C. Mann and L. Richard Hoffman, *Automation and the Worker* (New York: Henry Holt and Company, 1960), 272 pp.; Charles R. Walker, *Toward the Automatic Factory* (New Haven: Yale University Press, 1957), 232 pp.; U.S. Bureau of Labor Statistics, *Impact of Automation: A Collection of 20 Articles About Technological Change*, Bulletin No. 1287 (Washington: Government Printing Office, 1960), 114 pp.

where change has an impact on the blue-collar personnel of an enterprise. In large part, stimulus for using this approach came from observations made by Charles C. Killingsworth, as follows:

> . . . Throughout history, changing technology has changed man and his institutions. Many great dislocations in the past, like those accompanying the first industrial revolution, might have been avoided or mitigated if the nature of current changes and their consequences had been better understood. To increase our understanding of automation is an opportunity and an obligation for social scientists.
>
> How should we proceed? Some social scientists appear to have become disillusioned with the case-study method. Nevertheless, this method seems especially appropriate for research on some aspects of automation. Automation takes many forms. . . . Only by studying a variety of applications of automation in a number of industries can we answer such questions as whether automation fundamentally reshapes the nature of the human contribution to production. . . .[6]

The value of this study, as suggested by Professor Killingsworth, lies in the scope of its coverage. Examination of a miscellany of operations has permitted delineation of a variety of industrial relations problems caused by accelerated mechanization and automation, and this makes for broad understanding of the adjustments actually taking place in industry generally. By the same token, it has been possible to correlate with the problems the specific steps that have been taken, in both similar and differing situations, to smooth the inevitable adjustments to new production methods. Analysis on a somewhat broad base has also revealed some of the community and business problems and prospects on which major technological change has a bearing.

A review of the existing literature on the effects of modern technology was helpful in pointing to the areas in

---

[6] Charles C. Killingsworth, "Automation in Manufacturing," *Proceedings of the 1958 Meeting*, Industrial Relations Research Association, pp. 33–34.

which the conclusions of previous studies could now be examined on the basis of both a larger sample and a longer period of experience with major technological change. Consideration of other earlier writings also indicated the areas that had been filled with uncertainties, difficulties, and confusion, and to which investigation should be directed to throw the light of reason on the intellectual dilemmas that were presented.

Defining Major Technological Change

Early in the planning of the study, the authors surveyed a small number of manufacturing and service operations of several large companies which had introduced technological changes during the previous decade. This survey enabled the researchers to test out their ideas about the study and to set up guidelines for defining technological change for the purpose of the study. It became apparent that too rigid a definition of major technological change would exclude from the study situations in which significant employee relations developments had occurred, although the innovations were modest both in scope of application and in the type of technology adopted. In some, methods changes, plant modernization, and plant relocation were involved but these did not necessarily include the use of computers, feedback control systems, and other electronic devices popularly associated with automation.

Even though there had been little advanced electronic hardware involved in a change, the employee relations implications of such changes were frequently the same as those where automation had been introduced. Thus, to get at the "people problems" caused by change, an experimental definition was adopted, characterizing major technological change as:

1. The introduction of new or substantially different techniques and equipment, such as forms of "advanced mech-

anization," automatic processing and materials-handling, and automatic controls systems, or

2. Changes in methods of operations that had involved total or substantial alterations in existing facilities.

This definition was discussed with management representatives of the companies surveyed initially, and the indications were that it provided the best basis for examining the impact of major change on industrial relations in a larger number of companies. However, the preliminary survey had made it apparent that where rapid technological advances had taken place in segments of a factory operation they generally followed one of two extremes. They were either being intertwined with all other processes of the plant, or they were isolated from its other operating units. Unless this difference were taken into account, examination and evaluation of the impact of the respective changes on employee relations would be most difficult. With the brief definition previously cited as a guide, major technological change was defined more precisely as a basis for the contemplated research. In detail, the definition actually applied is as follows:

"Major technological change" refers to the introduction of new or substantially different techniques and equipment, involving a sizable financial investment, for use in the main and closely related operations of a company, plant, or facility, and designed to yield a *substantial* increase in output per man-hour worked. Such changes would encompass what is commonly referred to as "automation," as well as other innovations having pronounced impact.

Particularized, the changes encompassed by the definition are:

1. The integration of separate functions, the compounding of equipment, or some form of "advanced mechanization";

2. The introduction of automatic processing and materials-handling: automatic handling of parts between pro-

gressive production processes; utilizing the principle of feedback (closed-loop or servo-mechanism systems) to correct divergencies from the norm;

3. The introduction of automatic control systems: supervision and regulation of the production process by self-operating devices, such as computer regulation of raw material inputs to desired outputs, and communication of the results;

4. Changes in methods of operation, where substantial alterations in the utilization of existing facilities are involved, such as the use of master shipping containers to move materials between shipping points;

The changes may range in scope of application from an entire plant or other overall facility to a single operation, department, or function. They may be in either a primary production operation (such as assembly, finishing, and batch or continuous process) or in related operations (such as materials-handling, receiving and shipping, storage, packaging, quality control, production scheduling, and inventory management) which involve work by nonsupervisory production, operating, maintenance, and service employees.

Planning the Scope of Research

To gather meaningful experience on the impact of technological change on industrial relations, the design of the research was that it should embrace a sizable number of diverse operating situations where major technological innovation had occurred, yet not so large a sample as to be unwieldy for detailed analysis. Accordingly, some 70 companies were initially identified as prospective participants in the study, based on prior knowledge of the researchers and on information received as to developments in their operations. Among these companies, some were unable to cooperate during the time period allotted to the study, and in others, technological change was too much in flux to permit immediate study. A process of elimination brought the survey sample to 46 establishments (in 36 companies), in which predominantly blue-collar workers were employed.

While the sample of companies was not designed to be representative of industry at large, an attempt was made to select companies and plant operations engaging in a variety of industrial activities, at different geographical locations, and dealing with a cross section of unions representing blue-collar employees. Only 5 of the 46 operating units were not unionized. The operations in the sample were in various industries, mainly manufacturing, but also in transportation and public utilities. The industrial distribution of the establishments studied is shown below:

INDUSTRY	NUMBER OF ESTABLISHMENTS
Manufacturing: nondurable goods	
Food and kindred products	4
Printing, publishing, and allied industries	1
Chemicals and allied products	8
Petroleum refining and related industries ..	3
Rubber and miscellaneous plastic products	2
Manufacturing: durable goods	
Stone, clay, and glass products	5
Primary metal industries	3
Fabricated metal products	2
Machinery	4
Electrical equipment and supplies	4
Transportation equipment	3
Instruments and related products	1
Miscellaneous manufacturing industries ...	1
Transportation and public utilities	
Water transportation	1
Pipeline transportation	1
Electric, gas, and sanitary services	3
Total	46

As already noted, selection of the individual facilities of companies for study was based on their having introduced major technological innovations recently, but long enough ago to have passed the transitional period. Otherwise, appraisal of the impact of and adjustments to change would not have been possible to any extent. An attempt was made also to include situations in which employees had demonstrated resistance to the introduction of new technology.

Research Method

In each case, the focus of attention was on the industrial relations problems and adjustments associated with the nonsupervisory production and maintenance employees of the particular operation. Companies participating were asked for information on (1) advance company planning for the introduction of major technological change; (2) problems encountered in introducing change, and methods used in overcoming them; and (3) evaluation of the impact of the change on employee relations.

Field Interviews. The technique employed throughout was field research based on interviews, which followed the pattern set forth in the checklist shown in Appendix A. The plan of interviews was as follows:

1. There were interviews in depth with industrial relations and operating executives at corporate headquarters, to obtain a company-wide picture of technological change, and to determine the specific plant or other operating facility to be exposed to detailed study.

2. The top-level interviews were generally followed by intensive interviews at the plant or plants selected for study —with local managers, industrial relations personnel, first-line supervisors and, sometimes, nonsupervisory employees.

3. Where practicable, interviews were held with others concerned, such as engineers and union stewards.

Quantitative Data. In addition to the interview phase of

the study, an attempt was made to gather detailed statistical data on the impact of the particular technological change on specific aspects of the employment picture in each operation studied. It was soon found, despite the cooperation of company representatives, that it was possible to collect the data in the form requested (see Appendix B for the "Fact Sheet" submitted) only in a limited number of plants. However, the data which were available were valuable in illustrating employment trends.

In some cases the difficulties in data collection could be attributed to the manner of record-keeping; but in most situations, the difficulty of completing the "Fact Sheet" lay in the interrelation of many other factors with change itself.

For one thing, in many plants there was a steady employment turnover, resulting from retirements, deaths, voluntary quits, and terminations. In some, the turnover rate was less than 5 percent annually; in others, a rate of 20 percent was not unusual. Nevertheless, turnover distorted the picture of employment in terms of the age distribution of employees and their skill levels before and after a particular change. Moreover, in many companies, management anticipated turnover and, in planning to introduce labor-saving technology, timed its adoption to coincide with the expected separations, thereby narrowing the extent of displacement when change actually occurred.

In many plants, furthermore, a particular change studied did not affect the entire plant. In some cases, total employment in the plant increased after the introduction of the new technology, and in other cases it decreased. But in any event, except for the most gross measure, the impact of the change on the workforce could not be isolated from the normal ebb and flow of employment based on demand for a product. In some situations, plant, departmental, or occupational seniority clauses affected the relative job rights of workers in particular operations, and this further complicated a statistical study of the effect of change.

Lastly, the rapid changes in the types of product or the kinds of operation at specific plants also precluded a statistical picture. In most of the companies represented in the survey sample, various factors had caused considerable shifting and adjusting of operations in the past decades. These included such factors as a change in corporate organizational philosophy, the need to modernize plant facilities from a competitive standpoint, the rise of new products, or the importance of relocating an operation to harmonize with a shift in markets and raw materials. Each shift or change brought with it employment effects, sometimes calling for a reduction in the number of persons employed, and at other times for an increase. It became apparent, early in the research, that ongoing technological change could not be satisfactorily isolated, at least in plant operations, from the total and continuing operational process of a large company.

Form of Presentation. Because the study presumed only to explore the specific industrial relations problems and adjustments brought on by technological innovation, it is not a study of the total industrial and economic process. In presenting the findings, therefore, some developments that bear tangentially on, or are interrelated with, the effects of technological change are touched upon to that extent only. As indicated in the relevant discussions, some of these matters would require exhaustive study.

Furthermore, the study was not designed to elicit from employees their interpretation of the impact of technological change, in terms of the personal reactions and adjustments they experienced, although some information along these lines was gathered. Some work has been done in the area of personal reaction and adjustment,[7] but there still remains the need for a broad-based examination of individuals' views of their work situations. From the findings of such a study, it

7 Mann and Hoffman, *op. cit.*; Walker, *op. cit.*; William A. Faunce, "The Automobile Industry: A Case Study in Automation," in Howard Boone Jacobson and Joseph S. Roucek, editors, *Automation and Society* (New York: Philosophical Library, 1959), pp. 44-53.

would be possible to consider more rationally the individual adjustments new technology necessitates, and then to design educational, community, and public programs directed to alleviating the specific problems of employees and employers in periods of accelerated change. In any case, there were opportunities for discussion with some employees in the course of this study, and their reactions gave weight to specific findings.

With respect to union-management relations, the investigations were restricted to problems associated with the introduction of new technology in plant situations. However, it was not possible in this study to survey various levels of union organization as a basis for evaluating the thinking and philosophy of organized labor at large, relative to technological change. There were, of course, opportunities to observe the responses of local union leadership to change in specific plant situations and to infer from the positions taken some more or less prevailing union attitudes.

To the extent that meaningful statistical data on the employment implications of technological innovation were made available, these data have been presented in the appropriate discussions. Every effort was made also to quantify the findings with respect to other aspects of company experience with technological change, but very seldom did the information gathered in the interviews lend itself to such treatment. The problems involved were found to be quite pervasive, and any differences between one situation and another were in degree rather than substance. There was also great similarity in the routes taken by the companies to effect adjustments and to resolve problems.

For these reasons, company experience is more generally discussed in the aggregate, and representative or typical case examples are cited to illustrate the ramifications of some problems and the way they were handled. Each chapter deals with a recognizable area of industrial relations, but the sequence does not imply an order of significance.

CHAPTER II

Employment and
Current Technological Innovation

Fluctuations in the national level of employment—and of the counterpart, unemployment—have been as much a feature of a dynamic market economy as the spurts and lulls that have marked the course of technological innovation. Yet the movements in these two areas have not necessarily coincided. There have been periods in which rapid technological progress has gone hand in hand with full employment, others in which a decided lack of innovation has paralleled high unemployment, and still others in which the reverse of both these situations has occurred. Whatever the circumstances, there seems always to be a propensity to view with alarm the employment effects of technological improvement.

In this chapter, therefore, the employment scene in relation to current technological innovation is examined to see what connection there has been between technological progress and unemployment. In order to place this crucial issue in some perspective, the employment experience of the companies studied is brought to bear on this analysis. Account is also taken of the differential effects of technological innovation on communities.

FALLACIES AND FACTS

Technological innovation in the present period has induced a tremendous amount of concern—bordering on public hysteria—about the effects of "automation" on employment. Writers on "automation" have been haunting the public continually with the specter of mass unemployment resulting from new technology. This is a theme of one writer who foresees a situation in which "only an elite" will be allowed to work.[1] Another is concerned over the nation's ability to utilize its manpower as a result of technological innovation, and he cites and seriously discusses a proposal to export workers and their families to less developed nations, claiming that "it might be a better solution than letting the workers atrophy here."[2] These are indeed pessimistic assertions, and they should not go unchallenged.

The Broader Picture

Mounting concern over the consequences of automation is based on the incorrect premise that it will lead to widespread unemployment; it is not recognized that automation is but the newest phase of the continual process of technological progress. Fear of the impact of progress has accompanied every transition, and usually this fear has been accompanied by emotional resistance. It is interesting that this was so even in a more primitive stage of our society,

[1] Paul Jacobs, *Dead Horse and the Featherbird* (Santa Barbara: Center for the Study of Democratic Institutions, The Fund for the Republic, 1962), p. 62.
[2] Donald N. Michael, *Cybernation: The Silent Conquest* (Santa Barbara: Center for the Study of Democratic Institutions, The Fund for the Republic, 1962), p. 27.

when improved methods could hardly be characterized as new technology. As far back as the French and Indian War in the 1750's, there were just such reactions when the British turned to the use of oxen-drawn carts, instead of Indian labor, for hauling freight from boat landings and up the bluff of the Niagara River. To thus speed up delivery of supplies was undoubtedly vital, but the displaced Indians retaliated by killing the drivers and oxen and burning the carts—the historic "Devil's Hole Massacre."

In the ensuing centuries, other violence has erupted at various junctures in technological progress. Yet the entire history of the industrial revolution refutes this claim of permanent damage to the lot of the workforce. It is now an historical fact that technological progress contributes to the creation of more jobs and higher living standards for workers. Where labor-saving machinery is introduced in a particular operation, the resulting job dislocations may lead initially to a decline in employment. But the continual growth in demand for the goods and services of the economy should, in time, restore the level of employment and, in the long run, should increase it.

The indisputable facts about the so-called new industrial revolution are that it has been changing the composition of the labor force and, consequently, has caused special employment problems with respect to certain groups of employees. While the unemployment rate of about 5½ percent that the nation has been experiencing during the past few years is far from desirable, it is far removed from a situation in which "only an elite" is allowed to work. Still, the persistence of this unemployment rate during a period of economic prosperity has raised anew anxiety over the impact of technological change on employment. The Joint Economic Committee of Congress came to grips with the question in a recent study and interpreted, in particularly lucid terms, aspects of the current unemployment picture.

Explanation of the higher unemployment rates prevailing since mid-1957 has revolved around two major theoretical approaches which, for simplicity of exposition, we will refer to as the aggregate demand and the structural transformation theories. The aggregate demand theory maintains that recent unemployment rates are explainable by traditional supply and demand analysis. . . . The unemployment rate has been quite high since mid-1957, because the rate of growth in final demand has been low relative to the actual and normal rates of growth in potential supply made possible by increases in capital stock, labor force, and productivity.

The structural transformation theory maintains, to the contrary, that higher unemployment has been due not to inadequate final demand—and its concomitant in the labor market, an insufficient number of job opportunities—but, rather, to technological changes which are currently reshaping the American economy at an unusually rapid pace.[3]

The Joint Economic Committee concluded that there was little evidence for the structural transformation hypothesis, and supported the contentions of the aggregate demand theory.[4] It therefore looked to economic growth and increased demand to solve the problem of unemployment.

Comparative analysis of experience among the companies studied tends to support the conclusion that the *level of unemployment* is a function of the demand for the products of industry. Nevertheless, many of the plant situations studied reveal that *specific instances of unemployment* are due to structural transformation. It should be noted, however, that this conclusion rests on the study of a sample

[3] U.S. Congress, Joint Economic Committee, Subcommittee on Economic Statistics, *Higher Unemployment Rates, 1957–60: Structural Transformation or Inadequate Demand* (Washington: Government Printing Office, 1961), p. 6. The Committee took into account a third possible explanation of the rise in unemployment—a shift in the composition of the labor force "in the direction of those groups with the highest unemployment rate"—but this was regarded as having only a minor effect.

[4] *Ibid.*, pp. 78–79.

of individual operating units—not the total corporate or economic entity—and that no account was taken of labor force changes in peripheral white-collar or research and development operations. Further, the study did not consider induced employment in firms that supply new parts or equipment, or in service establishments that maintain equipment.

Structural transformation may derive from causes other than changing technology, such as foreign competition, shifts in demand resulting from altered consumer tastes, declines in the manufacture of particular products because of the exhaustion of raw materials, or government action in the forms of taxation, contract-letting, and fiscal and monetary policy.[5]

In some plants, moreover, management representatives insisted that declining employment was attributable as much to new methods of organizing work as to the introduction of new machinery. It was repeatedly pointed out that the same pressures which bring about the adoption of new technology also generate a more aggressive approach to the institution of efficient managerial techniques. In such instances, it is well-nigh impossible to distinguish the degree of employment reduction that resulted from each of the respective actions.

Another often obscured cause of employment reduction at the time of technological change is the remedying of uneconomical utilization of manpower which has prevailed over many years. Poor management, "past practices" clauses, and restrictive work rules in collective bargaining agreements contributed to labor "fat" in many operations. The introduction of new technology often creates an environment that makes a union more willing, or better able, to take a realistic attitude toward resolving problems of such overmanning. As a case in point, the introduction of containerized cargo in Pacific Coast shipping operations led to the famous 1960 labor-management agreement which eliminated many long-

[5] For a more detailed discussion of these points see International Labour Office (Geneva), *Unemployment and Structural Change*, 1962 (Studies and Reports, New Series, No. 65), pp. 11–14.

existing restrictive work practices in that industry. Any resulting decline in employment was, therefore, due partly to the elimination of the obsolete work restrictions, and thus only partly to containerization and mechanization.

One objective of this study was to explore the direct effects of technological innovation on the volume of employment in individual companies. To that end, as noted in Chapter I, the study was designed to cover only those company situations in which new technology had substantially increased labor productivity (output per man-hour), and this was true of all the cases examined. Companies which had instituted forms of technological improvement that were only capital-saving were excluded. On this basis, a major finding of the study is that as far as employment is concerned there was no uniform result among the plants studied. In fact, no correlation could be found between the extent of labor-saving machinery introduced and change in the level of employment in plants. In many cases, employment declined in the period following the introduction of labor-saving technology; in others, it remained stable; and in some, it rose. No relationship between the rate of increase in productivity and the movement of employment was observable. Illustrative is the comparison shown below of seven plants for which data were made available on *both production and employment* subsequent to the adoption of new technology:

Industry of Plant Studied	Percent Increase (+) or Decrease (−) Following Technological Change	
	In Production	In Employment
Petroleum (pipeline)	+ 1.5%	−29.0%
Chemicals (consumer)	+ 5.0	+ 1.0
Transportation equipment	+ 16.5	+ 6.5
Petroleum refinery	+ 18.5	−37.0
Chemicals (intermediate)..	+ 23.0	+ 2.5
Machinery (printing)	+ 25.0	−39.0
Machinery (industrial) ...	+100.0	No change

In these seven plants, the change in employment did not correlate with the degree of the technological improvement. The most advanced type of technology (various automated equipment and electronic computer-controlled machinery) was introduced into the plant producing intermediate chemicals. Yet its employment increased, simply because in this highly efficient operation product demand was growing even faster than productivity. Unrelated to the basic employment patterns examined in this study is the observation that technological change generally leads to greater plant capacity, as reflected in production increases cited in the above table.

A second major finding emerging from the case studies is that it is impossible to isolate employee displacements attributable solely to technological change, because of the interrelatedness of all the factors that determine the course of employment. Interestingly, the Joint Economic Committee has reached this very conclusion:

> . . . The concept of structural unemployment as applied to particular workers or groups of workers is theoretically meaningless and defies empirical measurement. There is no way to determine whether a particular worker has lost a specific job because of technological change, or the shift of demands away from the product his industry produces, or inadequate aggregate demand, or some other cause.[6]

It was found repeatedly in our study that plants were introducing new technology during the same period in which they were also experiencing economic stresses serious enough to have caused employment dislocations even in the absence of new technology. In some cases, fluctuations resulted from unfavorable swings of the business cycle; in others, from discontinuance of some products because of shifts in consumer tastes; in still others, from the development of new products never before made in a plant. There were also instances in which production of some items was lost to sister plants of

[6] Joint Economic Committee, *op. cit.*, p. 7.

the parent company because of their superior location with respect to raw materials or markets.

Specific Situations

In 31 of the cases examined, data were available for a comparison of employment in the periods immediately preceding and following the introduction of technological change. In 20 of the cases, employment declined; in 4, it remained the same; and in 7, the number of jobs increased, anywhere from 1 percent to as much as 34 percent. The extent of reduction in the 20 operations that suffered declines in employment was as follows:

Employment Reduction	Number of Establishments
Under 15 percent	10
15 to 29 percent	5
30 to 44 percent	3
45 per cent or over	2

These declines in employment were not due solely, or even primarily, to the increased output per worker that resulted from improved technology. Actually, in a very high majority of the plants, the most severe declines in employment occurred during the 1958 or 1960 recessions, and not at the time of the introduction of the technological change. Moreover, in many of them, production at the time that they were visited had not recovered to former levels. It was abundantly clear, therefore, that a rise in employment in these plants waited only upon an increase in demand for their products. These instances of depressed employment levels substantiate the premise that employment fluctuations are related to market conditions, and thus an increase in national economic growth would assist in reducing a good part of the current unemployment.

That employment declines were not necessarily related to technological innovation was most evident in the two plants that suffered the severest reductions in employment— 45 percent or more. In both of them, production was drastically cut back primarily because of a loss of markets: for one, the loss was attributable to foreign competition; for the other, to a shift in location of the major purchasing industry and to the rise of substitutes for its product. Indeed, in both cases, the programs of technological improvement were undertaken in an attempt to stem the market loss, and were partially successful in doing so.[7]

Focusing on individual plants, however, tends to obscure the more important trends within companies and industries; within the parent company of one of the 20 case-study plants in which employment declined, the experience is illustrative. During the period in which employment in this plant dropped, it increased at four other plants of the company, because they were better situated with respect to changed raw material sources and consumer markets. Moreover, an entirely new plant was opened at a separate location. The plant studied was the oldest operation of the company, and its survival rested on improving its competitive position by dispensing with obsolete production methods and automating the operation. This move resulted in preserving rather than destroying jobs.

The idea that technological change invariably reduces total plant employment derives from the popular misconception that it is introduced in one fell swoop throughout a

---

[7] Similar experience in a plant not included in this study was subsequently brought to the attention of the authors. The company was about to discontinue the operation because a foreign competitor was retailing a product of equal quality at less than the actual manufacturing cost at this plant. Complete restructuring of the manufacturing process drastically reduced unit labor costs, enabling the company to cut the price of its product by 40 percent. Although temporary layoffs were involved, a rapid increase in demand for the product not only absorbed all layoffs, but raised employment 25 percent above its former level.

plant. Actually, change is introduced by progressive steps, first in one department, and then in another. For this reason, the total employment situation in a period of plant renovation may vary considerably from one case to another. In the companies studied, there were instances in which employment declined within the department or operation automated, while it remained stable, or grew, in the entire plant. In others, employment declined within both the department and plant, and there were some in which jobs increased in number both within the department and throughout the plant.

While technological change in any given area of a plant may reduce the number of jobs available there, the increased efficiency of that operation may well boost employment in the entire plant. In a food-processing plant, for example, employment in one area of the operation dropped from 388 before it was automated, to 382 after completion of the change; but in the same one-year period, overall plant employment rose 34 percent, from 1,030 to 1,382. Similarly, in a chemical works, employment in the affected department dropped from 191 before the transition, to 168 afterward, but plant-wide employment increased 2.5 percent, from 1,777 to 1,819.

Another little-understood factor in the employment picture is that a worker does not necessarily become unemployed when he is displaced by the introduction of a labor-saving device. His services may be of value elsewhere in the plant. Proof of this lies in 11 of the cases studied; in each, employment remained at former levels, or increased, after technological change. Even in a situation of plant-wide decline in employment, workers are not necessarily laid off, for in a number of cases, especially where dislocations were of moderate proportions, normal workforce attrition had obviated the need for separations. Furthermore, layoff of an employee need not lead to his becoming unemployed if he is in a labor market that can absorb his skills.

DIFFERENTIAL EFFECTS ON COMMUNITIES

Situations of Persistent Unemployment

Much of the growing concern with unemployment is related not only to its incidence nationally but to its concentration in certain regions, making some labor markets "areas of substantial and persistent unemployment," in the classification of the Department of Labor. National attention has been brought to bear, in recent years, on the plight of these "depressed areas," culminating in the passage of the Area Redevelopment Act (1961), through which such communities may receive federal aid for retraining the unemployed, and for improving local facilities to attract new industry.

Many distressed communities are located, as one would expect, in the older centers of manufacturing,[8] some of which have lost their earlier locational advantages. One or another of several factors account for this: the rise of new products and markets elsewhere, depletion of the natural resources of an area, population movements, the changing structure of freight rates, shifts in forms of transportation, and, to some extent, the emergence of new technology. Particularly hard-hit are those areas formerly dominated by a single industry that has since declined or relocated. Some notable examples have been the coal industry of West Virginia and Pennsylvania, textile operations in New England, and steel production in the Pittsburgh area.

When technological change displaces employees in a depressed area, it compounds the unemployment problem in two ways:

[8] Actually, a recent study reports that some four-fifths of the 236 counties designated as redevelopment areas by the government were never important manufacturing centers, but in those areas where deterioration had already set in for other reasons, locational shifts in manufacturing have probably contributed toward creating and extending urban blight. See National Industrial Conference Board (New York), *Changing Location of Manufacturing Employment: Part I: Changes by Type of Location, 1947–1961,* 1963 (Studies in Business Economics, No. 83), 152 pp.

1. The displacement in such communities is often quite heavy. Because the plants are generally older, and hence, more obsolete, their modernization tends to be significantly labor-saving.

2. The displacement leads to unemployment for large numbers of workers, for there are few alternative jobs available.

Despite this unfortunate impact, however, it is a fact that only through technological improvement can a moribund operation be restored to usefulness and thus give a depressed community some promise of continuing job opportunities. If the improvements were not made, the plant would fall further behind newer and more efficient operations in its industry; and eventually competition would force its complete shutdown.

This study disclosed that technological change has a differential employment effect upon communities relative to their economic health, since the plants suffering the greatest drops in employment tended to be more heavily concentrated in depressed areas. This fact lends some credence to the structural transformation theory of unemployment. Fully one-half of the 28 plants[9] providing employment data for the periods before and after the introduction of new technology were located in labor markets that were characterized by the Department of Labor, in August, 1962, as areas of substantial unemployment.[10] But, when the 28 cases are sorted out according to the degree of change in employment, the relationship of the change in plant employment to the condition of the local labor market is highly illuminating. Of 9 plants, shown in the tabulation below, in which employment was significantly lower in the period after the introduction of new technology, 6 were located in areas of substantial unemployment. Only 5 of the 10 exhibiting moderate declines in

9 Of the 31 cases for which data are available, 3 cover multiarea operations and, therefore, are not pertinent to this analysis.

10 U.S. Department of Labor, Bureau of Employment Security (Washington), *Area Labor Market Trends*, August 1962 Supplement, pp. 10–13.

employment were in such areas, and only 3 of the 9 whose employment had remained steady or had increased were so located:

Employment Experience	Number of Plants	Plants in Areas of Substantial Unemployment
Large decline (15 percent or more)	9[a]	6
Moderate decline (less than 15 percent)	10	5
Steady or increased employment ..	9[b]	3
Total	28	14[c]

[a] Excludes a multiarea operation, which is not pertinent here.
[b] Excludes two multiarea operations.
[c] Includes five plants in areas of persistent unemployment.

It is even more noteworthy that among the 14 plants in areas of substantial unemployment, 5 were in labor markets where unemployment had been persistent (that is, in depressed areas). Interestingly, of these 5 plants, 3 suffered rather severe declines in employment (15 percent or more).

It must be emphasized that in reporting a correlation between the degree of employee displacement resulting from technological change and the state of the local labor market, no implication of cause and effect is intended. As has been pointed out, introduction of new production methods generally assures the continuity of the jobs that are provided by increasing plant efficiency. Yet it must also be recognized that it may in the short run intensify unemployment.

Mobility Factors

More than ever, the mobility of resources, including human ones, is of vital importance in keeping the economy dynamic and in fostering a rapid rate of growth. The increase in the number of depressed areas across the American landscape has focused attention on the need for greater mobility on two fronts: the movement of new economic activities into depressed areas, and the movement of population out of them. The desirability of increased labor mobility is emphasized by the availability in many communities throughout the nation of job openings for various skilled workers, including those with a background of blue-collar production work. Yet the persistence of high unemployment in many communities, through periods of national economic expansion as well as recession, suggests that only a minority of workers are willing to uproot themselves in order to pursue new job opportunities elsewhere.

The experience of the companies studied with interplant transfers would seem to substantiate this view. The managements found that employees were most reluctant to relocate to areas offering new job opportunities, preferring to take their chances, slim as they might be, in their home labor markets. This merely supports already existing evidence indicating conclusively that job changes from one local labor market to another are much less frequent than those from one occupation, or industry, to another in the same area.[11]

A significant body of literature on labor mobility has accumulated, and the findings of this study tend, in the main, to support the hypotheses already advanced as to the factors that influence employee decisions to relocate to areas where jobs are available. A case study of a 1954 shutdown of car production in a San Francisco plant indicated that only about one-fourth of the affected employees responded to an offer of transfer to another factory in Los Angeles, 450 miles away. The majority of acceptances came from employees who were most apprehensive about their chances of finding another suitable job in the home community—mainly Negroes and men with relatively low rates of pay and lim-

[11] Herbert S. Parnes, *Research on Labor Mobility: An Appraisal of Research Findings in the United States* (New York: Social Science Research Council, 1954), p. 76.

ited skill.[12] Similarly, one large company participating in this study, which has engaged in a great amount of inter-plant transfer of blue-collar employees, reported that generally the greatest willingness to transfer has been exhibited by young, unmarried Negro males, largely because they had the least to surrender in their home communities, including the expectation of alternative employment.

A prominent researcher, in his study of worker attitudes and behavior in relation to mobility, stated: "Younger workers showed a greater willingness to move than did older workers, and tenants were more willing to move than were home owners."[13] Studies in St. Paul and Minneapolis also found that "no clear-cut mobile type of worker is . . . discernible," but that those who appear to be more geographically mobile are males, renters, individuals who are not heads of families, and young people.[14]

Experience in the companies that have engaged in inter-plant transfers (see Chapter III), while not arguing against such a policy, does indicate that the results, in terms of labor mobility, are likely to be far under expectations, given the existing social attitudes of workers, and related factors. The findings in these companies tend to confirm a general assumption that employees of advancing age and those with family responsibilities are unwilling to relocate. They also concur with other studies holding that home ownership, children in school, friends and relatives in the home area, and liking for the community all militate against geographical mobility, and thus add to the problem of structural unemployment. The deeper the roots sunk by a worker in a community, the more reluctant he will be to seek jobs at

[12] Margaret S. Gordon and Ann H. McCorry, "Plant Relocation and Job Security: A Case Study," *Industrial and Labor Relations Review*, Vol. 11, October, 1957, pp. 13–36.

[13] Lloyd G. Reynolds, *The Structure of Labor Markets* (New York: Harper & Brothers, 1951), p. 78.

[14] Dale Yoder, "Manpower Mobility: Two Studies," in *Labor Mobility and Economic Opportunity* (Cambridge: Massachusetts Institute of Technology, 1954), p. 88.

plants located elsewhere. Trusting that his unemployment will be of short duration, he will often prefer unemployment at home to a job prospect in some other place. It may be expected that these factors will continue to impede labor mobility.

CHANGING COMPOSITION
OF THE LABOR FORCE

In many of the case-study plants, the drops in production that followed upon the introduction of new technology were attributable to a decline in demand for their products. In these instances, any increase in demand back to or above previous levels would, of necessity, raise total employment. This indisputable fact about the situation in these plants lends substantiation to the aggregate demand theory of unemployment.

Nevertheless, there was also evidence that new technology had brought about a restructuring of the labor force within plants, and that this had caused some degree of structural unemployment. For example, in some instances plants were laying off machine operators at the same time that they were hiring skilled craftsmen; and the displaced operators lacked either the qualifications or the desire to get the jobs which were available. To investigate this phenomenon of structural unemployment more fully, attention must be focused on the changing composition of the labor force.

Although it is impossible to isolate the total employment effects of technological change, its differential effects on types of employment are measurable. Without exception, the cases studied all conformed to the patterns noted by other observers of the impact of automation and other advanced technology. Such innovations have these effects: a relative shift from blue-collar to white-collar employment; within the blue-collar group, a shift from direct production to maintenance work; and within the direct production group, the continual elimination of unskilled jobs. More-over, these relative shifts occurred in all situations, regard-less of whether total employment was increasing, declining, or remaining stable. This restructuring of the labor force also occurred in all industries, though it was more pro-nounced in some than in others, depending upon the extent of "automation" involved in the technological change. The effect of such changes on the composition of plant work-forces will be examined in a sequence leading from the least complicated to the most revolutionary form of technological improvement.

1. *Advanced Mechanization*. The simplest form of cur-rent technological change corresponds to the definition of "advanced mechanization" employed in this study, as noted in Chapter I. Modernization of a small old plant manufac-turing printing machinery and inks, and the impact of the changes on the structure of its workforce, will serve as an example. In 1958, a good deal of materials-handling in the plant still depended upon human brawn—men lifted ap-paratus, shoveled sand, and wheeled things from one place to another, all by manual labor. Obviously, even a small-scale industry cannot remain permanently immune to better ways of operating; and when competitors modernized their establishments, this plant was compelled to follow suit.

The physical structure of the plant was altered; new machinery was introduced; and the handling of materials was mechanized through such devices as fork-lift trucks, con-veyor belts, buckets that automatically tipped liquids into pots, and the automatic feeding of sand. While none of the changes was revolutionary, and all of them were simply modern forms of operation which this industry had passed by for some years, they had a profound impact on the effi-ciency of the plant. By 1961—three years after the com-mencement of the modernization program—production had gone up 25 percent, despite a drop in total manpower re-quirements of 39 percent. Yet the structure of the plant nonsupervisory workforce was little altered; the only significant change was a relative decline in unskilled production work, as illustrated below:

Type of Work	1958 Employment		1961 Employment	
	Number	Percent	Number	Percent
Direct production work	140	79.5	86	78.9
Skilled	20	11.3	14	12.8
Semiskilled	85	48.3	55	50.5
Unskilled	35	19.9	17	15.6
Maintenance and technical work	36	20.5	23	21.1
Total	176	100.0	109	100.0

2. *Automatic Processing and Materials-Handling.* Gearing an operation for the automatic handling of parts between progressive production processes induces somewhat more marked labor force restructuring than does the mechanization of hand operations. The effects of this form of technology can be illustrated readily by the experience in a large plant manufacturing rubber tires. In this case, automation was not a startling development; rather, it was only the latest phase of the continual process of technological change that has been taking place since tires were first made. In earlier years, the manufacturing process went from hand to mechanical operation and control, and in recent years it began to go from mechanical to electronic operation and control. Consequently, no single technological change could be isolated for study, for there was a whole series of such changes. As a series, however, the technological improvements affected the composition of the factory labor force significantly, for the occupational requirements of the plant led to a shift in the distribution of its personnel from production work to maintenance and technical assignments.

In order to illustrate this shift, a comparison is made

between employment in the plant in 1955, which is about the time at which the newest types of equipment were first introduced, and 1960, the last full year for which data were obtainable. This comparison follows:

Type of Work	1955 Employment		1960 Employment	
	Number	Percent	Number	Percent
Direct production work	12,237	68.5	8,804	62.6
Maintenance work	1,949	10.9	1,782	12.7
All salaried employees (exclusive of office)	3,676	20.6	3,479	24.7
Total	17,862	100.0	14,065	100.0

It was unfortunate that a comparison had to be made between a year of national prosperity, 1955, and one of recession, 1960, which is reflected, in this case, in a drop in total employment of 21 percent. This does not, however, in any way affect the continuing trend in labor force restructuring from direct production work to maintenance and technical employment.

3. *Automatic Control Systems.* The most dramatic form of technological change is the introduction of automatic control systems, which have the most far-reaching effects on the structure of the workforce. With such systems, supervision and regulation of the production process is conducted by self-operating devices, as in the regulation by electronic computers of raw-material inputs and desired outputs. The revolutionary nature of this most advanced technology makes it apparent that no plant could switch *in toto* from a manually controlled operation to one that is computer-controlled. Rather, the process of change is in the nature of a continuum, along which a plant, already highly automated, becomes more so over time.

A natural-gas pipeline operation serves as an excellent illustration of this process of progressively moving toward more extensive automation, and of the fashioning of the workforce accordingly. The technological improvement began with the installation of five semiautomatic compressor stations, strategically located along 800 miles of a 30-inch main line. These semiautomatic stations required only 4 operators per station, as compared to 16 or more for the then contemporary stations of similar horsepower. As power requirements grew, five completely automatic compressor stations were added to the system. No operators were required for these stations; however, to maintain them, 25 skilled repairmen and 5 automation specialists were needed. These openings were filled through upgrading from other classifications and by new hires.

Later, automation was completed on the five original semiautomatic stations permitting *one man* to operate the system from a central control point. As a result, 20 operators were displaced. These men were transferred into the repairman classification and trained in that work. Thus, the continuous process of automation in this company has resulted in the shifting of men away from direct production and into maintenance activities, to such a point that there are virtually no "production" workers, as such.

The impact of two major technological innovations in a petroleum pipeline operation also illustrates this shift away from production-type jobs. The company installed improved pipes, designed to withstand higher pressures, which would permit the transmission of petroleum products in greater volume. It also introduced more centralized computer controls, which eliminated many intermediate pumping stations. These changes resulted in a gradual year-by-year chipping away of total employment, largely because the new technology reduced overall manpower requirements, particularly among the blue-collar crews; however, displacements were taken care of by normal attrition and transfers to other company operations. The reshuffling of occupations that has occurred may be seen in the following tabulation:

Occupational Classification	1948 Employment		1961 Employment	
	Number	Percent	Number	Percent
Production and mainte- nance employees ..	449	78.0	283	71.3
Technicians	2	0.3	8	2.0
Professional engineers ..	14	2.4	15	3.8
Managerial employees ..	52	9.0	38	9.6
Clerical employees	59	10.2	53	13.4
Total	576	100.0a	397	100.0a

a Totals do not equal 100 because of rounding.

Where automatic control systems are introduced into operations for the first time, they have an even more dramatic and immediately visible effect on the composition of the labor force. Illustrative is the case of a multiproduct food-processing plant, where automation revolutionized the manufacturing of one of its products. Laborious handwork and human judgment were largely supplanted by the introduction of centrifugal machines for mixing ingredients and of computer-controlled console panels for operation of the process. The data tabulated below reveal the altered composition of the labor force in the affected departments:

Type of Work	Pre-automation Employment		Post-automation Employment	
	Number	Percent	Number	Percent
Direct production work	211	77.9	99	51.8
Skilled	10	3.7	39	20.4
Semiskilled	61	22.5	40	20.9
Unskilled	140	51.7	20	10.5
Maintenance work	58	21.4	69	36.1
Technical work	2	0.7	23	12.0
Total	271	100.0	191	100.0a

a Total does not equal 100 due to rounding.

In this case, the most dramatic changes in the structure of the workforce were the extremely sharp decline of routine unskilled work, which was reduced to one-fifth of its former proportion of plant employment, and the even sharper increase in technical work. This increase stemmed from the new need for instrument technicians to control the automated operations. Although the total number of production workers declined precipitously, the number of skilled people within that group rose significantly. Additionally, there was an increased need for maintenance workers to service the more sensitive automatic equipment.

Of course, where an operation is already highly automated, additional technological change has less dramatic results, although the process of reconstituting the plant workforce continues. The experience in a chemical works after it introduced (in 1960) more refined instrumentation into one of its divisions illustrates the on-going shift among nonsupervisory employees, from production to maintenance jobs:

Type of Work	1960 Employment		1961 Employment	
	Number	Percent	Number	Percent
Direct production work	80	49.1	63	44.4
Skilled	67	41.1	58	40.9
Semiskilled	8	4.9	4	2.8
Unskilled	5	3.1	1	0.7
Maintenance work	60	36.8	59	41.5
Skilled	45	27.6	43	30.3
Semiskilled	7	4.3	8	5.6
Unskilled	8	4.9	8	5.6
Technical work	23	14.1	20	14.1
Total	163	100.0	142	100.0

4. *Changes in Methods of Operation.* Unfortunately, it was not possible to obtain precise data that would illustrate the impact on labor-force composition of the fourth form of technological change investigated, that is, instances in which

substantial alterations are made to facilitate the interfunctioning of existing facilities. An example of this type of change is the use of master shipping containers to move materials between shipping points. From case interviews, however, it was discerned that in such operations labor-force trends were following the pattern found elsewhere—the reduction of manual labor.

Comparative Experience

The data on labor-force composition become more interesting when company experience is compared on the basis of the form of technological change introduced. In all cases, the percentage of production workers declined, and there was some increase in the number of maintenance and technical employees. However, the greater the degree of "automation" in use, the more evident was this trend. Proof of this may be seen most clearly by a comparison of the effects in operations using less revolutionary technology with those comprising automatic control systems (see Form 3):

Type of Work	Percent of Blue-Collar Employment, by Form of Technology					
	Form 1	Form 2	Form 3			
			Plant A	Plant B	Plant C	Plant D
Direct production work ...	78.9	62.6	51.8	44.4	41.9	34.9
Maintenance and technical work ..	21.1	37.4[a]	48.2	55.6	58.1	65.1

[a] Includes some supervisory employees, but this does not affect the basic pattern.

Key: *Form 1*—Advanced Mechanization (Machinery Plant)
   Form 2—Automatic Processing and Materials-Handling (Tire Plant)
   Form 3—Automatic Controls Systems
       Plant A (Food-Processing)   Plant C (Petroleum Refinery)
       Plant B (Chemical)   Plant D (Petroleum Refinery)

A basic point to be recognized in the comparison is that the nature of the operation has much to do with the nature of the technology adopted. The more continuous the process of manufacture, the more adaptable it is to automation, and, consequently, the greater is the impact on the structure of the labor force. Accordingly, even after the introduction of new forms of mechanization in the machinery plant, almost four of every five workers were still in blue-collar direct-production occupations. But in the most advanced petroleum refinery, only slightly over one-third were still in such employment. In this latter kind of situation, those hardest hit —by the combination of reduced manpower requirements and a need for high-level skills and potential—are the unskilled and semiskilled workers. Since it is not often easy for them to qualify themselves for the growing proportion of maintenance and technical jobs, their displacement may constitute a form of structural unemployment.

Upgrading Within the Labor Force

Despite much discussion, little light has been shed on whether or not new technology upgrades the labor force. An answer cannot be given readily because it would depend on the kind of new technology that has been utilized, and, as has been demonstrated, this varies in both nature and impact from one situation to another. An answer would also hinge on exactly what is meant by "upgrading." If one takes a broad look at what is happening to the structure of the labor force, it can be seen clearly that the latest technology is upgrading the labor force. How else could one categorize the relative shift from blue-collar to white-collar work, the similar shift within the blue-collar classification from semiskilled production work to craftsman maintenance work, and the increased demand for many more technicians? Those who deny the upgrading process are considering not these broad changes but only the impact on direct-production jobs.

To the degree that new technology continues in its historical role of eliminating unskilled, routine, arduous jobs, it restructures the blue-collar workforce by advancing its status. This does not mean, however, that the *jobs* of the operators of more advanced machinery are necessarily upgraded. In the cases studied there was not, in the traditional sense, any general upgrading of jobs due to technological change. Furthermore, in the vast majority of cases, short-term, on-the-job training was sufficient to equip employees for the new requirements (see Chapter V). The content of the operator's job generally changed to require less machine skill and manual dexterity and to add new kinds of responsibility requiring the capacity for attentiveness, quick thinking, and alert action, as well as adaptability and the educational background for training. Do such changes in the bundle of required skills represent upgrading of a job? In terms of a company's job evaluation plan, usually they do not. But the people required for new hires will certainly have to be prepared to meet the new demands, and this has multiple implications— for business in terms of job evaluation, recruitment policies, and the like; and for society at large, in terms of the educational process. These will be discussed later.

In a few of the cases studied, the fact that job grades remained the same, on the average, has served to obscure changes in the skill levels of particular jobs. With respect to the latter, there were indications of two opposite trends. One represented a centralization of job grades—that is, a regression to the mean—and the other, a polarization of job grades. The first was observed in a steel mill that had undergone extensive automation. The change had the effect of downgrading the skills formerly required in the highest job grades, while upgrading the requirement of the bottom jobs. In terms of total plant employment, the effect was for the average job grade to remain the same.

On the other hand, two electrical equipment plants experienced polarization of grade levels: one form of technological change—the introduction of new complicated automatic machinery—required higher-level skills on the part of operators; the other type of change—concerned with mechanizing various routine procedures and simplifying set-up work or the wiring of control panels—downgraded the skill requirements. The effect of these two types of changes served, therefore, to eliminate the middle-level jobs.

In those instances in which, on the average, job levels were raised as a result of new technology, none of the upgrading was dramatic. It merely represented an evaluation of new or changed jobs at one or, at the most, two grades above their former level, because of slightly increased job requirements—mainly new forms of responsibility. In these situations, also, the degree of upgrading depended upon the type of technology introduced. Where the change was that of mechanizing former manual operations, through the introduction of materials-handling equipment (form 1, simplest of the three forms described above), the upgrading was that of converting unskilled-labor jobs to semiskilled, machine-tending jobs. The adoption of automatic processing and materials-handling (form 2), exemplified by the most advanced types of "Detroit automation" utilized in the metal trades industries, introduced new skills to set, operate, and maintain the transfer machines; also, it called for a degree of alertness on the part of operators not previously required of them, to assure proper functioning of the machinery. In the continuous-process industries, such as chemicals and petroleum refining, where fully automatic control systems (form 3) are in use, the very advanced nature of the technology generally made for greater complexity of work. In a chemical plant studied, fully 70 percent of the hourly-paid employees were performing highly complicated or responsible work and, consequently, were at the very top job grade.

In all cases, following technological innovation, maintenance jobs increased as a percentage of total plant jobs; and in many instances, they increased in absolute numbers as well.

Not all crafts benefited, however; the greatest rise in demand was for skilled electricians, particularly those with knowledge of electronics. Otherwise, the skills required of craftsmen did not change appreciably. This subject will be explored more fully in a later discussion of training and related problems.

Special Problem Groups

Certain groups of blue-collar employees—the less skilled, the inadequately educated, the very young, the aging, and Negroes, categories which are not necessarily mutually exclusive—present special employment problems. According to the Department of Labor, these groups stood out among the 600,000 persons noted in July, 1962, as having had unusually long spells of unemployment.[15] They have been most adversely affected by the shifts in labor-force composition and the demands of changing technology for workers with increased skills and education. Consequently, many of them join the ranks of the so-called structurally unemployed. At this point the problems of these groups, as related to the restructuring of the labor force, are considered. At appropriate points in the following chapters special problems or reactions of members of these groups will be discussed in terms of the case-study experience.

Low-Skill Workers. Analysis of the data on labor-force restructuring indicates clearly that a high proportion of displacement was attributable not only to skill deficiencies but to lack of appropriate background for learning the needed skills. In this regard, hourly-rated employees fared far worse than salaried plant personnel. Though this study focused on the impact of technological change on the blue-collar group in the factory, information secured from a number of plants permitted some comparison between the two groups, which

15 U.S. Bureau of Labor Statistics, "Employment and Unemployment Highlights, July, 1962," *Employment and Earnings*, Vol. 9, August, 1962, p. xxi.

substantiates the point. In almost every case of technological innovation, the skill level of salaried personnel who were displaced by technological change permitted their placement elsewhere in the company to a considerably greater extent than was true with hourly-rated employees.

This comparative result of skill requirements is particularly observable in the case of plant shutdown, because all employees are then displaced. The closing of a chemical plant located in a Middle Atlantic state serves as a good illustration. In that case, all of the technical, supervisory, and white-collar salaried employees had skills and training so in demand that they were offered transfers to other plants of the company; however, of a total of 538 hourly-rated employees, only 5 had skills not readily found at other locations, and consequently were transferred.

Within the blue-collar groups of all companies, problems of continued employment or re-employment were inversely correlated with the degrees of skill among the workers. In some instances, laborers and machine operators were being laid off in plants at the same time that a search was being made in the labor market for workers with maintenance-craft skills.

The Youthful and the Aging. Age, in terms of the two extremes—the very young and the aging workers—also has presented particular problems. Given the widespread institutionalization of seniority as the sole, or at least the principal, criterion governing layoffs, younger employees are generally the ones most immediately affected by displacement. Moreover, low-seniority personnel are given last consideration under programs of interplant transfer. The depth of layoffs in some plants visited had been so great that no one in active employment had less than fifteen years' seniority. It should be pointed out, however, that most of these plants were visited during the last recession and that undoubtedly many lower-seniority employees have since been recalled to work.

Younger employees are usually more willing to relocate,

however, and this factor advances their chances for transfer to job openings rejected by their seniors. Furthermore, once young workers are informed of impending layoffs, they tend to quit voluntarily in order to accept other jobs that may be available in the community, having relatively little to lose in the way of separation benefits if they do not wait to be laid off.

Although long-service employees are protected by their seniority standing, their situation becomes much less favorable when whole departments, job categories, and even entire plants disappear. They generally find themselves at a competitive disadvantage in the local labor market because of their age, particularly if there is a scarcity of job opportunities at their skill levels. Furthermore, they are most reluctant and often refuse to relocate.

In recognition of these factors, most companies have been quite liberal in offering special early and disability retirement benefits to older workers. But workers who are in their late forties or early fifties are clearly too young and too healthy to be pensioned off, and when their jobs disappear they can rarely find similar jobs. They must, therefore, either accept work that is inferior in pay and status to their former jobs, or join the groups that are regarded as structurally unemployed.

Negro Workers. Many companies have found that displaced Negro employees present the most formidable unemployment problem, even where the employer follows an unequivocal policy of nondiscrimination. The reasons for this are well known, although at the time of writing some changes for the better were taking place in the employment of Negroes:

1. Nondiscriminatory hiring policies are of rather recent vintage, and Negro employees are, therefore, invariably the low men on the seniority totem pole and thus most vulnerable to displacement.

2. Company efforts to aid displaced Negroes in finding

other employment locally often run into discriminatory practices in the wider home community, particularly among small companies, and among some craft unions.

3. Although Negro employees, particularly the younger ones, are most willing to accept interplant transfers, some companies have found the citizenry of the community to which they are being relocated quite vocal in its objections.

4. The employment of Negro workers in manufacturing industry has been concentrated in unskilled and semiskilled job categories—the precise areas that are shrinking the fastest.

5. Even where companies are willing to upgrade employees into the skilled trades, and engage in retraining to do so, they find that vast numbers of Negro employees lack the educational background to qualify for such training.

The experience of a chemical plant located in the South, in its attempt to upgrade Negro employees, is highly illustrative of the problem of inadequate educational background, even though this situation was one of expanding employment rather than employee displacements. Since the parent company was located in the North, the plant management was drawn from this area. Every worker was hired into the plant at the utility or unskilled-labor grade, from which he normally progressed up the occupational ladder. Historically, however, given the location of the plant and the attitudes of the local populace, Negro employees remained in the bottom labor grades indefinitely. Both corporate and plant management determined a few years ago to extend opportunities for moving into higher-rated jobs to Negro employees.

At this point, the management had to divide the utility labor category into two separate groups: (1) those who could read and write, and thus qualify for advancement, and (2) those who were illiterate, and thus could hardly hope to upgrade their skills. The latter group was entirely Negro. Meanwhile, increasing advances in the nature of the technology used in the chemical industry kept forcing the management to raise the qualifying standards required for promotion. By 1960, therefore, only high school graduates were being hired, and management found that a high school education enabled almost all white employees to move up the occupational ladder. This was not true for Negro employees, however. In fact, not a single graduate of the local Negro high school was able to pass the qualifying tests for upgrading, which may be less a reflection of lack of ability among the Negroes and more a silent commentary against the level of education afforded them.

It is indicative of the company's serious desire to upgrade Negro employees that even after this experience the plant was conducting an active search for Negroes who could not only meet the high-school standard for employment, but could qualify for advancement. At the time the plant was visited, these efforts had just been launched. The experience of this plant indicates that fundamental changes must take place in the larger social body before employment of Negroes can be enhanced throughout industry, particularly as jobs are becoming more and more technologically complex.

Women Workers. In some cases, advanced technology also has had an adverse effect on female employment, largely because of the decrease in semiskilled machine operator jobs —occupations in which there has traditionally been the greatest concentration of women factory workers. In a food-processing plant during a period in which employment declined slightly, from 3,000 to 2,700, the number of female employees dropped from 1,500 to 650. As women workers left the plant, they were replaced by more highly skilled men. Despite the decline in total employment, male jobs rose 36.7 percent, from 1,500 to 2,050 during the period of "automating" the plant.

Automation has tended to increase shift work, and, on occasion, female workers have consequently been affected adversely by state laws restricting hours of work for women. Moreover, when women are displaced, they will rarely relocate, and almost all are too young to be eligible for early retirement. In the main, when faced with displacement, they accept severance pay and thus terminate permanently their current employment. Some seek alternative employment, but others withdraw from the labor market.

* * *

It has been shown that in many cases job dislocations occur even when the employment level in a plant rises. The solutions to problems of dislocation and possible unemployment, which are attributable only in part to the impact of more complex technology, lie in two main directions. Basically, there must be an increase in the rate of national economic growth; this is the only basis on which enough jobs will be available to absorb the current excess of manpower, particularly workers whose limited capacities prevent their being retrained. Widespread creation of additional jobs will relieve the unemployment situation substantially, especially that occasioned by the yearly entry of large numbers of young people into the labor market. It is equally evident, however, that many in the problem groups can be and need to be retrained and thus equipped to take advantage of job opportunities that require new and special skills. These factors are discussed more fully in later chapters.

CHAPTER III

Dealing With Job Dislocations

The organizational dislocations that result from adoption of revolutionary technology, whether throughout a plant or in an area of a plant, are usually far-reaching. Their most sensitive point of impact is, of course, on the people who are presently employed, for new technology generally causes deep changes in manpower requirements—both as to the size of the workforce and the aptitudes sought in operating personnel. This study disclosed that companies have recognized the importance of having employees accept change and have therefore given much attention to reducing the magnitude of these "people problems" well before new technology has been introduced.

Managements have come to expect that employees—almost as a fact of human nature—will react negatively to change, whether they be production workers or executives. Because of this, it was quite generally anticipated in the companies studied that latent fears of employees would be reinforced whenever contemplated changes in operating processes were publicized at the planning stage. Further, speculation about the disastrous effects of the coming technology on the use of manpower would be encouraged, and this, in turn, would breed resistance among employees to adoption of the change.

Much of the conjecture about employee resistance to change derives from the increased productivity implied by technological progress. Accordingly, when new machinery is introduced into a plant, there may well be displacements in the workforce. Being aware of this and of employee proneness to see only the worst in any form of change, managements have applied their efforts, well in advance of the introduction of new technology, to correlating their current manpower situation with the projected needs of the proposed new production processes. The objective has been to decide upon ways in which the companies could shape their policies to accommodate the dislocations from technological change.

Dislocations induced by improved technology arise whenever—

1. New jobs come into being,
2. Some existing jobs change in character,
3. Other jobs are eliminated,
4. New skills are needed in the new jobs and in some changed jobs,
5. The supervisory function gains added significance.

Decisions concerning the utilization, retraining, or termination of currently employed personnel are crucial ones. Such decisions are of a different kind and often more complicated than the related financial and operational decisions. The latter are entirely within the province of management, but decisions affecting employees are generally hedged by regard for the individuals involved or by rights vested in those individuals under an existing union contract. Hence, even though a company could easily adapt to changes in work if it were free to adjust its workforce as it sees fit, that is never entirely feasible.

Dislocation problems were handled with relative ease in 11 of the companies, because sales increased enough to permit employment to either grow or remain steady. There was never any necessity, therefore, to consider the problem of separations, despite the introduction of new technology. Four of these companies, which had adopted the clear policy of "no layoffs due to technological change," were able to fulfill their commitment without undue difficulty.

On the other hand, among those companies in which technological change took place in a period of declining employment, three companies had also given "no layoff" guarantees. For them particularly, but also for all other companies that saw no prospect of an upsurge in their employment situation, technological innovation necessitated much advance manpower planning.

The experience of the companies studied substantiates the theory previously noted that it is the state of the economy in general which permits a company to avoid, or forces it to effect, employee layoffs, even when automation and other advanced technology are being installed. Where the sales of a company's products are expanding, the employment level of the company tends to remain stable, or even to improve, in the face of technological change.

Almost every company studied took an early look at the manpower implications of technological change, in the light of economic and business trends. In many instances company planning was designed to minimize permanent layoffs due to the elimination of jobs, to upgrade the existing workforce to meet the demands of new technology, and to ease the adjustment faced by employees who had to be terminated. Some company approaches were simply calculated to make possible the introduction of new technology with a minimum of conflict. In other companies, early planning flowed from deep convictions respecting the rights and needs of employees. It is significant, however, that in no case did the companies entertain the idea of alleviating technological dislocations by sharing available work among all employees in the existing workforce. Managements, and unions as well, rejected this route as inapplicable to the manpower adjustments occasioned by a changed technology. The limitations of work-sharing schemes are discussed in Chapter VII.

Treated in later chapters are the specific measures that were applied to qualify workers for new or changed jobs and to provide some income security for displaced employees. Also to be discussed later is the practice of advance notice to employees of impending change, which was found to be universal among the case-study companies. This chapter deals with the accomplishments of companies, through effective manpower planning, in lessening the incidence of outright layoffs when it was possible to anticipate that technological change would create an excess of personnel. Some companies proceeded on the basis of trial and error, and, consequently, their initial plans had to be refined or complemented by other procedures. In other companies where long-range manpower planning (see Chapter X) was a customary part of the management and industrial relations process, manpower adjustments were far more easily accomplished. On the whole, the experience of these companies should establish the value of advance planning.

When a company had a clear idea of the nature and impact of new technology, it was possible to prepare for change by bringing into play such controls as: (1) holding in abeyance the refilling of vacancies created by normal attrition in the workforce against anticipated technological displacements and thus averting further build-up of excess personnel; (2) mapping out possible employee transfers within the operations to be changed, and to other operations of the company; and (3) arranging for aid to employees through efforts toward job placement outside the company. These approaches are discussed below.

THE FACTOR OF WORKFORCE ATTRITION

Company experience indicates that one single step—allowing the process of normal attrition to trim the workforce before a change becomes effective—is most helpful in minimizing separations of employees. In most companies, there is a more or less predictable degree of labor turnover due to voluntary quits, normal retirement, and deaths. Obviously, therefore, if making replacements is avoided when these eventualities materialize, a gradual movement toward workforce reduction is started by natural causes. This approach was taken in most of the companies studied, and some also expedited the process by encouraging early retirement on pension among older employees.

Anticipating Normal Attrition

The rate of normal attrition in the workforce depends in large degree, of course, upon the composition of the labor force of a plant. Since both normal retirement and death rates increase with age, plants with a preponderance of older employees can anticipate a higher rate of attrition from these causes. Voluntary quits, on the other hand, are more common among younger employees, particularly those with the least service, and plants with a predominantly young labor force can expect a high rate of voluntary quits. Similarly, women enter and leave the labor force at a considerably higher rate than do men, and plants employing a large proportion of young women can also rely on having substantial turnover.

The rate of attrition experienced by a company also fluctuates over a period of time. Voluntary separations decline quite precipitously when jobs are scarce, as during the trough of the business cycle. In the low unemployment years of 1955 and 1956, the rate of voluntary quits in manufacturing averaged 1.9 per 100 employees; but in the recession year of 1958, the average was only 1.1.[1] Thus, the number of necessary employee displacements might be offset to some extent by voluntary separations if companies could time the introduction of new technology to coincide with periods of national economic expansion. This is not necessarily possible, however, for the competitive pressures to reduce costs are often heaviest in periods of business contraction.

The importance of attrition in preventing layoffs due to technological improvement becomes evident from the experience of the Kaiser Steel Corporation. The company reported that ever since it was established in 1943, Kaiser has lost far more employees through quits, deaths, and other natural causes than it has had to lay off because of technological change.[2]

Holding Down Hirings

Obviously, the occurrence of labor turnover, from whatever cause, would have little meaning in reducing layoffs if the resulting vacancies were filled without regard to the extent of displacements anticipated in a radically changed technology. To the contrary, by holding down the entry of new employees as replacements, the companies studied used the incidence of labor turnover to create vacancies for members of the workforce who would otherwise have faced layoff when technological change became a reality.

The case of a public utility offers a significant illustration of the way mass layoff of employees can be alleviated by

---

[1] U.S. Bureau of Labor Statistics, *Employment and Earnings*, Vol. 9, April, 1963, p. 47.

[2] Representatives of Kaiser Steel Corporation and United Steelworkers of America, *Joint Statement* on Kaiser Long Range Sharing Plan, before a Subcommittee of the Senate Labor Committee. Reported in Bureau of National Affairs (Washington), *Daily Labor Report*, No. 194, October 4, 1963, pp. E-1–E-5.

the suspension of hiring activities. The utility faced having a surplus of 1,500 workers when it converted its operations from the manufacture and distribution of producer gas, to merely the distribution of natural gas purchased from a pipeline company. Anticipating these manpower cutbacks, and continuing its adopted policy of no separations, the management drastically curtailed the hiring of new workers long before the conversion. Thus, it worked toward making room in its electrical operations for transferring the displaced gas employees.

Despite the intent of companies to hold down hirings when manpower reductions were in the offing, this course was pursued with widely varying degrees of finesse at the outset. In some cases, proper coordination was lacking: while one department of a plant was hiring new employees, another was at the same time laying off workers; a group of workers was laid off one week because of displacement by new machinery, only to be recalled the next week, when there was a normal seasonal pick-up in orders. Fortunately, experiences of this sort usually stimulated a better flow of information between production and marketing departments, and between higher management and subordinates. The improvement in communications led not only to better coordination of departmental plans but to more judicious timing of the introduction of new equipment. These are indeed essential ingredients of sound manpower management—setting objectives, communicating pertinent information, and coordinating relevant plans. Without manpower management, trying to prevent layoffs upon adoption of new technology is a vain gesture, and the concomitant fears of employees continue to grow.

Holding down hiring in anticipation of technological displacement carries with it the hazard of leaving a plant with manpower shortages, particularly with respect to critical skills. The most common approach in dealing with such shortages was to put existing personnel on overtime work when the demands of production required additional man-power. Some companies rejected this route, however, because of the costliness of paying overtime premium rates. Still, more and more managements came to the conclusion that overtime pay is cheaper in the long run than the hiring of new people for temporary assignments. These managements recognized that the layoff of employees, even very short-service ones, could have adverse effects on the morale of the workforce generally and on employee acceptance of techno-logical change. Even in the short run, overtime may be less expensive than layoffs, considering the cost of supplementary unemployment benefits and, of even greater significance, the disruptions to production caused by complex seniority bumping procedures every time a man is laid off. More will be said later about the impact of seniority practices.

Recourse to overtime work is not always feasible, how-ever, from the production standpoint, or in terms of employee and public relations. When former employees of a plant are on layoff, it is hard for a management to justify to them, their union, or the community, the increased earnings provided through overtime work for those who are still employed. This problem is particularly troublesome for unions in their re-lationships with both management and their members who are on layoff, which may explain the current union insistence on increasing the costliness to companies of overtime work.

The explosive nature of the problem is illustrated by an unpleasant incident resulting from such an attempted use of overtime, as described in an article by a shop steward in an automobile plant.[3] The plant was attempting to stabilize em-ployment by not recalling laid-off workers for temporary increases in production, using instead currently employed workers on Saturday overtime assignments. This was greatly resented by the men on layoff, who on their own initiative placed picket lines of the unemployed around the plant and

3 B. J. Widdick, "The UAW: Limitations of Unionism," *Dissent*, Vol. 6, Autumn 1959, pp. 449–450.

prevented the Saturday workers from entering the plant. Although the company obtained a court injunction to stop the picketing, it also changed its schedule to eliminate Saturday work, thus settling the problem. In this case, the laid-off workers backed up their resentment with action, which certainly tempered the company's thinking about overtime work.

Another approach taken to avoid accretions to the existing workforce is to hire workers only on a temporary basis in the period preceding the introduction of new technology. The success of such a policy depends, however, on the composition of the local labor market, because the most capable workers desire permanent employment and are not attracted to short-term jobs. A number of companies find that they can recruit a sufficient number of able temporaries within various labor markets in which they operate. Their main sources of supply are housewives and students, who have a tenuous attachment to the labor force in that they seek short-term jobs rather than permanent positions. Moreover, if temporary employees are recruited from such groups, their subsequent layoff seldom creates the problems of employee morale previously noted.

A further course taken by some companies to contain the size of the plant labor force when technological change is imminent is to subcontract particular types of work, rather than to expand the workforce to man them. However, this route has become increasingly difficult because of certain impediments laid down in collective bargaining agreements, by arbitration awards, and in decisions of the National Labor Relations Board and the courts with respect to the subcontracting of activities formerly carried out within a company. Even where a management retains the right to contract out certain operations (such as maintenance work), exercising that right might result in the company's becoming the victim of interunion strife. This point is discussed further in Chapter XI.

Accelerating Attrition Through Early Retirements

Retirement of many employees before their normal retirement date is getting to be almost a standard form of attrition in the workforce of companies. Provisions in pension plans for early retirement are becoming commonplace; and, in the interest of efficient operations, companies are encouraging early retirement for employees who are prevented by age, health, or job attitudes, for example, from keeping pace with the pressures of these times. Because any swelling of the attrition rate is advantageous to planning for technological change, 12 of the 36 case-study companies actively pursued the route of making the financial aspects of early retirement attractive enough for employees to seek it voluntarily, or to accept a decision to effect it in their own interests.

Experience indicates that a company may find it necessary to undertake an intense program of "selling" the benefits of early retirement to employees, if it seriously wishes to increase the number of early retirements. Companies employ two basic approaches with respect to early retirement. The first calls for maintaining a fixed policy in that regard and for keeping the door open to older employees by constantly bringing forward their privilege to retire early. The second calls for a one-shot drive to encourage early retirement by offering special inducements to those who are eligible to retire immediately. An example of a limited-period offer is the program of a petroleum company, which permitted an employee who elected early retirement by June 1, 1963, to receive a higher pension than that normally established for his age. Where special one-shot offers were made, they were found to stimulate employee interest in seeking early retirement more promptly than might otherwise have been the case.

One danger in pushing older employees into considering early retirement, without exercising selectivity, is that a company may thereby lose employees whose experience is still needed. With this possibility in mind, some companies allowed employees to opt for early retirement only with the permission of their supervisors. The discriminatory aspect of such a proviso is obvious, and it can create employee relations problems on that score. If it is advantageous to offer inducements for early retirement, in planning against technological dislocations, the best policy—apparent in the experience of the case-study companies—is to allow employees complete freedom of choice.

Though some pension plans do not provide for early retirement based on attainment of a specified age, they do permit disability retirements before the normal retirement age. The route of urging early retirement for reasons of health or similar incapacity was heavily traversed by all managements to help in offsetting excess manpower. As a case in point, a public utility retired more employees on disability benefits than on early retirement pensions when it closed down its manufacturing of gas. In such instances, managements simply interpreted "disability" quite liberally when less able older employees showed a willingness to retire. It must be recognized, of course, that liberalization of retirement provisions, whether through reducing the actuarial discount for early retirement or broadening the interpretation of disability, will materially increase pension costs.

Other factors than company efforts may contribute to the drive for early retirement of older members of the workforce. Among these is the constant pressure exerted by younger workers on their elders to retire rather than face the need to adapt to technological change. One form of pressure is exercised through work-group interaction, as witnessed in some companies, where young workers have displayed their educational attainments to hint at their greater capacity for learning new assignments. In one instance, a worker in his mid-thirties who was a ham radio hobbyist flaunted his self-accredited knowledge of electronics to impress his elders and told them that their technical knowledge belonged to the era of the "Model A" Ford.

Military service training is also used as a status symbol by the younger members of work groups. In still another gambit, the younger worker exhibits his physical strength or stamina in ways that discredit the efforts of older workers. However manifested, younger workers display their fear that there are not enough jobs for all; they therefore are concerned with preserving available jobs for themselves. They consider it quite equitable for an employer to pension older employees whose children are no longer dependents, rather than to terminate employees who are in the prime of life and have heavy family obligations.

In some companies, the hiring pattern of a particular plant over the years has led, unfortunately, to an imbalance in the proportion of old and young people in the workforce. Because the hiring practices of companies have been shaped by the earlier economic depression, wartime conditions, and the ups and downs of the business cycle since the war, the age distribution of their workforces may be greatly skewed, and may be even bimodal or trimodal. Seniority practices further contribute to a distortion of the age distribution of plant employees. These factors work toward the amassing of a particularly heavy cluster of employees who are just below retirement age, and retiring them on pension would contribute significantly to allaying the need for layoffs.

It is in such circumstances that the subtle social clash takes place between younger workers, who face layoff because of low seniority, and older employees, who may be eligible for early retirement but are also protected against layoff by their seniority rights. Where this form of rivalry existed, companies found many cases in which older workers accepted early retirement because they had actually been pressured into doing so by their younger colleagues.

Unions also plump for early retirement in concrete situations so as to save jobs for younger members, despite occasional philosophic comments to the contrary. In this matter, the unions obviously are guided by the realization that their older members will soon withdraw from active employment anyway, and that future membership allegiance depends on the attitudes of the younger workers.

Though effecting early retirements helps to solve the problem of excess personnel, some companies attempted to steer clear of the practice because of the resulting increase in pension costs. It is interesting, however, that quite a number of these companies eventually had to liberalize early retirement pensions and thus speed up workforce attrition. Moreover, companies found that such increases in pension costs were balanced by the savings in supplementary unemployment benefits or severance payments to younger employees who, but for early retirements, would have been displaced. Details of early retirement provisions are discussed in Chapter VII.

Reported as even more important, though there is no substantiating proof, is the likelihood that early retirements resulted in lower production costs. This probability holds because the younger workers were generally better educated and more adaptable to learning new ways of doing things; hence, they could be expected to be more productive, more quickly, than older workers in situations of technological change.

TRANSFER OF EMPLOYEES

It is obvious that transferring displaced employees to other jobs in a company is possible only if there are genuine vacancies in the various areas of the organization. If employees whose jobs have disappeared are only added to already adequate departmental workforces, the transfer method becomes no more than a system of work-sharing, which managements invariably reject. Nevertheless, in the companies studied, effecting transfers was a principal element of advance manpower planning to prevent loss of employment due to technological dislocations.

Opportunities were explored for transfer of employees not needed for their customary plant jobs to fill vacancies that occurred within their own departments, in other departments of the plant, or, in the case of multiunit companies, in other plants of the company. All of the case-study companies effected intraplant transfers, even though in a number of cases there were several obstacles to such transfers. Furthermore, transfer of employees to other jobs within the same plant contributed substantially to minimizing employee separations in many operations. It should be noted that opportunities for transferring employees to other departments or plants highlight the very uneven incidence of technological change within companies, as well as the influence of certain successful products in creating jobs. In general, transfer of employees was not all smooth sailing, as shown in the following discussion of the experience and the attendant problems.

Intraplant Transfers

The ability to effect intraplant transfers smoothly is highly dependent upon astute management, for so many facets of industrial relations practice are involved, including recruitment, job training, placement, transfer rights, and seniority practices. Because of the need to interlock several personnel procedures, effective coordination among departments, as to expected vacancies and manpower shortages and surpluses, is essential to fulfilling the objective of minimizing job loss through intraplant transfers.

A particularly good program of this sort was that of an electrical machinery plant. The management followed the practice of keeping all departments informed of impending technological change well in advance of its occurrence. The company's development engineers then calculated the reduction in crew size that would result from adoption of the new technology, and the industrial relations department was informed of their findings. On the basis of this information, the industrial relations staff identified the individuals who would actually be displaced, and compiled a list of those employees, showing their qualifications and seniority standing. This roster was circulated among all departments of the plant and served as a notification to hold off on hiring new employees in the expectation that openings could be filled from the projected displacement list by employees having the qualifications needed. In addition, a management "surplus committee," composed of the supervisors of the various operations in the plant, met regularly to identify vacancies into which displaced employees could be fitted. This program worked exceedingly well; no employees were separated as a result of technological innovation, as all displaced employees were transferred to other jobs within the plant.

A similar type of program was carried out at a petroleum refinery, which for some years so aggressively modified and improved its operations that change became known as the order of the day. A "manpower committee" with representatives from each department met weekly for the purpose of encouraging and facilitating transfer of employees from points where there was an excess of personnel to departments that were in need of additional employees. This program of manpower planning, integrating intraplant transfers, early retirement, and extensive retraining, enabled the refinery to undergo vast technological improvement without the involuntary separation of a single employee.

Even though effective utilization of the transfer method as a solution to the displacement problem is often blocked by seniority rules, adjustments can be adopted to prevent seniority applications from hindering the transfer of displaced employees to other jobs. The ramifications of the seniority problem in relation to technological change are discussed in the next chapter.

An even more formidable barrier to the transfer of displaced employees is their lack of qualifications for other available jobs. One way for overcoming this difficulty is to lengthen the learning time on new jobs allotted to displaced employees. Retraining is a second means of meeting this problem, as will be shown in a later chapter. On the strength of experience with the skill limitations of employees and the need for them to learn new processes, the companies, in general, concluded that selection processes should favor the worker who has qualifications that are broader than those needed in the particular job for which applicants are being considered.

At the time of the study a few companies already were linking their labor recruitment to the recognition that technology of the future will require versatility in workers, based on their having diverse skills. These companies, therefore, were following the policy of selecting employees with multiple skills, and thus they experienced a reduced need for separations caused by obsolescence of skills when new machinery was introduced. In a sense, all companies surveyed were moving in this direction. Their recruitment standards were beginning to stress general intelligence and ability to learn in new areas of work, rather than acquired skills alone. This approach was moving hand in hand with higher educational requirements, and many industrial plants operating with more advanced technology demanded a high school diploma as the minimum attainment for entering any blue-collar job.

Interplant Transfers

In the typical multiunit company, opportunities for transfer of employees from one plant to another derive from the changing volume of employment at the various company facilities. This volume may be moving in different directions at any given time for a number of reasons, of which the more controlling usually are: an uneven pattern of technological innovation within the company; a decline in the demand for particular products and a rise in the sale of others; and shifts in the manufacture of products from one plant to another because of locational advantages. Moreover, it sometimes becomes necessary for a company to shut down an entire plant permanently in response to the rise of new products and markets, the depletion of natural resources, the movement of population, the changing structure of freight rates, and the rise of new forms of transportation.

The emergence of new technology is generally regarded as also a contributing factor, but the interaction of technological change and plant and product relocation is somewhat complex. The case studies tend to indicate that the adoption of new technology is seldom the cause of plant relocation, but is often the occasion for it. To illustrate: the market for the product of a plant may have shifted well before any change in technology was contemplated; and although the company has recognized that savings in transportation costs could be effected by getting closer to the new market area, it is not impelled by that consideration alone to effect a move. But when it finds that the introduction of new technology demands the extensive overhaul of the plant, the management may be spurred to build a new plant at a more advantageous location.

In other cases, an old plant may be abandoned because it is too obsolete for modernization and its site is inadequate for the building of a modern structure. Rarely, however, was it found that labor relations considerations contributed significantly to any management decision regarding the relocation of production from one area to another. Among the companies studied, such decisions were based primarily on economic factors.

Whether a company faces plant relocation or a decline in job opportunities at a given plant, the question that arises, from an industrial relations standpoint, is whether or not it has the responsibility to transfer displaced employees to other plants. The ruling of the federal courts in the Glidden case,[4] under which employees retain employment rights when a plant is relocated, has brought the issue to the fore. But the question is much broader than that. It encompasses the right of displaced employees to transfer to other plants of a company, even though there has been no relocation of facilities, when there has been simply a decline in employment due to technological change or any other cause.

Of the 32 multiunit companies participating in this study, 18 did not engage in interplant transfer of displaced blue-collar employees. They refrained from that course for one or another of three reasons: (1) there was no problem of separation in any plant; (2) employment was declining at most plants, and, consequently, there were no opportunities for transfer of employees; (3) the management was opposed to such a policy, either on principle or because of complicating factors involved in attempting to effectuate it.

Those who are opposed as a matter of principle hold that an employer makes jobs available to the people of the community in which he operates, and that when he no longer can provide jobs for them there, his responsibility to them ends. Most companies having this philosophy would be willing, however, for practical reasons of staffing, to accept former employees as new hires at other locations, and some would even extend preference to such employees.

Other companies hold no principled opposition to interplant transfers, but reject this route as leading to more industrial and community relations problems than it solves. They point to the major problem of accrued seniority: if transferees cannot retain their seniority standing upon transfer, they are aggrieved; if permitted to do so, employees at receiving plants become resentful. Transferring workers meets dis-

4 Industrial Relations Counselors, Inc. (New York), *Plant Relocation— Industrial Relations Implications: A Review Based on the Glidden Case*, 1962 (Industrial Relations Memo No. 142), 51 pp.

approval in many communities, the sentiment being that all job openings should be filled from within the local labor force. Community attitudes toward interplant transfer policies become even more antagonistic when they result in an influx of people from unaccustomed ethnic groups.

Despite these obstructions to interplant transfer of displaced employees, 14 of the case-study companies engaged in the practice, on one basis or another. Preferential hiring within a given labor market was one of the forms used. Others included outright transfers within a given area, setting aside a specific share of jobs at new locations for those at other plants who sought transfer, or a combination of more than one of these approaches. In some cases, relocating employees to other plants was done at company expense. Some companies adopted formal policies regarding interplant transfers, but the more typical approach was to act on an *ad hoc* basis. When a particular problem of dislocation arose, management negotiated a supplementary agreement with the union, covering transfer rights of bargaining-unit employees.

Specific Practices. Company experience with respect to the relocation of blue-collar employees differed as between nonunion situations and those in which employees were organized. In unorganized companies, the managements had much greater freedom to reassign and transfer employees to suit changed manpower demands. Moreover, where employees were not organized, the companies felt committed to protecting job security, particularly for those with long service. In some cases this solicitousness created additional problems beyond that of the initial relocation, for transferred production workers were not always satisfied with their moves. They then expressed the desire to return to their original communities, and in such cases most companies felt obligated to aid them in doing so. Many companies that encountered this problem took particular care subsequently to impress on employees the difficulties of acclimating themselves to new communities; employees were urged to weigh well their decision to accept transfer, as they would get no company assistance for return to their former location.

The extent to which interplant transfer of unionized employees can be so effected as to maintain the seniority rights, job classifications, and wage rates of employees depends largely on the number to be transferred relative to the total labor force, and on the frequency of transfer. For example, a petroleum company estimated that technological advances at one of its refineries would lead to a maximum displacement of from 65 to 75 employees. Since the number was relatively small, management planned to absorb the displaced elsewhere. The union was informed that refinery employees would be given first consideration for jobs in other company plants in the immediate area, and that opportunities for transfer to plants located elsewhere would be afforded those who could not be placed locally. The plan was introduced on management initiative; and no formal negotiations were conducted with the union, though suggestions from the union were invited and considered. About two dozen employees were actually moved to company locations in other areas, and the rest were absorbed locally. All transferees retained their seniority rights, job classifications, and wage scales, and their moving expenses were paid by the company.

In the automobile industry, on the other hand, where transfers have occurred often, and on a mass basis, managements of necessity have negotiated the details of the transfer program on each occasion of transfer. During the past decade, many thousands of employees in that industry have actually transferred from one plant to another, and elaborate agreements covering seniority rights, recall rights, and the like, have been negotiated in dozens of cases. In fact, the most detailed programs of negotiated interplant transfer rights have emerged in the automobile industry.[5]

---

[5] Under the 1961 contracts, workers transferring to plants more than 50 miles distant from their customary place of employment get moving allowances of up to $580, depending on the exact distance.

One approach taken in the automobile industry has been to grant blue-collar employees who are laid off at one plant employment preference at other of a company's plants in the same area. This system was applied in the Ford Motor Company, where, in one decade, over 27,000 laid-off employees were placed in jobs, under the company's "Detroit Availability Agreement" with the United Automobile Workers.[6]

A second approach in this industry, as well as in others, has been to offer interplant transfers to other company locations to employees of plants that are closed. The way in which this policy is put into practice varies from case to case depending upon the situation at the company's other plants, for if there are employees on layoff at the active plants, it is extremely difficult to carry through transfer of displaced employees. Even preferential hiring is usually contingent upon prior recall of all former employees at a receiving plant. Moreover, though the national leadership of a union may be anxious to place dislocated workers, the local unions at the respective plants may be loath to accept them until all their members are back on the job. This was the case in one of the companies studied. The management reached agreement with the national union for one of its plants to extend preferential hiring rights to displaced high seniority employees from another operation, although the plant affected by the agreement still had employees on layoff. But the program had to be abandoned within a year, mainly because of the strong influence of lower seniority people on the local union at the receiving plant.

One of the devices produced by collective bargaining to establish interplant transfer rights is that of reserving a fixed proportion of jobs at new locations for employees from older plants. A company in the glass industry followed such a practice. When the company opened a new automated

6 Malcolm L. Denise, *Statement* before the Subcommittee on Unemployment and the Impact of Automation of the House Committee on Education and Labor, April 7, 1961 (Washington: Government Printing Office), p. 531.

plant in response to the growing demand for its products, employees at its other plants showed no particular interest in transferring to the new operation, since there had been no cutback in production at these older plants. During the subsequent business recession of 1958, however, layoffs were heavier at the older, higher-cost plants than at the modern, highly efficient operation. In fact, as a result of intensified competition in the product market, the older plants never returned to their former manpower levels, even after a pick-up in the national economy. The decline of jobs at the outmoded plants, combined with the prospective opening of other new facilities, led to a union demand at the next negotiations for transfer rights for production employees, to which the management acceded.

The resulting contract obligated the company to offer employment at a new plant to regular bargaining-unit employees at its other works. The provision called for reserving for them 25 percent of the original manning requirements at the new plant or, if the number of applicants for transfers fell below that level, until the list of applicants was exhausted. An employee who accepted employment at a new plant forfeited his seniority and recall rights at his former place of employment, unless he was disqualified by management during the probationary period on his new assignment. In that case he was returned, at his own expense, to the plant from which he was transferred, with reinstatement of his full seniority rights. The company guarantee to permit employees to try for one-fourth of the jobs at new locations did not include any provision for relocation allowances.

The structure of unionism within a company is an important factor in applying a policy of interplant transfers, as exemplified by the contrasting experience of two public utility companies. Both faced the problem of employee displacement due to conversion from the manufacture of producer gas to the distribution of natural gas; but in one of these companies all production employees were in the same bargaining unit, and the company engaged in system-wide bargaining. This facilitated accomplishment of the management's desire to use present employees in other operations. Through negotiation with a single union, representing all employees, the company was able to transfer all displaced gas employees to the electric generating stations, with full protection of their seniority and job status.

In contrast, the other utility had many separate bargaining units and dealt with six different unions, each of which refused to grant transfer rights to the members of other unions. As a result, the company could not effect interplant transfers of surplus gas workers, except on the basis of their entering employment as new hires. Within this company's electrical department, however, management bargained with various locals of the same national union, and, although each location legally remained a separate bargaining unit, system-wide bargaining existed in practice. This facilitated adjustment to technological change within the electrical department, because those displaced from one station could be transferred to another without any sacrifice of either seniority or job status. The fact that the company operated within a limited geographical region obviated one problem that often arises in interplant transfers—employees did not have to relocate their homes, as they were able to travel by car to any of the company's plants.

Negotiating interplant transfer rights for bargaining-unit personnel does, of course, increase the likelihood of organization of new plants by the union that had represented the transferred employees at the older operations. Indeed, some companies have found it necessary to expedite union recognition in the new plant in order to make an interplant transfer policy practicable. Yet, it is evident from the experience of one of the companies studied that the transfer of union members into new plants may not necessarily lead to their organization. The glass-producing company referred to earlier, upon the opening of its second automated plant, transferred to that operation (in conformance with the previously negotiated provision for allocation of 25 percent of jobs in new plants for transfer purposes) a substantial number of bargaining-unit personnel, particularly younger ones. Although the union that represented these employees at their former location sought representation rights at the new plant, it lost out in a National Labor Relations Board election. The transferred workers, smarting under the union's rigid seniority arrangements at the older plants, which had operated to their detriment, apparently contributed to rejection of the union.

Inherent Problems. Assuming optimum favorable conditions for effectuating an interplant transfer policy—that is, no interunion deterrents, and room for transferees in other plants—still many other problems remain. First, a method of distributing transfer rights must be determined. The standard practice is to survey displaced employees as to their willingness to transfer, and then actually offer transfer, based first on the needs of other plants for particular skills, as determined by management, and beyond that, on seniority, as long as the worker has the ability to perform available jobs. Since the jobs at different plants are usually similar, ability to perform seldom presents a formidable barrier to transfer, except for very low-skill individuals. Typically, production-line employees and skilled maintenance groups are considered separately, and this further reduces difficulties growing out of ability to perform.

A second set of major problems concerns the integration of transferees into the new workforce, particularly with respect to seniority rights. The case studies indicate that employees who move from one plant to another always retain their seniority standing for fringe benefit purposes. But their retention of seniority status for purposes of layoff and recall varies from one situation to another, depending very much on the attitude of the union local at the receiving plant.

Often national union leadership favors retention of seniority status for transferees, while local union leaders do not.

The strongest objections come from local unions at newer plants, where their members have relatively few years of employment with the company. These locals usually refuse, therefore, to allow the seniority ranking of employees transferred from older plants to apply to layoffs in the newer operations. One of the case-study companies was subjected to wildcat strikes by workers at receiving plants because the union leadership agreed to allow transferees to retain their seniority standing. On the other hand, some companies carried out such transfer policies with more amicable results.

When, however, interplant transfers are made as a convenience for a company, the management usually does everything possible to protect full seniority rights for the transferred employees and provides liberal relocation allowances. For a glass-container producing company, the interplant transfer problem revolved about the need to find a sufficient number of skilled employees to man and train production workers at new plants. When the company opened a new facility, therefore, it sought key personnel from among the blue-collar forces at its existing operations. The company's industrial relations department conducted the recruiting, but the management of the new plant reviewed the qualifications of the applicants for transfer and selected those most suitable for its needs. Top management recognized that relocation posed economic difficulties for employees, as well as the inevitable family readjustment. In order to encourage applications, therefore, the company paid moving expenses, plus reimbursement for out-of-pocket expenses, such as travel costs, living expenses in the transitional phase of the moves, and extra costs connected with selling homes or breaking leases.

A third major problem encountered by managements in effecting interplant transfers is that of guarding against seniority practices that would interfere with efficient operations or would penalize long-service employees. This is a particularly difficult problem where a plant is being closed down or a department is being shifted from one plant to another. If transferees do not retain their seniority status upon transfer, senior employees are at a disadvantage, in relation to short-service workers in the plants from which they move. Since the latter are laid off first upon the closing of an operation, they get the first opportunity to bid on vacancies in other plants, because the more senior workers are transferred later.

On the other hand, if employees are permitted to transfer on the basis of seniority, the old plant may be left with only less-experienced short-service workers during the phase-out period. A solution to this dilemma has been found in the use of "pegged" seniority dates, whereby the starting date for seniority credits at the receiving plant is the same for all transferees, even though some arrive later than others. In this way, a company can insist on retaining employees who are needed during the phase-out of the old operation, without any sacrifice for such employees of seniority credits at the plant to which they will later transfer.

Another aspect of the integration problem involves the jobs to which transferees will be assigned. In this connection also, local unions at receiving plants have more generally insisted that transferees be placed in the lowest-rated jobs, but some companies have been able to transfer workers with their full seniority, job classifications, and wage rates. Public utilities have been better able to do this than manufacturing companies, because they employ a heavy proportion of highly skilled workers; but, even in the latter companies, it is the skilled employees who have been most often protected against job or wage downgrading upon transfer.

The question of the right of employees to transfer back to their old plants poses another dilemma for management. If they are denied this right, a plant may find itself saddled with a group of unhappy employees. If employees are allowed to return to their former plant, that may result in job-hopping on a national scale, with complete confusion of seniority rights. The problem is intensified further when transferees subsequently become displaced at their new locations. Almost invariably, managements have denied to their workers who are laid off, after having accepted transfer, both the right to return to their home plant, even if jobs subsequently become available there, and the right to the separation benefits that they could have decided to take in lieu of transfer. The withholding of these privileges does not arise from vindictiveness, but is a necessary control to avoid fractious decisions about transfer on the part of employees. Transfers are always on a voluntary basis, and employees are made to understand that their decisions are final. If these terms were violated in individual cases, employees would come to regard transfers as merely experimental; and all of the problems connected with interplant transfer would be compounded. However, employees are frequently given a trial period of from one to three months at a new location, during which they may elect to return to their former plant or to accept separation pay.

The right to transfer back to one's old plant, as well as the holding of multiple seniority rights, does obtain, however, in situations in which employees are given preference in hiring at other company plants within a given area. In such cases, the employee may remain on the recall list of his old plant, while acquiring seniority at his new location. A problem arises only if and when the employee is recalled to his original plant, at which point he must make a choice between the two operations and then surrender his seniority rights at one or the other.

In one case of employee transfer, a pipeline company ran into an unexpected problem connected with employee housing. Its generator stations had been in the remote countryside, and to attract employees to such locations the company had built houses, for which it had charged only nominal rents. When it centralized the control of its generator stations at one point along the pipeline, close to 50 surplus employees were transferred to other operations. At their new locations, the economic situation of employees became less advantageous because they had to secure private housing at market rentals. This result of transfer bred discontent among the employees, even though they were in comparably rated jobs, had retained their seniority status, and the company had borne all the costs of moving them. Moreover, the company was left with the problem of disposing of the houses they had occupied.

Employee Response to Transfer Offers. It is reasonable to postulate that company policies for interplant transfer would be conducive of greater mobility of labor. But company experience with employee response to opportunities for transfer does not support this thesis. Experience in the automobile industry shows that, despite company willingness to relocate employees, a relatively small percentage of them actually avail themselves of the opportunity. With the closing of an automobile assembly plant in a Middle Atlantic state, for instance, management and the union negotiated a plan to assist the 1,247 hourly employees to adjust to this severe dislocation. All of them were offered transfers, with retention of seniority, to other company plants—mainly to one located 115 miles away—but as the following tabulation indicates, less than one-fourth accepted transfer:

Employee Decisions Upon Plant Closing	Employees Displaced	
	Number	Percent
Accepted transfer	290	23.26
Accepted retirement	137	10.99
Accepted separation pay	592	47.47
Declined transfer (but did not apply for separation or retirement benefits)	228	18.28
Total	1,247	100.00

Of the 137 employees who preferred to accept retirement, 18 were at normal retirement age, and 119 elected special early retirement. Close to half of the group accepted separation pay, thereby severing their employment relationship with the company. Between one-fifth and one-sixth of the employees declined transfer. They did not, however, apply for separation or retirement benefits, preferring to remain on layoff status even though they had virtually no prospect of being recalled to a plant that had been closed. Moreover, within four years after the transfer program had started, 100 of the transferees had left their new plants to return to their former community and go on layoff status, thus reducing the proportion transferred to 15.24 percent.

A chemical company, which in 1954 began to modernize an old plant in the East North Central region, had still less success with respect to the willingness of employees to relocate for new job opportunities. As a result of technological improvement, 56 of the 523 plant employees had been displaced by 1956, and management anticipated that within another year an additional 100 would be laid off. In the hope of relieving the impact of change on its employees, the company in June, 1956, offered to transfer surplus personnel to another of its facilities in the same region—some 500 miles away. Transferees were to be permitted to retain their accumulated seniority, and the company was to pay their moving expenses.

Despite the liberality of the transfer policy, a mere eight employees were willing to accept management's offer to visit and look over the other community, and of those, only two actually accepted jobs there. This was most disappointing, since alternative employment opportunities were very scarce in the home community, which had been classified by the federal Department of Labor as an area of substantial and persistent unemployment. The lack of interest displayed by this group of employees deterred the company from again offering workers the opportunity to move.

In the modernization of the petroleum refinery previously referred to, the company embodied a transfer policy within its program of manpower planning for technological change. Employees and union representatives were informed that the change would place the refinery in a more competitive position but that it would also reduce manpower requirements. They were assured, however, that employees would be given first consideration for jobs in other company plants in the area. They were also informed that the company would watch for opportunities for transfer to its operations in other areas. Employees accepting transfer were guaranteed retention of all rights, including accumulated seniority.

The transfer program was handled on a company-wide basis, and at other refineries new employees were hired on a temporary basis. Thus permanent job opportunities were retained for workers yet to be released at the refinery undergoing technological change. In the first two years of the modernization program, employment at that refinery was reduced by 75, but without any layoffs. Displacements were offset by normal workforce attrition, early retirement of some older employees, and acceptance of transfer to other company locations by 23 employees. Further reductions in personnel were anticipated, and other transfer opportunities were offered. But employees preferred to wait until the job situation at the refinery became clearer, in the hope that they would be able to retain employment at the same location. Excerpts from a company policy on employee transfers appear in Appendix C.

An entirely different approach to interplant transfers was taken by a multiplant company with a number of small facilities scattered throughout the New York-Northern New Jersey metropolitan area. The company did not engage in the preplanning of transfers, and it did not extend transfer rights, as such, to employees. It operated instead on a *post facto* basis. After displacement occurred at a plant, company headquarters notified its other plants, listing the job qualifications of its surplus employees. The local managements then informed the company's industrial relations department if they had suitable job openings for specific personnel. That department then determined whether or not the displaced employees in question wanted the available jobs. Those accepting them were, however, generally treated as new hires, except for those having skills the company was anxious to obtain at the new plant.

Although this method is unique among the companies studied and may seem cumbersome, a surprisingly large number of displaced employees were transferred to jobs in other plants by this means. At the plant visited, 24 of the 54 employees displaced by technological change were transferred; and 5 of them, having skills that management required at the new plant, were paid relocation allowances. In this company's experience, those who were successfully transferred were high-skill and younger personnel. This result conformed with overall company experience with interplant transfers: there were usually more openings in plants for young, skilled workers; and it was generally such employees who showed greater willingness to transfer, particularly when the move entailed relinquishing home ownership or other well-established living arrangements. This pattern of employee response to transfer seems to be a prevailing one. Evidently, the attitudes of employees, and the factors that influence their attitudes toward transfer are the same, regardless of the region of the country in which they have set their roots.

AID TO DISPLACED EMPLOYEES
IN FINDING JOBS

In view of the many problems associated with interplant transfers, managements often take a further approach to ease the impact of technological change on employees. This calls for helping the displaced to find alternative employment in their home communities. Such action is seen as having great value in supporting employee morale during the transition

to use of new technology and in getting the fullest cooperation from employees.

Some companies gave only sporadic and informal aid to
displaced employees, merely relaying information received
concerning possible job openings with other employers. One
company simply capitalized on its participation in the
regional manufacturers' association to circulate to all association members a list of its displaced workers, showing their
experience and skills. As a result of that effort, a number of
the employees, particularly those with maintenance-type
skills, received job offers, and they were released ahead of
schedule so that they could accept the jobs.

In a few cases, however, elaborate outside-placement
programs were carried out, based on surveys of the local labor
market, inventories of skills available among the displaced,
employee interviewing and counseling, and the virtual operation of placement services. A petroleum refinery engaged in
the most extensive program found in this study. Modernization of the refinery's facilities in 1960 required a permanent
cutback in employment. The management was concerned
about the situation of the employees who had to be laid off,
and there were no opportunities for transfer to other company operations. It was decided, therefore, that the company
would aid them in getting placed in other jobs in the large
metropolitan area surrounding the small community in
which the plant was located.

Only 254 of the displaced—one-third of the total not
eligible for early retirement—applied to the company for aid
in finding alternative employment. The applicants were interviewed three months before their scheduled layoff, beginning with those who were lowest on the seniority roster; and
their skills, interests, and experience were evaluated. This
information was then kept available for transmittance to
some 600 employers who had been contacted by the company's industrial relations department. Two private employment agencies also were hired by the company to supplement

the activities of that department, but their efforts were far less productive than the company endeavor.

The proportion of employees who availed themselves of this opportunity to secure employment was surprisingly low, but the actual placement activity was nonetheless successful. A total of 109 workers, 43 percent of those requesting aid, were placed in jobs through company assistance. Company representatives felt that the percentage of placements would have been even higher, had the displaced employees been more zealous about finding employment immediately. Many displayed inertia in exerting their own efforts to seek jobs, and often they refused jobs that did not pay quite as much as they had become accustomed to earning. Some even rejected comparable-paying jobs, simply because the prospective place of employment would have necessitated a longer drive to work. The company also offered displaced employees the opportunity to run their own gasoline stations; and when there was only negligible acceptance of this offer, the management was surprised at the lack of enterprise shown. In addition, work was offered in company-owned stations in the area, but here, too, there were few acceptances.

Perhaps the generous severance allowances provided all the displaced employees accounted for the dilatory attitude shown by such a high proportion toward getting placed in other jobs. Apparently, as long as their severance pay held out, they tended to be "choosy" about accepting proffered employment. But even so, these displaced employees behaved in an astonishing manner. Many of them, it was learned during the visit to this refinery, used severance pay for new cars although they had no employment in the offing. Since it is beyond the scope of this study to probe the response characteristics of workers, suffice it to say that the company felt its efforts were repaid by the employees' acceptance of change and by their recognition of the company's efforts toward helping them.

Decidedly less success with outside job placement was

experienced by a plant in the metal trades, which operated in the same large metropolitan area. The company closed down the obsolete plant in 1961, and its other facilities had insufficient job openings to absorb the 2,000 people displaced by the shutdown. Only 384 employees (140 managerial, 104 salaried, and 140 hourly-rated) were transferred to other operations. In view of the internal employment situation, the industrial relations department tried to place terminated employees with other companies. It contacted 750 outside employers and also worked closely with the state employment service in a search for alternative job opportunities. Lists of job openings were made available to employees, and they were given extensive counseling, as well as assistance in arranging interviews with prospective employers. Although the program extended over a period of years—prior to, during, and after the shutdown—the management reported that the number of job openings found was low relative to the displacements.

The very limited success of this placement effort, as contrasted with that of the refinery in the same area, was ascribed by the management to a number of factors that were outside the company's control. The labor market of the area had already suffered an increase in unemployment when the heaviest phase-out of the plant took place; the skills of the great majority of the workforce were decidedly less transferable than those of refinery workers; and a large proportion of the employees were in the higher age groupings.

Another rather successful outside-placement program was conducted in conjunction with the 1957–1958 shutdown of an obsolete polychemicals plant in the East. Of the total of 737 plant employees who were in service when the placement activities started, 199 were pensioned, 6 died, 72 (mainly salaried) were transferred to other plants of the company, and 460 were terminated. Extensive efforts were made before, during, and after the shutdown to place the terminated employees with outside employers. Management representatives wrote to and telephoned employers in other local industries. Industrial relations department personnel helped employees write personal job application letters in answer to newspaper want ads. Placement prospects were posted on the plant bulletin boards; and interview appointments were arranged, many of which were held in the plant. Employees who located employment were permitted to move up their termination dates and receive their normal dismissal benefits early, in order to accept the jobs; between 60 and 70 employees took advantage of this procedure.

Although the onset of the 1957–1958 recession reduced the effectiveness of the company's outside-placement efforts, the skill levels of the terminated employees enabled 83 of them to find other jobs through contacts made by the plant management. Of these, 51 were hired by the company that purchased a part of the abandoned facilities; and following the actual shutdown, 55 additional employees were placed with the successor occupying the plant. This brought the total placed to 138—exactly 30 percent of the terminated group.

A similar placement program was conducted in 1958 by another plant of this very company. The dislocations at the plant resulted from both technological change and product change. A representative of the industrial relations department was assigned full time to the job of trying to place laid-off employees with other companies, and he maintained constant contact with local employers and with some outside the local area as well. In terms of numbers, this placement experience was the most successful one reported in this study, in that the majority of displaced employees were able to locate other employment. In terms of the comparability of the jobs they found with their former assignments, however, placements were much less satisfactory. Their new jobs were mainly as service station attendants, store clerks, and farm laborers—occupations that were below their levels of skill and customary pay. Some of the displaced employees would not accept such jobs, apparently believing that they would be recalled to the company after a short time, and that their severance pay would tide them over until then.

The plant was the major employer in the town, accounting for the lack of a sufficient number of comparable job opportunities for the laid-off employees. In addition, the management found that employers who might have provided better jobs were reluctant to hire the laid-off workers, fearing that they would return to their former employer when and if recalled.

It is clear from company experience that opportunities for outside hiring of displaced employees depends primarily on what is transpiring in the surrounding community at the time of termination. This may be illustrated by contrasting two layoff situations in the same metropolitan area. At the obsolete chemical plant described earlier the shutdown coincided with a national business recession. At a food-processing plant the timing of layoff was more fortuitous. At this plant, extensive technological improvement and loss of products combined to cause two series of terminations, one in early 1959, and a second a year later. In both instances, the largest group of displaced employees consisted of female assembly-line machine operators. The layoffs in both years occurred, however, just before a drug company in an adjoining community expanded hiring of such types of workers. In each year, consequently, about 50 percent of the women who were laid off were able to get jobs at the drug plant. The food processor, knowing of the imminent expansion of employment at the drug firm, referred all laid-off employees to that plant, where management chose from among them those with the occupational skills and abilities it needed.

One route well worth exploring more often in the placement programs of companies is that of tying in the efforts of management with the work of community agencies, in order to widen the scope of job information. Cooperation with state employment services is very often ignored by employers as impractical, because, as noted by one observer, some employment services face a constant burden in having to match "hard to place" workers with "hard to fill" jobs.[7] This is not universally true, however, and where these agencies are utilized by significant numbers of employers their personnel have a greater range of knowledge of local labor-market conditions and more extensive contacts with employers than would representatives of a single company.

In seeking jobs for displaced employees, discussions with the unions involved may also yield some results. Such discussions may be of particular value where unions maintain employment services of their own, as in the case of many craft unions. Also, where a union's jurisdiction cuts across industry lines, the leadership may know of job opportunities in areas of the labor market with which the people in a given company or plant are not familiar, as was the situation in one of the case-study companies.

On the basis of the cases reviewed, it appears that outside-placement programs of companies for aiding displaced employees are well worthwhile. It is also evident, however, that the success of such activities does depend largely upon external factors, including the state of the local labor market, and the characteristics of the displaced workforce. These factors are beyond the control of a company, for it can neither create outside employment opportunities in the community nor endow employees with abilities they do not have. But the placement efforts of companies are valuable in reducing frictional unemployment. An outside-placement program is justified because a company can fit together available jobs and displaced workers more quickly and efficiently than is possible through the normal workings of the labor market.

* * *

The evidence is conclusive that a variety of means can be found and used effectively to minimize the effects on em-

[7] Lloyd G. Reynolds, *The Structure of Labor Markets* (New York: Harper & Brothers, 1951), p. 58.

ployees of the dislocations brought about by technological change. The measures that have been tested by company experience, as reported here, have real advantages for exploitation by a company adopting new operational processes. The core of this experience is planning ahead of change, for only thus can forward-looking action be taken to ease the personal anxieties of employees and to help those whose jobs will be affected. It is unquestionable that effective advance planning eases the task of introducing new technology.

CHAPTER IV

Labor-Management Relations in Adapting to Changed Technology

A dvanced planning does much to ease the handling of job dislocations arising out of the introduction of new technology in a plant. But it does not mean that a company will thus escape having to deal with critical issues in labor relations. The changes that result alter existing patterns of work organization, the numbers and kinds of jobs, and the locus and distribution of work. Consequently, they disrupt the established relationship between management and labor.

Where employees are represented by a union, technological change invariably involves the collective bargaining process. Some issues arise in the application of existing labor contracts and must be handled at the time technological change is introduced, either through recourse to grievance-arbitration processes or by negotiation of special supplementary agreements or understandings. Other issues may not arise until after new technology has been in operation for a period of time and its consequences have been evaluated; then either labor or management, or both, may see a need to rewrite contract clauses.

Unions may be committed to the necessity of technological change for the health of an enterprise, but this does not preclude their viewing union interests and roles as being at variance with those of management. The overriding responsibility of management is to maximize the profitability of the company by increasing its efficiency; the role of the union is to protect the job security and income of its members. In the case of major technological improvements, the two goals may seem to conflict, at least as related to a particular situation.

It is not surprising, therefore, that among the companies studied labor-management relations in the face of technological change have not always been characterized by spontaneous agreement between the parties as to the necessity of change and the nature of the accompanying adjustments. There have been clashes of interest and specific areas of conflict. What these were, how they were resolved, and the guides that may be drawn from the overall experience are set forth in this chapter.

AREAS OF CONFLICT BETWEEN LABOR AND MANAGEMENT

Opposition to change by employees and their bargaining representatives can hamper the very ability of management to introduce new production processes. They do so, not by directly stopping innovations, but by making the undertaking exceedingly costly and erecting many roadblocks to effective utilization of the new technology.

The situation is not new, for the introduction of new

technology has caused discord between labor and management ever since the emergence of industrialism. Consider, for example, the Luddite movement in England, in 1811–1812, when new machinery was smashed by textile workers. Similarly, early mechanization of some American industries brought strikes, disruption of existing collective bargaining relationships, splits within unions, and the collapse of some unions. The turmoil that accompanied the revolutionary changes in glassmaking at the turn of the century[1] is a case in point.

In some instances, union opposition to change has been backed with strength formidable enough to block the use of technological innovations for decades, a most famous example being the refusal of painters in the building trades to use spray guns. In other situations, unions have not resisted technological improvements, but their insistence on maintaining outmoded work crews has partially nullified the anticipated labor-cost savings—a current example being the retention of railroad firemen in diesel locomotives. Resistance to change, moreover, has also manifested itself in nonunion situations.

In the present period of technological innovation, union conflict with management over the necessary readjustments has been more often obstructive than violent. Certainly, newspaper headlines have featured dramatic illustrations of clashes on the railroads, on the docks, and in various manufacturing industries, when workers and union leaders sought to offset the impact of new technology through featherbedding and make-work practices and restrictive work rules. Such adherence to outmoded practices has been tantamount to outright resistance to technological change.

Some of the companies studied also have experienced forms of labor conflict incidental to the introduction of new technology, and occasionally the controversies erupted in strikes, mainly wildcat in origin, and sporadic. In these cases,

1 See George E. Barnett, *Chapters on Machinery and Labor* (Cambridge: Harvard University Press, 1926), 161 pp.

however, the impetuous actions of groups of employees have been designed less to forestall the installation of new machinery than to secure protection against any effects unfavorable to their interests. For example, disputes over speed of operation of new equipment have led to strikes; yet the employees involved have never attempted to prevent the installation of the equipment.

In fact, labor-management conflict over new technology has been largely concentrated in four major areas: (1) deciding who should run the new machinery—jurisdictional issues; (2) determining the number of people who should run it—manning requirements; (3) establishing how much they should be paid—wage rates for new or changed jobs; and (4) solving the attendant problems in upgrading, downgrading, or laying off employees as a result of the job shifts entailed—seniority considerations. These areas of conflict are discussed separately.

Jurisdictional Issues

New technology often serves to dilute skills and to blur existing jurisdictional lines among unions; consequently, the transition from old to new production processes sometimes becomes embroiled in matters of union rivalry. The problem is particularly acute in those companies which bargain with craft unions, each of which guards its domain jealously and aggressively.

Because of jurisdictional barriers, severe problems arise even though management desires to be fair. It becomes virtually impossible for a management to transfer workers displaced by new technology into departments organized by unions other than the one to which the displaced members belong. Furthermore, whenever a new method of production results in an overlap between two or more unions in the area of job control, management is inevitably caught in the middle of an interunion jurisdictional dispute. Where warfare ensues between the competing unions, it can result in strikes. These problems are best illustrated by citing some specific cases.

A company in the stone, clay, and glass industry had developed over the years highly mechanized production operations. Only the cutting of the finished product into sheets had remained a highly skilled hand operation, manned exclusively by members of a small craft union. For many decades there had been no significant change in the nature or style of the product, and this had contributed to management lethargy in extending mechanization to the cutting process. Eventually, however, the intensified pressure of foreign and domestic competition in the mid-1950's forced the company to adopt automatic cutting machines as another means of more efficient operation.

The first major hurdle before the new machinery could be utilized to the best advantage was a jurisdictional dispute between the craft union and the industrial union representing the production workers as to the manning of new machines. The new machines had significant advantages: they were both labor-saving and space-saving, and they permitted a better flow of production through the plant. Management concluded that machine-tending jobs were not in a craft classification and, therefore, properly belonged within the province of the production workers' union. Accordingly, the jobs created by the new mechanized process were assigned to members of that union. At this point, the craft union went on a one-day strike, and the jurisdictional question then had to be submitted to the National Labor Relations Board. The decision of the Board was to apportion the jobs between the two unions—an unhappy outcome, requiring members of separate unions to work side by side within one operation, even though their conditions of work were governed by two collective bargaining agreements, with differing provisions.

Another facet of the jurisdictional problem was found

in a publishing company. The management ran into considerable union resistance stemming from attempts of craft unions with very narrow jurisdiction to gain exclusive control of new jobs arising from new processes. When new technology in its shipping operations overlapped the jurisdictions of two unions, the company faced strike action by the union that lost out when control was awarded. Once the award was made, a strike did ensue; and the company was forced to obtain an unfair labor practice injunction to halt it.

In plants organized by industrial unions, it is generally easier for the management to introduce new machinery, because of greater contractual freedom to assign work, combine or eliminate jobs, and determine crew sizes. But even these plants have a form of jurisdictional problem which stems from union attempts to preserve craft demarcations (as, for example, pipefitter, electrician) in the face of new technology that requires new combinations of skills.[2] On the whole, the insistence by plant-wide unions upon precise skill differentials is a major impediment to the efficient use of labor. Few companies have had any success in relieving their operations of these restrictive lines of demarcation, and in many plants valuable manpower is being wasted because three or more men are assigned to a task that one could do. One observer has stated the problem well:

A typical machine repair job, for example, may require the use of seven or eight trades, most of them performing simple incidental tasks, such as connecting or reconnecting pipe, removing guards and using hoists, all of which could

2 It is interesting to note that the recent settlement ending the longest strike in the history of the petroleum industry gave the management of the Shell Oil Company's Houston refinery and chemical plant more flexibility in using workers for several duties under certain conditions. Under the agreement with Local 4–367 of the Oil, Chemical and Atomic Workers, operators can be used to perform minor running maintenance and adjustment work as a part of their normal job responsibilities, and during an equipment maintenance turnaround, operators may be utilized as craft helpers; also, craftsmen can be assigned to do the work of other crafts, when that is incidental to their primary tasks.

be accomplished easily and conveniently by the skilled employee whose skill is actually necessary to the work.[3]

Another variant of the jurisdictional problem involves union claims to types of work that management feels justified in assigning to nonbargaining-unit personnel. Such a dispute arose in the plant of an aerospace manufacturing company. This factory integrated numerically-controlled machines into its production process. Subsequently, it was bombarded with union complaints that some of the set-up work with tapes, which was handled by nonbargaining-unit technicians, properly belonged to the production workers. The issue was yet to be resolved at the time of the study.

The very same type of problem was encountered in the automobile industry when the General Motors Corporation assigned the programming of such machines to engineers. The United Automobile Workers protested the company policy and carried the case to arbitration. General Motors argued that its action was a proper exercise of management's contractual right to "maintain efficiency" and determine "methods, processes, and means of manufacture." However, the arbitrator, Nathan Feinsinger, ruled that the work of programming a new tape-controlled multipurpose machine should not have been given exclusively to process engineers, who were usually outside the bargaining unit. He pointed out that programming was traditionally part of the toolmakers' activities, apparently involving the highest skill of the trade.[4] He refused, however, to say how much of the work should be given to toolmakers, and he did not forbid overlapping of duties between bargaining-unit and nonbargaining-unit employees.

Professor Feinsinger based his award in this case on the recognition clause of the labor contract, but the merit of his

[3] Leonard A. Keller, "Automation and the True Causes of Unemployment," *Personnel Journal*, Vol. 41, July–August, 1962, p. 334.
[4] Bureau of National Affairs (Washington), *Labor Policy and Practice*, October 12, 1961, p. 2.

decision has been seriously challenged by other attorneys.[5] Beyond that, the ruling may become a precedent for similar arbitration cases in other automobile companies and in other industries. The UAW reported that it would seek compliance with the ruling throughout the automobile industry, claiming that the jobs of 100,000 tool and die makers in the industry would be affected over the next ten years.

Sometimes the jurisdictional issue between the bargaining-unit and nonbargaining-unit personnel concerns production workers and their supervisors. A rubber plant ran into conflict over whether a supervisor or a production worker should man an electronic console board which replaced a mechanical operation that had required an operator and one supervisor. Management contended that it was the operator's functions which had been eliminated and, therefore, that the panel board should be run by a supervisor. This contention was upheld in arbitration.

Manning Requirements

Aside from disputes over union jurisdiction in assigning men to new machinery, unions and management sometimes disagree on the extent of manning requirements for new operations. In adjusting to technological change, companies have repeatedly faced the problem of union attempts to retain more men than were needed on a new operation.

One approach taken by some unions to block workforce reduction is to negotiate a demand for contract wording that will restrict management's right to reduce manning requirements as a result of technological improvements. In a food-processing plant this issue brought on a five-day strike. The source of the dispute was the elimination of loaders' jobs in the plant warehouse. Originally, fork-lift trucks had brought pallets to a platform, to be removed by loaders. A new fork-

[5] F. A. O'Connell, "Automation Issues and Arbitration: A Management View," *ILR Research*, Vol. 8, No. 2, 1962, p. 5.

lift truck permitted its operator both to carry and discharge the pallet onto the platform without assistance. The greater efficiency of the new machine changed the process from a two-man to a one-man operation.

The power base of the union involved was in another industry, in which the union had a long record of success- fully thwarting company moves to reduce crew sizes in con- formity with technological advances. In this case, however, strike action did not result in a similar victory. The manage- ment refused to accede, and the union finally signed a new contract which preserved the company's right to eliminate outmoded jobs.

A similar problem arose in a printing and publishing plant. Automation of the foundry process of making the casts of the type rolls that go onto the printing presses reduced the needed crew size from four men to one. No lay- offs were contemplated, and the displaced stereotypers were transferred to other jobs. But their union nevertheless chal- lenged management's manning decision. The case then started up the ladder of the grievance procedure, and was probably on its way to arbitration. The management held the position that it would prefer to work out the problem on the shop floor, rather than have an outsider make a superficial judgment of the issue, but that it would not retreat from its decision, because experience had taught it that any such compromise only breeds future problems.

Flexibility for management in the handling of work- force adjustments has been achieved in some situations by guaranteeing to unions that none of their members will be laid off as a result of technological changes. This course had been followed in plants with several bargaining units and where various craft unions had continually attempted to regulate crew sizes. The danger of the no-layoffs guarantee is, of course, that a company might find itself saddled, for a time at least, with excess manpower. However, the manage- ment of a company that has made this guarantee considers it preferable to carry one or two extra people for short periods of time—until they can be properly utilized somewhere in the operations—than to become involved in union disputes over crew sizes for new machines. A guarantee of no layoffs gives a company a free hand not only in determining how best to utilize the employees whose jobs have disappeared but in effecting reductions in the total labor force gradually, through normal attrition.

Joint determination of crew sizes, on the other hand, can lead to long-run freezing of unnecessarily inflated manpower quotas, as unions are prone to insist on retention of crew sizes, once established. Experience of employers in the East Coast longshore industry is the best-known example. The union refused to agree to a reduction in the traditional work gang size, despite the use of improved machinery.

A variation of the manning problem relates to the distribution of work among employees. Obstacles to the introduction of new machines sometimes grow out of the language of a labor contract. In one case, the labor agreement with a craft union stated that all work had to be equally shared among the members of the union. This meant that the work had to be spread out so thinly among the men that there could be no long runs, and, as a consequence, economic utilization of the machinery was effectively barred.

Sometimes employee resistance to technological changes does not take the particular focus of insisting on the size of crews, but it stems, nevertheless, from a similar objective. Employees tend to think in terms of the "lump of labor" concept of employment—that there is just so much work available and that it has to be conserved by spreading the work out as long as possible. To illustrate: a company introduced high-speed presses as an efficiency measure, only to be faced with a slowdown by the employees on the new presses. The intent, obviously, was to offset any possible layoffs because of time-saving through use of the new machinery.

In this case, the fear of displacement was entirely unwarranted, since there was no threat of any personnel layoff.

The experience at a petroleum refinery, which undertook a thorough modernization of its operations, indicates that in manning changed operations even violent union opposition can be channeled into constructive effort. The refinery management gave the union advance notice of an impending layoff of 200 employees as a result of the new technology. When the union called a strike to protest and forestall the layoff, management stood firm on its decision. The union had to accept the uselessness of the strike route, and after a few days, the strike terminated. Once the atmosphere was less charged with resistance, it was possible to explore means of adjusting to the layoffs. Eventually, the union turned its efforts to cooperating with management in working out a program to help the displaced employees in finding other jobs.

Wage Rates for New or Changed Jobs

The most frequent, though not generally the most serious, bone of contention between labor and management has been that of establishing rates of pay for the new jobs that emerge through technological innovations. Controversy in this area has arisen even in plants where the unions concerned have cooperated well with management in adjusting to new technology. Commonly, unions take the attitude that the introduction of labor-saving machinery should automatically lead to higher rates of pay for operators, regardless of whether actual job requirements have expanded, narrowed, or remained unchanged.

The majority of case-study companies met the problem of pay for new or changed jobs head-on, by evaluating them as fairly as possible, raising rates when job requirements were increased, and refusing to capitulate under union pressure for higher rates when it was clear that rate increases were not justified. Those which achieved a short-term gain in acceding to union demands usually found that surrender to unjustified demands created significantly greater future problems.

Obviously, upgrading of new jobs merely because they are new will produce an imbalance in a plant's entire wage structure. Historical rate differentials within the plant are upset, and management is besieged by complaints from workers in other classifications who claim that their jobs are not properly evaluated relative to the new ones. Usually at this point management recognizes the fallacy of having departed in the face of pressure from the basic principle of setting wage rates according to job evaluation standards. Then it becomes necessary to refuse to revise established rates, so as to prevent an unwarranted spiral of the entire wage structure. Comparative experience among companies shows that taking a belated stand against unjustified rate levels leaves a greater residue of unhappiness among employees than does management's refusal of a demand for elevating rates at the time new jobs are evaluated.

Vacillating on the issue of pricing jobs according to their relative value constitutes a denial by management of its regard for the job evaluation process, and it opens the door for future complaints and demands. Among the companies studied, the prevailing opinion is that a sound course for management is to be as objective and conscientious as possible in pricing new or changed jobs according to accepted job evaluation methods, and to hold firmly to the rate set. But even the wage administrators who set out to follow this course find that the way is not easy, for modern technology has introduced new factors or new combinations of factors in specific jobs, which require delicate weighting in evaluating the jobs. Moreover, modern technology raises basic considerations about responsibility in jobs, a factor which many job evaluators have not yet resolved; where this is so, it may not always be possible to be decisive in evaluating jobs after technological change. Problems of this kind are discussed in Chapter VI, which deals more comprehensively with company experience in adjusting employee compensation to the necessities of new technology.

Seniority Considerations

Of all the matters that induce conflict between labor and management as operations are increasingly mechanized, probably the most troublesome is that of seniority applications. Many managements have found that strict adherence by unions to established seniority rules, of whatever type, complicates the adjustment to new technology. From a company's standpoint, serious problems derive from such considerations as these:

1. The application of seniority to broad units can be both very costly and disruptive of normal work groups because multiple bumping follows automatically upon the upgrading or displacement of an employee.

2. The most senior worker is not necessarily the best equipped to handle certain types of new machinery.

3. When new operations carry higher wage rates and improved working conditions, the most senior workers are likely to bid for them. Assignments to such jobs solely by seniority may leave only inexperienced work groups in the old operations.

4. Where seniority rules are on other than a plant-wide basis, long-service employees may sometimes be denied the right to bump into other jobs, thus they are left jobless while shorter-service employees continue to work.

5. Rigid application of departmental or occupational seniority rules often adds to the difficulties of transferring employees displaced by new machinery to other jobs.

Qualifications Versus Seniority. Typical of the conflict that arises over the staffing of new operations is the experience in a steel mill undergoing some rather extensive adaptations of automation to its operations. The issue is the need to assign workers on the strength of their qualifications, but the current labor contract prescribes seniority as the sole determinant. In other words, automation demands skills and aptitudes that were not required at the time the contract was drawn. Some aspects of the new technology are quite revolutionary, as compared with the former methods of producing steel, and the management is convinced on the basis of its experiences so far that many of the older workers are not qualified to operate the new machinery and never will be able to do so efficiently. Looking to the future, when other operations will be automated, the company is attempting to devise fair and realistic criteria and methods for measuring ability and performance, geared to the requirements of automated operations. It plans to staff the next such operation with the best qualified people, as determined by the selection process being evolved. Although the management anticipates difficulties with the union, it feels that the company's position will be entirely defensible if contested by the union and carried to arbitration.

In practice, companies have more often retreated than advanced along this front. At an electronics plant, for instance, the management originally had freedom to upgrade the most efficient worker, for the contract had stated that promotions would go to the "best qualified" worker with the most seniority. Under union pressure this clause was later amended to read "amply qualified" worker. Now the union is insisting on straight seniority as the governing factor in promotions. Because of the increasing complexity of its automated operations, the company will resist this demand, feeling that it must retain some discretion in judging qualification for promotion, to prevent progressive deterioration of plant efficiency.

Seniority Base. The composition of the seniority unit is often a cause of union-management disagreement. This study confirms the often-made observation that unions will try to widen seniority units, while management will seek to oppose such efforts. Broad seniority units are regarded by companies as detrimental to efficient plant operation because layoffs and transfers under seniority rules disturb the manning of departments that are functioning efficiently. Pressure by unions for broader seniority units is based frequently on the claim that technological change tends to blur departmental lines.[6] The pertinent cases studied indicate that this outcome has been generally more imagined than real, for new technology has very rarely had that result.

There have been cases in which both management and unions reversed their positions—management attempting to broaden seniority against union resistance. Such instances indicate that the attitudes of both parties toward seniority applications are based not upon an inviolate principle but on the pragmatic views of each side in concrete situations. A few examples from company experience will illustrate this point.

In the case of a chemical works, the management sought and secured a widened seniority base, with the precise purpose of protecting the job security of old-timers in the plant workforce. Conversion of the plant, from the manufacture of one product to another, made defunct an entire department which was not needed in making the new product. Because departmental seniority prevailed in the plant, a group of long-service employees was threatened with layoff. In planning for the change, management foresaw this development and wished to protect the jobs of the long-service group—hence, its drive for plant-wide seniority. Although the union resisted at the outset, mainly because of the internal political power wielded by the various departments, it eventually yielded to a revision of the seniority base from an occupational and departmental system to a two-group plant-wide basis, the division being only between production

---

[6] John H. Fanning, "The Challenge of Automation in the Light of the Natural Law," *Labor Law Journal*, Vol. 11, October, 1960, p. 877.

and maintenance jobs. Safeguards against multiple bumping were built into the plant-wide seniority system, by making it possible for a displaced employee to bump only the employee with the least accrued plant seniority in the particular work group. The management gained this concession by stressing the possibility that the plant would undertake manufacture of additional new products which would benefit all departments.

A telling example of the circumstances under which plant-wide seniority becomes onerous for a company was found in a rubber factory. Upon the establishment of a metal products division within the plant, the union insisted that the new division be included in the plant-wide seniority unit. Before long, management faced the problem of an undermining of efficiency in the metal products operation. Employment in the rubber division was subject to greater seasonal and cyclical fluctuations; and, consequently, whenever there was a layoff high-seniority rubber workers automatically displaced metal workers whose seniority standing was lower. Workers from the rubber division were being constantly shifted into and out of the newer metals operation, as production in their own division dropped and rose. With efficiency thus damaged, the situation became untenable. The management then notified the union that it would be forced to move the metal products division to a separate location to escape the effects of the plant-wide seniority application. With this word, the union agreed to separate seniority units for rubber and metal product workers.

Management's objection to very broad seniority units also emanates from its concern over the costliness of the bumping procedure. In most plants, technological innovation usually leads to multiple job moves. And often this chain of personnel adjustments adds considerably to costs, because of the need to train workers up and down the line. Some companies find themselves in a position similar to that of the Pittsburgh Plate Glass Company a few years ago. The long strike against this company in 1958–1959 was due in part to union refusal to relax seniority practices that had become established at its Creighton works. An article on the PPG dispute sums up the problem:

> The unlimited right to take any job held by a less senior man had converted the concept of job security into a special privilege for the most senior workers, irrespective of injury to the company or to less senior employees. This "straight seniority" system was extremely costly to the company because of constant "bumping" and because of management's inability to assign individuals to the work for which they were best suited.[7]

The company found that the practice of "instantaneous" seniority created serious operational problems and high costs. In its experience, the application of plant-wide seniority moved people in and out of jobs so erratically that often a worker's stay on a job was shorter than the period required to complete the training on which he had been started.

Most companies have been careful to avoid being led into such difficulties under the guise of protecting worker security. Some have been able to steer clear of the multiple bumping problem without jeopardizing the job security of long-service employees. At a small machinery manufacturing plant, for instance, a senior worker is protected against layoff resulting from technological change by a form of plant-wide seniority that allows him to displace only the worker with the least service in the plant.

Other companies have attempted to strike a balance between job security for long-service employees and plant operating efficiency. One approach has been to preserve seniority on a departmental or occupational basis, and then make subject to plant-wide seniority certain designated "labor" jobs for which almost all employees can qualify.

[7] Irwin L. Herrnstadt and Benson Soffer, "Recent Labor Disputes Over 'Restrictive' Practices and 'Inflationary' Wage Increases," *The Journal of Business,* Vol. 34, October, 1961, p. 457.

Thus, a displaced employee can be readily transferred to one of these jobs without upsetting the efficiency of plant operations.

In a food-processing plant, employees displaced by automation were given a form of superseniority to bid on new jobs *if they could pass a qualifying test.* Once a man qualified, he had the opportunity to advance up the job ladder without further tests. For the first year he had a "red-circle" rate, whereby his pay was maintained at its former level even if his new job was at a lower grade. At the end of that time, he was paid the job rate.

The 1961 national agreement between the General Motors Corporation and the United Automobile Workers provides for seniority "by noninterchangeable occupational groups within departments, group of departments, or plant-wide, as may be negotiated locally in each plant. . . ." In order to protect high-seniority workers against possible job loss due to change, however, the agreement stipulates that:

> When changes in methods, products or policies would otherwise require the permanent laying off of employees, the seniority of the displaced employees shall become plant-wide and they shall be transferred out of the group in line with their seniority to work they are capable of doing, as comparable to the work they have been doing as may be available, at the rate for the job to which they have been transferred.

PROCEDURES FOR RESOLVING ISSUES

Along with the steady movement in industry toward increased adoption of improved technology, there has been a decline in the use of raw power in labor-management relations when issues arise over adapting to change. It is interesting to consider the areas of conflict in terms of their effect on the union as an institution versus their effect on the membership. In general, the greatest difficulty in dealing with unions is apparently on those issues which touch their established power position. Union leaders respond most aggressively when they fear that their sphere of influence may be weakened. Those who represented employees in the plants studied were more readily constructive when pay-rate adjustments or severance-pay formulas had to be worked out than when jurisdictional issues, for example, were involved. Of course, when the membership brings pressure on union leadership, this becomes a clear threat to the union hierarchy, and the fears of the membership are welded with the threat to the leadership into a powerful force for management to counter.

Typically, the process of reconciling conflict and achieving accommodation is initiated when a management notifies the union, as well as employees, of impending change—an action found common to all of the companies studied. The exact timing of notification to employees and unions of impending change is a pragmatic issue to be decided on the basis of the particular circumstances in each situation. This is well illustrated by the cases of two multiplant companies, where the lead time in communicating change was determined with due regard to the climate of labor-management relations in the respective operations.

One of the companies, a public utility, has both unionized and unorganized establishments. In preparing to introduce technological change at a unionized operation, the management notified employees and their union long in advance, regarding it as advantageous to work out the details of the necessary adjustments with the union. In introducing change in another operation, the notification period was shortened, for two reasons: (1) the operation was not unionized, and, therefore, an allowance of time for two-party collaboration was unnecessary, and (2) shortening the notification period to the necessary minimum would reduce the likelihood of unionization activity before the possible disruptions of change could be ironed out satisfactorily.

A transportation equipment company, all of whose plants are organized, varies the lead time in its notification of change according to expected differences in the reaction of union locals. Where local union leaders have been cooperative, long advance notice is given. But where others have demonstrated a proneness to resist change, the notification period is shortened, so as to forestall any concerted efforts to deter the introduction of new technology.

Usually, however, the resolution of issues flows from having established a nonthreatening climate in dealing with employees and their unions, with the result that accommodation on both sides has become the most general course. Unions accommodate themselves to the realities of technological change, even when there is job displacement, and seek various compensatory measures. Managements accommodate themselves to the realities of union power, and work out with union representatives procedures for easing the worker's adjustment to change.

Consultation

The experience of a food-processing plant indicates that open discussion of the problems attendant on the adoption of new manufacturing processes can lead to realistic decisions. It has been the policy of this plant, as soon as decision to introduce any new technology is made and its consequences evaluated, to inform the union business agent and shop stewards of the decision and to invite them to cooperate in effectuating the inescapable adjustments. The management has built a reputation of discussing frankly with the union the impact of technological and other changes, and this approach has given the union confidence in management's good faith. In one instance, this constructive relationship paid off in collective bargaining negotiations when the plant could not afford a wage increase in line with that of the wage pattern-setting company in the community. The latter company had made a very high wage settlement in exchange for union acceptance of automation. When the management of the food-processing plant presented the facts honestly, the union permitted the breaking of the pattern by accepting a smaller increase.

In only one company, another food processor, was it found that mandatory consultation with the union was demanded, and that the management had acceded. Under the terms of the labor contract, management is obligated to notify the union "as soon as possible" after reaching a decision to install labor-saving automated equipment. Both parties aim for a target date of one year in advance of installation, but this is not always achievable.

The notification and consultation procedure in this company works in the following manner. First, the personnel department arranges a meeting with the local union committee, at which an engineering representative explains the new technology in laymen's terms, and with models, including its purpose, principles, and the contemplated methods of operation. Management then provides the union with its tentative plan for staffing the changed department or process and with a list of the employees affected. Since selection of employees for new jobs includes qualifying tests, the union may, if it so wishes, be a party to the administration of the testing program. Throughout this procedure, the union may make suggestions, but acceptance or rejection of the suggestions remains solely a management decision. The program has been in effect for only a short period, but the early experience with the consultative process has been most satisfactory.

The management of a 200-man machinery plant—organized by the craft union that is dominant in the industry which uses the machinery—holds that it could not have carried out its program of plant modernization without the cooperation of the union, as achieved through consultation. Before attempting to introduce the new equipment and methods of operation, representatives of the company's industrial relations department met with the union business agent who serviced that plant (the local union was too small to have full-time officers). The business agent was informed of the proposed changes, their urgency, and the possible consequences of delaying them. The industrial relations men convinced him of the soundness of the undertaking and, with him, formulated a program of adjustment. They also jointly and successfully impressed on the plant employees the need for the change, with assurances that the employees' interests would be protected.

Joint Committees

The practice of giving advance notice of impending change sometimes leads to the setting up of *ad hoc* labor-management committees to handle anticipated or actual adjustment problems. When the management of a transportation equipment plant prepared to introduce the type of new technology that has become known as "Detroit automation," it invited the local union to help in working out the details of the people-adjustment program. In the interest of protecting its members and improving labor-management relations, the local union, a militant affiliate of an equally militant national industrial union, cooperated.

Joint committees met daily during the transition period to hammer out a program of mutual benefit. The management members of the committee acceded to union requests for special protection of workers against downgrading and for extension of learning periods for new jobs. In exchange, by furnishing proof and explanations of the necessity for changes, they gained local union consent to relaxation of certain provisions of the national labor contract that restricted the ability of plant management to effectuate the change-over to a new method of operation. The transition meant that production lines using both the old and new technology had to be operated simultaneously, and it was necessary to have experienced personnel in both places. Rigid adherence to the seniority provisions of the contract with respect to new jobs would have prevented this advantageous use of personnel, and would have severely hampered the break-in of the equipment. But the union was willing to work out the necessary deviations from the normal seniority pattern.

Establishment of a joint committee also proved to be the best means of solving an issue over seniority in a machinery plant. To facilitate technological change, the management sought relaxation of rigid seniority rules on a *quid pro quo* basis. Automation aroused union fears that the number of particular types of jobs would be severely curtailed, and that the employees affected would lack sufficient protection because seniority was occupational. Management, on its part, needed assurances that certain types of skills would be available to handle new technology, regardless of seniority. In order that the mutual interests of both sides would be served, management agreed to substitute plant-wide seniority for occupational seniority, specifically "to protect the jobs of employees who might otherwise be displaced." At the same time, it secured union agreement to the establishment of a joint union-management committee empowered to determine special-skill occupations that would be exempt from seniority rules and thus insure efficient operation of the plant.

Grievance Machinery and Arbitration

Some problems of technological change involve application or interpretation of an existing labor agreement and cannot be solved through consultation. Then the union's resort is to the grievance procedure and, ultimately, to arbitration. This study found that very few disputes relating to technological innovation have actually been arbitrated. It was apparent that neither management nor unions have wished to tolerate the delay entailed in resolution of issues by that route. Generally, only disputes over rates for new jobs have gone all the way to arbitration. Even so, it was found in some situations that after one or two experiences with arbitrators, the parties settled cases of rate assignment between themselves.

There are types of grievances, generally involving the question of management rights, which companies are reluctant to carry to arbitration lest the arbitrator's awards set undesirable precedents. This aversion to arbitration has stemmed from the experience of some companies with arbitrators who avoid settling a case on its own merits. These arbitrators take the easier road of "splitting the difference" between the parties concerned, or render awards that hamper management in modernizing work practices. Too often, arbitrators have gone beyond contract interpretation relative to technological change and have initiated what they believed to be solutions to problems in areas in which the collective agreement was silent. Managements are particularly concerned about such attempts to use the arbitration process of a grievance procedure to rewrite agreements regardless of the wishes or intentions of the parties.

Companies also see a risk in having to abide by the off-hand judgment, on an operating matter, of an outsider who may not be aware of the full consequences of his decision. Thus, even after a grievance has been certified for arbitration of such issues as proper crew size, and the like, managements still hope and prefer to work it out with the union on the shop floor, if this can be done without creating other problems.

Supplementary Agreements

Adjustments incidental to technological change often raise issues that are not covered by the existing collective bargaining agreement, or which call for solutions that contravene its terms. In these circumstances, companies have most often followed the path of negotiating a supplementary agreement between plant management and the local union. Where a plant is part of a company-wide bargaining unit, and technological innovation is very broad in scope, preliminary discussion of proposed adjustments usually takes place at the higher level—between the corporate industrial relations staff and the national union leadership.

Whether to initiate discussion with the union at the local or at the national level has been decided by management on a pragmatic basis. If the local union is cooperative, management prefers to deal with the local leaders, since they are directly involved in the implementation of decisions. Where a local union is obstreperous, management considers it wiser first to consult with the national headquarters of the union and leave it to the national officers to force local compliance with decisions reached at the top level. On the other hand, there are times when local officers, although willing to cooperate, are reluctant to do so because of their concern with local internal relationships. Then they may subtly encourage management first to pursue discussions with the national union, to avoid compromising the situation of local leadership if the resulting agreement proves unpopular with the membership. While this may not be a very forthright approach, it is understandable since unions are political institutions and management has to deal with them on that basis.

In plants where advanced technology introduces jobs requiring new skills, the traditional seniority rules often become unendurably restrictive for effective manning of the new jobs. In such situations, special supplementary agreements are negotiated at the local level to relax existing contract terms or otherwise accommodate the new technology. Illustrative of the way in which this form of accommodation takes place is the experience at a plant manufacturing automation equipment, where seniority had been applied on a plant-wide, occupational basis. New techniques for the wiring of electronic control panels threatened to wipe out a number of plant wirer jobs. Normally, this would not have been a problem, as displaced workers would simply have pre-empted other jobs in their occupational category held by employees of lesser seniority elsewhere in the plant. In this case, however, there were no similar jobs to which the surplus wirers could be transferred. With the resultant threat of layoff of long-service employees in upper job grades, the union began to pressure management to widen the seniority unit, but this would only have intensified the management's problem of manning the factory efficiently.

Discussion between management and union representatives of the problems on both sides led to the mutually acceptable solution of providing for a retraining program that would enable the displaced wirers to qualify for other types of jobs in the plant. The retraining procedure was formalized in a plant supplementary agreement, designed, however, to protect only long-service employees in high job grades who were displaced by technological change, and for whom there were no comparable jobs to which their occupational experience would entitle them. The agreement gave such employees an opportunity to train for better jobs as they became available. With these exceptions, seniority remained the standard whereby displaced workers might qualify for training to fill jobs in any occupational category.

This problem of conflict between seniority applications and the need for special skills on new technology differs among companies both in degree and in the solutions. In a food-processing plant, the management and union resolved the problem by the simple expedient of agreeing to disregard the plant-wide seniority clause whenever necessary to retain the services of people with specialized training, even though low in seniority.

When an obsolete plant in metal trades manufacturing was closed, the negotiation of a series of special supplementary agreements was of paramount significance in formulating a program to ease the impact on employees. These agreements derived from continuous discussions with the union. The major agreement covering the closing of the plant provided a special seniority placement application procedure, which guaranteed that first consideration would be given to the displaced workers for all new jobs at other plants of the parent company. It was also agreed that a displaced employee, when hired by another plant of the company where employees were represented by the union to which he belonged, would be treated as a transferred employee for all purposes *except seniority*. Furthermore, employees were permitted, if necessary to accept other employment, to quit voluntarily before the scheduled termination date without sacrificing their rights to separation pay.

Numerous other special supplementary agreements were negotiated for this plant. One made it easier for employees to qualify for early retirement benefits. Another provided special arrangements with respect to supplementary unemployment benefits, making additional funds available sooner to displaced employees. A third froze wage rates for computation of separation pay at the levels prevailing immediately before the start of the shutdown, in order to protect employees against any downgrading that might occur as a result of staggered layoffs. In addition, the management cooperated with the union, the state employment service, and the company's other plants in the area in an attempt to place surplus employees promptly.

In a few situations both the management and the union regard the labor contract as sacrosanct. They shun the negotiation of supplementary agreements as a medium for resolving the special problems of technological change; and they do not reopen any area of agreement during the life of an existing contract. For them, the simplest solution is to postpone dealing with the problems that develop until the negotiation of the next contract. This was the situation at a machinery plant where departmental seniority practices posed problems with the introduction of new technology. The seniority rules of the contract were rigidly adhered to, even though discontinuance of a malleable iron operation resulted in the layoff of men with up to 35 years of service, while newcomers in other departments continued to hold jobs.

It was not until the next negotiations that the union and the management sought to remedy the situation. The new contract retained departmental seniority as the general rule, but provided the needed flexibility by designating 18 types of "labor" jobs as being subject to plant-wide seniority. This solution proved to be too expensive, however, as subsequent experience showed that some of the jobs required qualifications which not all employees in the categories could meet. Upon normal contract reopening two years later, the number of jobs subject to plant-wide seniority was reduced to nine.

Deferring resolution of the immediate problems of change until negotiation of the next contract is, unfortunately, not always the best course, for some problems do not lend themselves to postponement without damage to either company or employee interests, or both. And yet, broader collective bargaining considerations also sometimes deter managements from taking needed action in time to accommodate to the changed circumstances. This was true of a company in which there had never been layoffs and, therefore, no contractual provisions for severance pay.

Looking forward to the introduction of new technology, the management had foreseen the possibility of layoffs and wished to aid the employees who would be displaced. But it faced a dilemma. If the management unilaterally instituted termination benefits during the life of the existing agreement, the union could charge the company with an unfair labor practice. If it initiated discussions with the union to establish a system of severance pay under the contract, it might set a dangerous precedent; the implication would be that negotiations can take place during the life of an agreement, whenever either of the parties becomes dissatisfied with any of the contract terms. The company's way out of this dilemma was to intensify its efforts to prevent layoffs. Through careful advance manpower planning and the offer of jobs at other company facilities to displaced employees, it was possible to achieve adoption of the new technology without layoffs.

That there are dangers in reopening agreements is undeniable, for experience has shown that unions do take advantage of a contract reopening to press issues that have nothing to do with the problem at hand. As in the case just cited, and in others, overall bargaining considerations sometimes interfere with what management sees as the most realistic way of protecting both employee and employer interests in adjusting to technological change. On the other hand, internal politics in a union situation can subvert reasonable attention to the welfare of employees affected by new technology.

Illustrative of the latter point is the experience in a machinery manufacturing plant. In this case, too, there had been no previous severance pay arrangements, but the company expressed its willingness to reopen the agreement to negotiate such benefits in the face of technological dislocations. During the negotiations, the union would not agree to a proposal that the retirement clause be reworded so as to prevent retirees from becoming eligible for both severance pay and pensions. Without this change, severance pay would have become a grab bag for the older employees rather than a source of benefit to those for whom it was intended—the employees who faced technological displacement.

It was clear that in this case the union catered to the special interests of the more powerful segment of the employee group, to the detriment of the other. The leadership refused to agree to a ban on the dual collection of severance and retirement benefits; the severance pay negotiations collapsed; and the contemplated plans for displaced employees did not materialize at that time. Thus the plight of individual workers who are adversely affected by technological change may be ignored because of the weight given by either a union or a management to securing its institutional goals. Fortunately, however, this was rarely the case.

COLLECTIVE BARGAINING EXPERIENCE

Technological change has obviously had a great impact on many facets of industrial relations. Yet its effect on the content of collective bargaining has been modest, being found mainly in an expansion of emphasis from wage demands alone toward the provision of new and liberalized benefits when jobs are threatened by new technology. This greater interest in employment security extends, however, into such other related areas as seniority procedures, job classification and evaluation, and wage structures. There has also been some novel experimentation with provisions for interplant transfers, protection of employees against downgrading of rates, and retraining, as well as the incorporation of specific "automation" clauses into a few labor contracts.

Many prognosticators have tried to anticipate the impact of change on labor-management relations, and they have been borne out on some issues but not on others. Aronson predicted that with automation would come demands for a broadening of the coverage of bargaining units,[8] but this has not been the experience of the companies studied. There were cases, as already cited, in which unions claimed that certain work being done by nonbargaining-unit personnel properly belonged to their members. But in few instances did a union contend that other personnel belonged in its jurisdiction; nor were there serious attempts to organize beyond established units.

Aronson thought also that unions would be forced to re-examine their policies with respect to occupational wage

8 Robert L. Aronson, "Automation—Challenge to Collective Bargaining?" in *New Dimensions in Collective Bargaining,* Industrial Relations Research Association Publication No. 21 (New York: Harper & Brothers, 1959), p. 58.

differentials, in order to stimulate worker interest in up-grading themselves into the ranks of skilled craftsmen.[9] This, too, has not materialized. On the contrary, if there has been any trend, it has been toward setting up restrictions to prevent machine operators from becoming craftsmen. In one of the companies studied, for example, an industrial union negotiated a change in the labor contract to specify that workers in production operations could not transfer to maintenance jobs unless they already had craft experience or had completed training in an authentic, approved, apprenticeship program. The point of this demand was that the union sought to still the fears of craftsmen within its ranks over possible dilution of skills. Although the management questioned the wisdom of the union's move, it was not seriously inclined to resist the demand.

Furthermore, this study has revealed no evidence that unions are re-evaluating their occupational wage differential policies; actually, industrial unions continue to favor a narrowing of differentials. Where they have succeeded in winning special increases for skilled workers, the concern of union leadership has been not with reappraising union policy in relation to new technology, but rather with satisfying craftsmen and thus preventing growth of splinter groups.

It is also noteworthy that no examples were found of union demands for the preferential hiring of displaced workers for technical jobs outside the bargaining unit. This is interesting, in view of a request by Walter Reuther to 20 companies with which the United Automobile Workers bargains. Reuther asked that displaced blue-collar workers be given first crack at available white-collar jobs, as one means of reducing dislocations stemming from technological and economic change.[10] Actually what he proposed has already been taking place in many companies, but on management initiative alone, not in response to union pressure. In numer-

[9] *Ibid.*, pp. 58–59.
[10] *New York Times*, March 25, 1962, p. 1, Col. 2 and 3, p. 46, Col. 4.

ous companies, former production workers are now filling white-collar and supervisory positions.

Many unions have talked about the need to negotiate special "automation clauses," in order to meet the challenge of technological change, but at the bargaining table they have been hard-pressed to specify what such clauses would say. A public utility was confronted in negotiations with just such a demand, but the union was unable to define "automation" and had no specific ideas as to what it wanted, other than to secure protection of existing jobs and rates. The proposal for an automation clause was eventually withdrawn, but the company anticipates a renewal of this demand, because of the existence of an undefined fear of "automation" among workers, provoked by the nation's press.

In the main, so-called automation clauses appear to be nothing more than promises by management to try to ease the burden of new technology on workers, a policy which most companies follow without contractual obligation. An example of this type of clause was found in the contract of another public utility. The job security clause simply re-affirms management's policy of effecting change without lay-off, to the extent possible.

Among the companies studied, there are only two instances, both in nondurable goods manufacturing, in which special automation clauses negotiated into the agreements encompass something specific, rather than vague intentions. In one case, the clause was inserted in the article governing the establishment of base and hourly rates of pay. It reads:

> It is not the intent of the Company to apply the provisions of this Section to new jobs resulting from automation without consideration of the earnings levels of the jobs eliminated by such automation.

The effect of this commitment is that the company cannot reduce the job rate, even when a new machine so simplifies the content of the job as to place it at a lower grade.

In the second case referred to, a special automation article of the labor contract binds management to give the union notice, as soon as possible, of proposed installations of automation that would entail a decrease in the employee force. It also obligates management to furnish the union with a tentative proposal for staffing the changed operation, as well as a list of the employees affected. Workers in departments affected by automation are given the first opportunity to bid on new jobs, provided they pass a qualifying test of general intelligence. Those with three or more years of seniority who do not qualify for automated jobs are given preference, on the basis of their seniority, for other job openings in the plant for which they are qualified. The wages of transferees are "red-circled" for a year; that is, their pay stays at former levels even if their new jobs are at lower ones.

From the findings of this study, it may be said that technological innovation has brought no revolutionary changes in the process or results of collective bargaining, and, indeed, none appear necessary. Apparently, the inclusion in contracts of automation clauses, as such, has not been universally demanded by unions. And where such clauses do exist, their terms, in most cases, are but a generalized expression of company policy. The more common approaches to cushioning the impact of change on workers are toward working out, at the plant level, adjustments to specific problems, liberalizing benefits, and developing special programs. Some of these programs have already been reviewed, and others will be discussed in later sections.

SOME RELATED OBSERVATIONS

As publicity is given to the dramatic instances of union resistance to technological innovation, there is a tendency to conclude that such resistance is widespread and acute. Experience in the segment of industry covered by this study gives scant support to this idea. The fact is that technological progress has been taking place constantly, and with overt employee or union resistance to the change itself arising only in isolated cases. Several factors account for this greater repetitiveness of change without, rather than with, extreme conflict:

1. For whatever reason—the desire to do the right thing or to gain acceptance of change, or both—management policy in effecting changes has been one of playing squarely with employees and their bargaining agents. Companies, and unions also, are sensitive to public opinion and about the image they project in the community—hence, their careful attention to public relations in handling matters connected with technological innovation.

2. Unions in general have recognized the futility of resisting progress, and the majority of employers have refrained from dictatorial approaches when contemplating the introduction of new technology. Both sides usually have sensed that antagonistic attitudes simply will not work with respect to technological change, for they are not conducive to constructive adjustments in employee relations matters.

3. There has been a maturation in the relations between labor and management; solutions to problems have been found when the approaches taken were reasonable and the rights and positions of both sides were mutually recognized. Furthermore, bargaining power in most situations is too evenly matched for either party to be able arbitrarily to dictate terms and conditions to the other.

Overt resistance to change has been blunted, moreover, by the play of economic forces on the situation of a company or industry. Strikes, slowdowns, loading of the grievance procedure, and adherence to outmoded job classifications have often delayed the most efficient and economical use of new technology. But the economics of the market has inexorably forced accommodation to reality. Where successful and prolonged efforts on the part of employees and unions have blocked new methods of operation, in the hope of preserving jobs, they have always been self-defeating. The result has usually been the company's loss of markets to competitors offering lower-priced products. And then jobs have disappeared even faster than if the effect of innovations had been allowed to run its course.

It may be said, therefore, that although labor-management relations in a period of technological change have not been characterized by sweetness and light, and there have been major areas of conflict, they have reached a new level of maturity. Considering the differences in outlook between unions and management, the extent of accommodation that has been achieved through the process of collective bargaining is remarkable. In this regard, the approach of unions has been described by one observer as "the union's three-stage collective bargaining defense against automation":

> Stage one is implemented by the negotiation of provisions designed to maintain existing jobholders in their jobs at existing levels of earnings. The second line of defense represents a recognition on the union's part that jobs and earnings attrition can no longer be resisted in *toto* and that the union position must shift toward transitional measures "to cushion the shock of displacement." The third line of defense (perhaps coexisting with stage two) is the assertion of the claim that the loss of jobs and job perquisites should be compensated by a financial settlement, in return for which the employer is permitted greater freedom for maneuver.[11]

To the degree that companies have been able to afford it, they have, in the main, accommodated themselves to stages two and three of this union strategy, just as the unions have accommodated themselves to new technology. The unions have been able to lay the basis for sympathetic and cooperative dealing on the part of the management when they have ceased to direct their efforts to obstructing the installation of new machinery and have centered instead on

---

[11] Jack Barbash, "Union Response to the 'Hard Line,'" *Industrial Relations*, Vol. 1, October, 1961, p. 27.

assuring that such changes would be accomplished with minimal disruptions and separations and with provision of compensatory income to employees displaced by technological innovation. In some cases, the mutual regard of union and management for the problems of each other entirely precluded arbitrary resistance and lasting conflict over change. The unions have cooperated with plant management in working out programs to ease the transition period, in the interests of both getting the new equipment operating efficiently and protecting employees against adverse effects.

It cannot be said, of course, that unions welcome new technology and do nothing to hinder management's efforts to increase operating efficiency. But the findings of this study indicate that instances of overt resistance from unions were isolated and sporadic, and had no aspect of calculated, preconceived campaigns to thwart management efforts to improve plant efficiency. Apparently, the employees and unions concerned were sophisticated enough to recognize that the continued existence of jobs depended upon the ability of their employers to remain competitive, which, in turn, required the introduction of the latest methods of production.

It is perhaps a symbol of the quality of labor relations in the companies studied that the accommodations between labor and management with respect to technological change were achieved through the normal processes of collective bargaining. Typically, these accommodations grew out of healthy labor and management attitudes toward their problems. But it must be pointed out that companies cooperating in this study were not burdened by the fetters of overly onerous lines of craft demarcation and union concepts of workload limitations, as are characteristic of the construction and transportation industries, for example. Though this study embraced only one company in those industries, its overall finding relative to union-management adaptations to change is clear. The necessity to take aggressive and timely action consistent with current economic pressures exerts the greatest influence on the parties to achieve reasonable solutions to the attendant problems without costly strikes.

Extraordinary difficulties can arise, of course, when a management inherits a situation in which union pressure has traditionally led to company concessions that have been damaging to efficiency in running the business. In at least two situations studied, this was the case. In both, before operations could be geared for the new technology, the managements had to face up first to the necessity of regaining their control over certain operational matters. Upon attempting to do so, they were forced to take strikes over unreasonable union demands. Once the unions realized that even in the face of a strike the managements were determined to be firm in not acceding to the unreasonable demands, they were far more willing to find reasonable solutions to the dislocations arising out of technological change.

The general experience seems to contradict even the view that adjustment to technological change is so difficult as to require the development of some form of trilateral collective bargaining.[12] In only one company were public representatives drawn into labor-management deliberations on the adjustments to be made. And there, the inclusion of these neutrals did not materially contribute to a solution of the problems encountered with automation, though their participation did reduce union-management tensions. There is, further, no indication from the experience of the companies studied that there is any widespread need for special industry or company-wide joint study committees to deal with the dislocations brought about by automation. On the other hand, some of the companies that participated in *ad hoc* joint committees at the plant level found them useful in formulating solutions to *specific problems*.

In certain situations, of course, company-wide bilateral

[12] See, for example, George H. Hildebrand, "The Use of Tripartite Bodies to Supplement Collective Bargaining," *Proceedings of the 1961 Spring Meeting,* Industrial Relations Research Association, pp. 655–663.

study committees can be most helpful in dealing with problems of adjustment to technological change. This is attested to in the reports of progress that emanated from the Human Relations Committee operating in the steel industry, and in the resulting 1963 collective bargaining agreement, as well as by the successful Pacific longshore experience. It should be noted, moreover, that the new approach developed in the longshore industry did not originate with formal demands served by one party on the other during contract negotiations, but stemmed from discussions and negotiations over a period of years.[13]

The use of third-party neutrals and of joint labor-management study committees may represent a useful form of accommodation by the parties to a particular problem or set of problems. But the success of either device as an aid in reaching viable solutions will rest upon the quality of relationships that has developed between the parties over the years.

The finding of this study that new technology has scarcely altered the traditional course of collective bargaining serves to contradict the oft-made assertions that the bargaining process would have to undergo fundamental change upon the rise and spread of automation. That the experience belies the prophecies should not be surprising, however. Automation, it must be remembered, is only the latest phase of the continual process of technological change that has characterized most American industries, and to which unions and managements have grown accustomed.

Although collective bargaining has proved quite successful as a means of adapting to technological change, it obviously cannot handle all aspects of the accompanying adjustments. The scope of some of the attendant problems goes well beyond the confines of any plant, company, or industry,

13 Charles C. Killingsworth, "The Modernization of West Coast Longshore Rules," *Industrial and Labor Relations Review,* Vol. 15, April, 1962, p. 299.

and involves action on a national basis, through government effort. Thus, industrial and labor-force restructuring has led to passage of the Area Redevelopment and Manpower Development and Training Acts within the past few years. Since this study is concerned with the impact of change only at the plant level in companies, it makes no analysis of the government role, except where our findings hold pertinent implications.

GUIDES PROVIDED BY COMPANY EXPERIENCE

The experience of the companies studied in introducing new technology, and in resolving the resulting labor-management conflict, provides lessons which others may find valuable. There are, however, no direct guides for universal application; the points enumerated below are meant to suggest areas for consideration when change in technology is contemplated.

1. The first and most important step is to give advance notice to employees and their bargaining representatives of impending change. Through advance notice management gives recognition to employee anxiety over any innovation and also brings about employee understanding of the reasons for the change. Frequently, notice is also followed by an invitation to the unions to assist in working out the necessary adjustments.

2. It is best to keep discussions with the union informal and to avoid any semblance of bargaining, for two obvious reasons: (a) decision-making with respect to technological change is a management responsibility that cannot be shared or surrendered without loss of control of operations; and (b) there may very well be occasions on which management, for technical and other reasons, will wish only to inform, not to consult.

3. Never should the informational nature of management contacts with a union be allowed to carry any inference

of seeking union permission to adopt new methods. In practice, consultation has meant that management notifies the union of firm decisions and solicits its cooperation in achieving a smooth adjustment to whatever changes are entailed.

4. It is only good sense to recognize that union cooperation may be essential to the accomplishment of improved efficiency through new technology, particularly in small companies bargaining with powerful locals of national unions.

5. Where *ad hoc* labor-management committees are established to deal with adjustments to technological change, their activities must focus exclusively on the specific problems involved, to keep them from attempting to deal with the whole gamut of labor relations matters.

6. In some situations, it may be easier to gain the cooperation of national rather than local union leadership. This is so because the national leaders are usually more aware of the economic considerations that move a company to introduce new technology. Moreover, they are able to view the problems in true perspective because they are not in direct contact with individual employees who are laid off, transferred, downgraded, shifted from day to night work, or affected adversely in any other way. They may be in a position, therefore, to consider what is best for the most in the union membership. Local leaders are in the unenviable position of having to face daily the concrete human problems arising from change and the resulting unhappiness of the employees. Having to cope with the "beefs" of individuals, the shop steward or other local union officer sees the problems in a narrower light.

Being a step removed from the scene of conflict, a corporate industrial relations department and the national leadership of the union may be better able to erect a framework in which cooperation can take place; then each party can use its influence with its subordinates at the plant level to effectuate the details of the program agreed upon.

7. In other instances, however, plant management can

play a successful role in gaining the cooperation of a local union while introducing change, based on the recognition that give-and-take by both sides is a necessary ingredient of such cooperation. The achievement of cooperative endeavor at the plant level is, moreover, particularly desirable because it enables experimentation with new programs designed for adjustment to change. This approach is not generally favored by national union leaders and company executives, however, for fear of establishing precedents or sacrificing "principles."

8. Joint union-management efforts can be most valuable where widespread dislocation is involved, as with the discontinuance of a whole department or the closing down of an obsolete plant.

9. At the time a collective bargaining agreement is reached, particularly if it is of long duration, all future developments cannot be foreseen and taken into account. Technological change, therefore, may bring to the fore new issues that require immediate resolution. Experience has shown, from both the management and the union standpoint, that in these circumstances there are only two recourses: a reopening of the contract or the signing at the plant level of a local supplementary agreement to the national contract. However, there are hazards involved. With respect to contract reopening, a union may use the occasion to press for unrelated concessions which it could not obtain at regular negotiations, but a company can avert this by maintaining a firm position.

In the case of supplementary agreements, unrestricted independent action by plant management can bring about an erosion of the company's position at the plant; the safeguard here is to keep the development of such agreements under the scrutiny of corporate management.

10. Extensive use of arbitration does not appear to be the best means of solving the day-to-day problems of adjustment to technological change, for several reasons. First, there is the inherent danger that an arbitrator may go beyond the

confines of the existing collective bargaining agreement and create new contract terms. Second, being unfamiliar with the technical complications of new machinery, the arbitrator may render decisions having ramifications that serve to hamper efficient operations. Third, habitual reliance on a third party for solution of problems chokes off the efforts that labor and management themselves should make to work out the necessary accommodations to technological change.

11. Underlying all that has been accomplished in smoothing the way for technological innovation is the success of advance notice and discussions with the union of the attendant problems. Such discussions can lead to the development of mutual trust, which creates an atmosphere in which the parties solve problems as they arise and, in most cases, in the best interest of the health of the enterprise and the well-being of its employees.

CHAPTER V

Training and New Technology

Many early observers held that automation and other technological innovations of this decade would lead to unprecedented workforce dislocations. They foresaw the emergence of a whole range of entirely new skills which would disqualify large numbers of employed workers. There seemed to be the further presumptions that job requirements would be so highly advanced that on-the-job training could not produce the needed skills, that the new jobs would go to fresh ranks of specially trained technicians, and that displaced workers would have to be retrained en masse to qualify for re-employment. The concept that retraining of workers on a mass basis would be needed was based on the a priori reasoning that automation would lead to a wholesale upgrading of skill requirements.[1]

Each of these assumptions contained a grain of fact, but as a broad premise each has been refuted by experience.

[1] See, for example, Peter F. Drucker, "Integration of People and Planning," *Harvard Business Review*, Vol. 33, November–December 1955, p. 38.

Today, most observers have come to see training as having a more selective and specialized role, still highly important, in easing the impact of technological change on employees. General retraining programs have been launched, however, under the federal Area Redevelopment Act of 1961, and broadened in coverage by the Manpower Development and Training Act of 1962. Various state governments and local communities have also undertaken independent programs.

The hazard of setting up broad training programs unrelated to specific needs is that in the end there may be quite a disparity between the kinds and quantity of available skills and the needs of industry—at the plant level, at given locations, and at given times.

Another difficulty is that there are always ideas on the drawing boards of engineers which will alter skill requirements in the future. According to an industrial engineer, ". . . automation is evolving, and . . . even those skills presently identified as necessary for automation are only transitional."[2]

In all likelihood, these considerations have caused both management and union representatives to be often unenthusiastic about massive retraining programs. It would be unfortunate indeed if a hard and fast division of views were to develop in our society with respect to the value of training as a medium for developing the talents now needed for jobs in industry. Some flexibility in attitudes is imperative, for it is only on the basis of a body of accumulated experience, and through cooperative efforts of labor, management, government and educators, that training concepts can evolve and be developed to meet the precise requirement of a changing employment situation.

An example of the problems encountered in company training efforts was that of Armour and Company, following

2 Louis E. Davis, "The Effects of Automation on Job Design," *Industrial Relations*, Vol. 2, October, 1962, p. 55.

the 1960 shutdown of its Oklahoma City operations.[3] The Automation Committee, provided for under the company's 1959 union agreements, prepared a program, in cooperation with the Oklahoma State Employment Service, to enable displaced employees to acquire training for other types of jobs. Of 431 former Armour employees, only 170 completed the necessary tests and counseling. Of these, only 60 qualified for some form of vocational training, and only 58 of them actually enrolled for training. Since this was a period of rising unemployment in the area, a mere 7 were able to find work in their new skills.[4]

With respect to the experience of companies in this study, there are several general observations regarding the impact of technological change on training needs and dislocations. In the first place, the contractual protection afforded industrial workers provides safeguards against job loss by arbitrary or indefensible employer action. Moreover, industry needs the experience, aptitudes, and demonstrated adaptability of the large body of its already seasoned workers. In our dynamic American economy, facing up to innovation has long been a way of life, and skill requirements have continually changed, over time, in conformance with changed industrial techniques. Also, the general level of education has been rising over the decades, and the majority of workers

[3] The Automation Committee of Armour and Company and the United Packinghouse Food and Allied Workers AFL-CIO and the Amalgamated Meat Cutters and Butcher Workmen of North America AFL-CIO (Chicago), *Progress Report*, 1961, 29 pp.

[4] A later progress report of the Armour Automation Committee recounted job retraining experience following the closing of Armour's Fort Worth, Texas, plant in 1962, which was much more favorable than that at Oklahoma City. Of the 117 displaced employees who completed retraining courses, 91 (77.5 percent) found new jobs, though, for many, at considerably lower earnings than their former jobs. Most important, the relative employment experience was decidedly better for the retrainees than for those displaced workers who were not retrained. According to the Fort Worth results, it appears feasible to retrain displaced workers who have limited educational and occupational backgrounds. For more details on this report, see "The Fort Worth Project of the Armour Automation Committee," *Monthly Labor Review*, Vol. 87, January, 1964, pp. 52–57.

today are quite well equipped, by their educational achievement and training during military service, as well as by past employment experience, to meet a wide range of new job requirements within a reasonable period of preparation.

Industry has already had almost a decade of experience with "automation," and the findings that have resulted with respect to training needs and how they have been met are suggestive of the actual problems to be dealt with. There are but little grounds for the concept that the technical skills needed are beyond the capacity of most experienced industrial workers and craftsmen to learn. The propensity for learning and for being adaptable to change is, however, quite another matter. On this score, it appears that ability to adjust is undoubtedly greater among younger employees than among the older group. But seniority applications protect the latter; and where they have had the inclination and perseverance to adapt themselves, they have adjusted.

All of this is not to say that companies have had no problems in manning changed operations, for they have had to balance their obligations to employees against their responsibility for maintaining operational efficiency. Many interrelated factors have impinged on the development and supply of needed talents and skills, and often on the proper placement of employees in the new operations. In this chapter, an attempt is made to clarify these problems, as indicated by the experience of the companies studied. The discussion treats the skill levels required by new technology as related to utilization of the normal workforce of companies, and specific cases are cited to illustrate the retraining and training procedures companies have followed and the problems they have encountered.

SKILL LEVEL OF NEW JOBS

The evidence from this study indicates that the worker skills demanded by advanced technological change are not fundamentally different from former job demands and that they are, therefore, well within the learning capacity of the majority of the regular workforce of a company. Although modern technology has sometimes led to a reshuffling of skill requirements, the rise of some new skills, and a drop in the need for others, these necessities have not precluded the upgrading of workers through on-the-job training. To the contrary, both management and unions have striven to protect the jobs of employees in the face of new technology. The compromises made on both sides to accommodate employee training in the operation of newer and more complicated machinery have helped maintain job security.

The new jobs do, however, require new combinations of skills. Employees must adapt to the new bundle of job requirements, even though they remain at a comparable skill level. In the main, production workers have been found to be adaptable to the changed requirements.

Earlier investigators reached conclusions similar to those of this study, and their analyses are noteworthy in the light of subsequent experience. As early as 1958, Bright concluded that automatic machinery does not result in higher workforce skills.[5] Although Davis cautioned about the evolutionary nature of modern technology, he also commented: "Indications so far are that the levels required for semiskilled, mass-production jobs will be suitable for operators of automated equipment."[6] In relating automation to skill requirements, Crossman[7] pointed out that automation demands a shift in emphasis from manual skills to the ability to absorb, organize, and interpret information. He distinguished three types of automation, and these differentiations are useful for discussion of the present study's findings:

5 James R. Bright, "Does Automation Raise Skill Requirements?" *Harvard Business Review*, Vol. 36, July–August 1958, p. 85.

6 Davis, *op. cit.*, p. 68.

7 E. R. F. W. Crossman, *Automation and Skill*, Problems of Progress in Industry, No. 9 (London: Her Majesty's Stationery Office, 1960), pp. 4–5, 35, 38, 42–43.

1. Continuous-flow production, including both transfer machines and automatic control processes, which, though technologically different, require similar types of skills,

2. Programmed machines, including electronic data processing and electronically-controlled machine tools,

3. Centralized remote control, including railway control centers, process-control rooms, and continuous strip mills.

The type of automation most frequently encountered in this survey of blue-collar work was continuous-flow production, and the findings, coinciding with those of Crossman, were that the operator needs control skills—sensing, perceiving, predicting, familiarity with the controls, and decision-making. Despite the change in the types of skills required, the vast majority of pre-automation operators were found to be capable of adapting to the new processes without great difficulty.

The use of existing workers as programmed machine operators also presented no difficulty, for this type of job is also learned quickly. In fact, as Crossman pointed out, programmed machine tools enable an operator who is not a skilled machinist to do accurate complicated work. The main qualifications for the operator are a flexible, logical mind, and resourcefulness—qualifications which companies have found widely among blue-collar workers.

The situation with respect to remote control operators is somewhat more complicated. Nevertheless, most such operators have been recruited from former operators on the outmoded production lines, and they have become skilled in remote control operations. The skills required are of the "information-handling" type, requiring selective vigilance, translation of data, decision-making, and sharp short-term memory.

In one respect, however, some former operators have not been able to adapt readily to remote control systems. They develop and are unable to overcome an anxiety resulting from their new role in overseeing an entire operation. These behavior patterns led a public utility to adopt the policy of strongly advising individuals whom management had recognized as psychologically unfit for the new type of work not to transfer to such jobs. Since the collective bargaining agreement granted the employees the right to move into such jobs, regardless of any determination by management as to their psychological fitness for the work, some employees ignored that advice. Eventually, however, management's original evaluation was confirmed, as most of those who were so counseled found that they could not bear up under the strain of controlling operations in automated power-generating stations. They then accepted transfer back to older, nonremote-control stations. The plight of such employees will present grave problems throughout industry as older operations disappear from the scene and some employees find it difficult to adjust to the new types of work.

In considering the skill demands of the latest technology, it is well to emphasize a point made earlier. Although actual company experience so far indicates clearly that almost all new production jobs are within the abilities of present employees to perform, generally without extensive training, modern technology could take new turns, bringing greater demands on employee talents. Moreover, skill attributes, in the traditional sense, are not controlling. Job requirements are changing in such a way as to outmode conventional concepts of "skill." Greater capacities for concentrated attention and process conceptualization are needed than ever before, as well as more intensive application of the basic skills of reading and writing. These are the new dimensions to be considered in correlating worker skills with job requirements. There is also the factor of changes in the work environment, which may be far more significant than job requirements for worker adaptability to advanced technology (see Chapter VIII).

TRAINING AND RETRAINING MEASURES

In discussing company experience with retraining of the regular workforce for jobs in automated operations, a distinction must be made between employees who have been in production operations and skilled craftsmen who have been in maintenance work. The two groups present significant differences, affecting the problems companies have faced in gearing to new technology.

Production Operations

With respect to production workers, companies have found, as noted earlier, that employees have proved to be equipped for learning the new tasks in a changed technology as a result of their skills, qualifications, and experience acquired before operations were modernized. In the great majority of companies, the skills required of operators of new machinery have not differed significantly from those required before, and extensive retraining of personnel has therefore been unnecessary.

New equipment has often been developed and "debugged" on the factory floor, contributing to the ease of training workers. In this process, line management has worked closely with the engineering force. By the time the automatic machines have become operational, supervisors have known how to run them and, in turn, have been able to teach their subordinates right on the job. Often, the employees who were eventually to operate the machinery have worked in proximity to the debugging process and, therefore, have learned a good deal about its operation by observing the new processes during the break-in period.

In situations where fairly standardized machinery has been purchased, supervisors have learned about the new processes either by visiting the plant of the equipment manufacturer and familiarizing themselves with the machinery, or from instructors sent by the vendor to the buyer's factory. The supervisors have then been in a position to teach the members of their work crews how to operate the new equipment.

In the minority of cases in which significantly different skills have been required as a result of new technology, managements, recognizing a responsibility to employees and desiring to allay employee resistance to change, have been willing to retrain employees, despite the costliness of this more basic retraining. Retraining is often more costly than hiring new workers, for the latter are generally younger, are better educated, and bring with them more up-to-date skills; they also start at the low end of the wage scale.

Four factors have militated against the most expeditious retraining of production workers in new and more complicated skills, and thus have added to the costs. First, older and long-service employees have often lacked the basic qualifications that would fit them for such training. Second, seniority considerations have sometimes obstructed the best selection of employees for training in particular skills. Third, older workers have generally been slower in learning and have required more intensive or prolonged training. Fourth, employees and their unions have often been unenthusiastic about the programs companies devised for upgrading of the workforce. The problems and the solutions that have obtained in reconciling these deterrents with operational needs are best seen by considering illustrative cases of company experience.

1. *Inadequate Basic Qualifications.* The lengths to which some companies have gone to overcome the handicap of deficient qualifications among employees is demonstrated in the action taken at a plant in the South. The operations were converted from the manufacture of one fabric to that of another, to meet a shift in consumer tastes. The conversion brought a need for a new set of skills in the labor force, and the plant management planned to undertake whatever

retraining was necessary to provide these skills. It found, however, that about two-thirds (200) of the long-service employees could not pass the qualifying test for the program. The fundamental cause of these failures was found to be a lack of basic reading and writing skills on the part of the older workers.

Management then set about remedying the situation. The company decided to work through the local school board and secured its assistance in aiding the employees to acquire the basic education they needed. Classes were arranged on company property to provide an elementary education course through the fifth-grade level. The classes were conducted during the employees' off-hours. All employees were given the opportunity to participate, and the response was overwhelming. The costs of instruction, including salaries of teachers and materials used, were assumed by the company. The results of the program were favorable, for at its conclusion, most of the formerly disadvantaged employees were able to qualify for the new jobs.

This is an extreme case. But it highlights the way in which the utilization of workers in a changed technology is often thwarted by basic educational lacks rather than by difficulties with the degree of skill involved in new jobs.

2. *Seniority Consideration.* Retraining long-service employees to protect them against technological displacement, whether because of contract obligations or on management initiative, has generally required much more time, money, and effort than companies originally contemplate. A number of companies have also discovered that broadening plant seniority units and relaxing restrictions on job transfers for displaced employees have multiplied their training needs. At a petroleum refinery, extensive modernization of the operations resulted in excess personnel and, consequently, a heavy layoff of employees, including skilled workers in the maintenance division. The employees having longest service were protected from layoff by plant-wide seniority, and the skilled

workers displaced employees in the production division on the basis of their seniority. There were large numbers of such employees, for the maintenance division had disproportionately more high-seniority men. The management was forced, therefore, to undertake a fairly extensive program to retrain them to handle operating jobs.

Led by its concern for high-seniority employees about to be displaced by technological change, the management of a food-processing company explored ways of opening new job opportunities for them. It took the course of permitting them to apply for jobs requiring capacities beyond those for which their past experience qualified them. The result was that the employees had to be given rather concentrated retraining, which entailed substantial expense. However, the company preferred to incur the extra cost rather than to lay off senior employees as an alternative.

Technological improvements in a chemical plant introduced a whole new family of job skills. About 160 long-service employees were released from their regular jobs to undertake one month of training on mock equipment. Although requiring more time, money, and effort than had been originally contemplated, the undertaking proved highly successful. At the end of the course, all but 35 of the employees qualified for the new jobs. Management did not then take the easy course and separate the 35 failures for lack of ability; instead, it offered them an additional month of training. At the conclusion of that period, only 8 still could not qualify, and they received another month of training, after which only one employee could not measure up to the work requirements.

3. *Age and Learning Ability.* In the experience of a number of companies, employees of fairly advanced age have presented particular retraining problems. Recognizing the developing shift in manpower requirements from production to maintenance, a transportation equipment manufacturer decided in 1957 to increase opportunities for its more senior

production employees by eliminating the age limit for undertaking apprenticeship training for skilled maintenance jobs. Within two years, about 200 workers over age twenty-eight began training in skilled trades, but few employees past age forty-five even applied. Experience indicated, however, that some older workers were still capable of learning new trades when the opportunity was presented.

On the other hand, a petroleum refinery engaged in a great amount of retraining over an extended period and found age to be a severe handicap to learning. With the shutdown of some obsolete equipment, operating personnel were reassigned to other jobs, but it was quickly discovered that they were not prepared to handle the new work. Specialized training was then provided for 34 operators, mainly in the younger age groups, and this met the problem to a considerable degree. Management maintained, however, that its problem of manning the new operations could not have been resolved by retraining of older workers, for they were, in the main, incapable of grasping the new concepts of operation. Fortunately, it was possible to retire the older operators under the company's early retirement program.

The problem of retraining older people to meet the responsibilities and challenges of current job opportunities is a pervasive one. It has arisen and is being studied in a steel company with respect to engineers, and any findings from this study will probably have broad application to the company's entire labor force.

There is a body of opinion holding that the ability to learn does not necessarily decrease with age, although the rate of learning may slow down somewhat. Perhaps the oldsters in the cases cited had training difficulties because the level of education in their youth was well below the standards of today, and because educational achievement was not a factor in selection for the jobs they entered. Even though such employees were able to gain skills on the job through slow accretion over the years, they did not prove to be favorable subjects for rapid retraining under pressure.

4. *Employee-Union Reactions to Training.* In some situations, union relations have been of crucial importance to company retraining plans. Some of the companies studied have found that unions and workers do not always respond favorably to management offers of retraining. When the automation of the shipping operations of a printing and publishing concern necessitated the conversion of the department's common laborers into machine operators, the management sensed that a company retraining program would be resisted. It accordingly encouraged the union representing these workers to run a training program on company premises. Preparatory to inauguration of the training sessions, the union's instructors were trained by a man obtained by the company, who had helped to install automated equipment in other printing establishments. The program, as presented to the workers, was given two emphases—that it offered an opportunity for them to acquire "skill" and that it was directed by the union. The management remained in the background, which served to allay fear of the forthcoming technological change and to eliminate possible resistance to the necessary training.

In one instance, a union almost scuttled a retraining program, because management refused to conduct classes on a segregated basis for Negro and white employees. In another, the management virtually had to force the union to take the initiative in impressing on its members their training needs, in order to gain worker acceptance of the retraining program. On a more national scale, the International Union of Electrical Workers, in its 1960 negotiations with General Electric and Westinghouse, turned down the companies' offers to provide retraining or reassignment to selected employees facing layoff.

On the other hand, a local union in the electrical manufacturing industry in one of the case-study plants accepted a variant of the retraining plan refused by the IUE the year before. At this factory, men in high labor grades were displaced from their jobs by a simplification of wiring procedures, and there were no comparable jobs to which their occupational experience would entitle them. Seeking a solution to the problem of obsolescent skills among these long-service employees, management signed a supplementary agreement with the local union, granting these workers an opportunity to train for other jobs. Under the program, the persons to be trained were selected by management, and they received 95 percent of their former grade rate during the period of training. The workers were allowed one week of training for each year of service.

5. *Training Versus Contracting-out Work*. An interesting training procedure was followed by a public utility that converted from producer to natural gas. The management undertook to combine training within an integrated program designed to accomplish a number of management objectives. When the company stopped manufacturing gas in its own plants and switched to buying natural gas from pipeline distributors and selling it to local customers, there was a reduction in its manpower needs. The company, as many others in similar circumstances have done, hired an outside contractor to accomplish the conversion of gas appliances in the homes of its customers. Upon completion of the conversion in one district, management was dissatisfied with the arrangement from both a cost and a public relations point of view. Realizing that outside labor was being used in its operations, while the company itself faced a large surplus of manpower, management decided not to contract out any more of the conversion of the home appliances.

In order to do the job internally, however, the company had to train its employees for the work. First, management combed its files to select employees with mechanical backgrounds who could qualify for short-run training. Then a training school was set up on company property. Training took only a few days per man, and was offered on company time. It was designed to acquaint the employee with the various types of appliances used in homes throughout the area, and the methods of converting them for the use of natural gas. The employees were also instructed in ways of conducting their work in private homes with dispatch and decorum. Only the simpler home conversions were entrusted to employees who had worked formerly in the gas and coke plants, and the more complicated ones at industrial establishments were assigned to special skilled staffs that were already within the company.

At the conclusion of the conversion program, management was most pleased with its results. The employees had willingly accepted the training measures, which enabled the company to utilize its own manpower and thus helped to avert layoffs. The conversion work, moreover, had gone much more smoothly than that performed by the outside contractor, particularly from the standpoint of relations with customers, a most important consideration for a public utility.

Skilled Maintenance Work

According to the experience of most of the companies, maintenance skill requirements after the introduction of new technology have, in general, remained comparable to those utilized in former operating processes. As mentioned earlier, this conclusion is in line with that of Bright, who in 1958 maintained that the levels of skills of many of the crafts are little affected by automation.[8] The exceptions to this more general experience have arisen in companies where advanced technology has increased the complexity of some jobs requiring certain of the craft skills. An automobile manufacturer reported that the increased importance of the

8 Bright, *op. cit.*, p. 95.

maintenance function upon the introduction of intricate and expensive automatic transfer machinery necessitated extensive training of its maintenance craftsmen. This supplemental training entailed up to 200 hours of individual instruction in the areas of electronics, hydraulics, welding, and lubrication. At a rubber factory, automation had varying effects, depending upon the craft. It reduced the skill requirements of mechanics and riggers, while those of electricians and pipefitters were raised.

The increased need for preventive maintenance in the upkeep of automatic machinery has raised skill requirements for those craftsmen who are members of trouble-shooting crews and, therefore, must be adept at diagnostic techniques. As an example, 20 of the 524 maintenance jobs in one highly integrated continuous-process chemical plant now require a college degree. In some integrated operations, new technology has also tended to create a need for multiskilled maintenance men. Crossman's research also uncovered this fact, and he pointed to the seeming development of the *polyvalent* craftsman, who can service modern equipment in which electrical and mechanical parts and controls are interlocked.[9] This study reveals a continuing trend in that direction, but developing individual craftsmen to acquire the several related skills needed in some operating situations is being retarded by union insistence on preserving older skill demarcations.

Even where unions have acceded to the establishment of broader skilled trades definitions, there has been a serious problem of adaptability of the worker to the broadened scope of his activities, even though the skills required of him remained comparable to his accustomed level. During the study this problem was found to be prevalent with respect to general mechanics in petroleum refineries. The men were competent to carry out all assignments, but because of past work habits they frequently had difficulty in

[9] Crossman, *op. cit.*, pp. 48–49.

quickly shifting their frame of reference as they moved from an assignment involving one type of skill to another requiring a different skill.

Supply of Skilled Workers. Despite company training and utilization of employees from the established crafts for the servicing of new technology, an emerging problem has been to secure an adequate supply of craftsmen. More skilled employees are needed to maintain and repair automated machinery. The rising importance of craft skills in maintenance work has created serious manpower shortages in such trades in some labor markets.

Most of the companies studied have been able to fill their maintenance manpower needs adequately, and in a few situations heavy employment cutbacks, resulting from a combination of factors, have even caused displacement of some craftsmen. However, the short supply of skilled labor in some labor markets has meant that certain plants have experienced shortages in particular craft occupations. Some companies have tried the route of moving production workers into skilled maintenance jobs, but with little success. For skilled work, production men have lacked either the basic qualifications or the desire to transfer to maintenance jobs. This was the experience of a chemical plant in the South that underwent product and process change. The management had to hire 43 craftsmen from outside the plant, despite widespread cutbacks among production workers. Similarly, a New England machinery plant which had employees on layoff suffered, at the same time, a shortage of highly skilled workers, such as turret lathe operators. There, too, displaced machine operators could not qualify for such work, and many, particularly the older ones, lacked the educational background to even train for such jobs.

A food-processing plant in the Middle Atlantic region reported some success in transferring surplus production workers to maintenance jobs, but even in this case it was frequently necessary to hire skilled craftsmen from the outside to work with new equipment. An electrical manufacturing plant in a major industrial center in the same region reported that machinists and mechanics were always in short supply, and that the management had to rely on its own continuous training program to fill its needs.

The problem of shortages was being resolved in a different way in a continuous-process operation on the West Coast, where it was reported that highly skilled mechanics would be hard to find. The servicing of the company's computer equipment was being performed by the manufacturer of the new machinery and by other special maintenance service corporations in the area. Contracting-out was also resorted to where periodic peak maintenance work required, for short periods, a much larger skilled force than that regularly employed in a plant. This was particularly true of petroleum refining operations during major "turnaround" of equipment for cleaning and repair.

Problems in New Plants. Recruitment of craftsmen has always been a problem in the establishment of new plants. The difficulties have been particularly great in areas that have not been highly industrialized in the past and, hence, lack pools of skilled labor from which to draw needed manpower. In-company training of employees has been the course most often followed by companies facing this problem, though a company in the glass industry resorted to recruiting workers with certain skills from its other plants to man a new facility in the South.

On the other hand, a machinery manufacturer, in relocating an operation to the South, found it unnecessary to transfer any hourly-paid workers. Within a year preceding the plant opening, it was able to recruit and train at the new location its entire complement of 400 employees, including those for the skilled crafts. For most large companies, however, a year would hardly be enough time in which to train workers in the variety of high skills that would be needed. An automobile company representative indicated that from two to three years would be the minimum period needed to develop workers for the highly skilled jobs in his company.

Programs for Development of Craftsmen. Some plants have avoided shortages of skilled maintenance employees, despite an increase in their need for such workers, because they have had the foresight to undertake special training programs in advance. A steel-producing company coordinated its apprenticeship training program with its research and development activities. It has for years maintained a highly effective apprenticeship program to develop individuals with skills that would be required by the company in the future. The company believes that its in-service training program has been most fruitful. Those employees who have been so trained have demonstrated the ability to adapt to the demands of various new pieces of equipment for constant repair and operation at a highly skilled level of maintenance work well beyond that required in the past.

Similarly, a petroleum refinery in the Southwest has engaged in special employee training for assignments to instrument and mechanical work. The program has been conducted on a formalized classroom basis and over an extended period. It has resulted in a material improvement in the understanding and capability of these highly-skilled employees, and they, consequently, are efficient in handling new manufacturing processes.

Many other companies have had similar experience. One, for example, has developed special production and engineering training groups for the combined purposes of training men for eventual rise to positions of responsibility, for meeting emergencies, and for balancing production. Unfortunately from management's point of view, there are provisions in the union contract that limit management's use of the employees so trained. Preference, on the basis of the group training experience, is not permitted in the filling of job vacancies.

Companies reported mixed experience with respect to

the response from employees to tuition-refund programs designed to encourage them to improve their skills. Some had decidedly poor results upon extending tuition-refund programs to blue-collar employees, finding that no matter how liberal the policy very few took advantage of these opportunities.

A few companies reported that a number of craftsmen were willing to take advantage of tuition-refund programs in order to prepare themselves for new developments in their areas of skill. A food-processing company found that increasing the reimbursement for outside educational courses, from 50 percent of tuition to 100 percent, encouraged workers to devote spare time to upgrading their skills. In addition, some production-line workers took advantage of the company's new policies in order to learn the mechanical and maintenance skills which increased in importance as a result of new technology.

Apparently, disregard of such opportunities stems in part from lack of employee initiative, about which management can do little. Also, employees cannot adequately gauge the type of educational training they should seek; in this regard managements can take effective action in guiding employees, as happened in one case. The management of a machinery manufacturing plant, realizing that certain of its maintenance craftsmen were not adequately equipped to handle new technological developments, cooperated with the local trade high school in establishing training courses in electricity and electronics geared to the plant's needs. When these courses were offered to the company's employees on a tuition-refund basis, a sizable number took advantage of the offer.

This form of cooperation in the area of training between a company and community schools is not uncommon in industry at large, but the case just cited was the only such example found among the companies studied. There is some similarity, however, in the previously cited case of cooperation by a local school board in establishing an elementary education program for production employees. Many companies also have worked closely for decades with the Bureau of Apprenticeship of the United States Department of Labor in conducting apprenticeship training for the skilled trades.

IMPLICATIONS OF TRAINING EXPERIENCE

Actual company experience in the past few years with the requirements of advanced technology disproves early thinking that automation would vastly upgrade jobs and thus disqualify large segments of the workforce, with a resulting need for mass retraining of industrial workers on a formal basis. The companies included in this study have all undergone extensive technological change, and their experience offers some important insights into the entire question of training and retraining of blue-collar personnel. The essence of the findings from this experience is as follows:

1. New technology has not led to any great degree of job upgrading for blue-collar workers. In the typical plant, therefore, short-term, on-the-job training has been adequate to prepare employees to operate and maintain more advanced machinery and equipment.

2. Where new technology does require new families of job skills, particularized retraining programs, some on an extensive scale, have been the chief means of teaching current employees those skills.

3. To be successful, retraining programs have called for a willingness to expend sufficient time, effort, and money to meet the objectives. Many workers, particularly those far removed from their school years, have required more instruction than is normally assumed; older workers have taken longer to regain the knack of learning. Many workers have lacked the basic qualifications for learning new skills, and at times retraining efforts have had to start with providing elementary education. In some situations, these factors have

made the training task more complicated than had been anticipated.

4. The broader the seniority unit in a plant, and the looser the restrictions on job transfers for displaced employees, the more training management has had to provide.

5. Workers and their unions have sometimes been hostile toward management training proposals. Gaining union cooperation in conducting training programs has been valuable, therefore, in helping to allay employee fear of displacement and suspicion of the aims of new technology. Union cooperation has sometimes been achieved more easily at the local than at the national level because the need for training is understandable to both the employees and the local union, in terms of specific plant problems.

6. Tuition-refund programs, designed to provide the basic education needed to qualify for highly skilled jobs, have yielded good results when the courses of local schools have been coordinated with the specific job needs of local plants.

7. Although new technology has seldom raised job requirements in production work, it has demanded extensive maintenance and has therefore drawn heavily on the supply of skilled craftsmen. Already shortages of such workers have been felt by companies, and the situation could well worsen.

* * *

It may be said that within industry training activities have been adapted to the specific needs of particular operations. They have been conducted with the combined objectives of utilizing the regular workforce to the fullest extent and of maintaining efficiency and continuity of production. These efforts have been costly, but they provide realistic guides for the future.

The dearth of skilled workers in some communities, scattered throughout all regions of the nation, demonstrates that some of the present unemployment is structural in nature. Here is a basis for specific exploration of training needs and remedial programs, geared to the demands of present-day work opportunities. It would be rather ironical if a serious shortage of skilled workers were to develop in the face of greater craft opportunities through advanced technology. The problem, then, is not that most jobs under automation require unprecedented skills, but that the new technology has created considerably more skilled jobs.

Since workers must continually bring new skills and better educational backgrounds to their jobs, much of the training responsibility lies with educational authorities. Industry cannot reasonably be expected to provide the basic skills which employees have customarily brought to their jobs. So far, many of the on-going vocational training programs have not met the actual needs at the plant level in industry. It is incumbent on educators, therefore, to re-examine present school programs to insure that they are providing youth with the types of skills that will be required in this age of rapid technological advancement. The task is not merely to teach skills that are needed at the moment, but to look to the future as well. A like responsibility rests upon industry to take the initiative in giving encouragement and guidance to the educators. At the same time, companies would do well in their own training efforts to achieve the best possible coordination with their research and development activities.

There are a growing number of community facilities which can be utilized by both management and employees for supplementary training. In fact, smaller companies, without adequate resources with which to conduct their own extensive retraining, may find that federal funds are available under the recently developed area redevelopment and man-power training programs. Even where companies are not interested in utilizing these resources, it would be desirable for management to point out to displaced employees how they might avail themselves of the opportunities thus afforded to learn new skills that would qualify them for new types of jobs.

Change seems to be the only constant on the industrial horizon. Consequently, one of the major tasks facing this country today is to reshape its educational institutions so as to equip people with a greater ability to adapt themselves to continuing technological change. Certainly, workers at all job levels will have to regard education as a lifelong process, not an activity that ends at the twelfth grade.

CHAPTER VI

Revising Pay Structures

E mployees find it easiest to articulate their general dis-
turbance over the dislocations of technological change
by focusing on matters of pay and earnings. Unions, too,
very often concentrate on wage issues in a period of change,
though their real concern may be the matter of control of
other aspects of work and jobs. This chapter deals with two
aspects of pay structure revision. It treats with, first, specific
problems that arise in applying job evaluation standards to
the new and changed jobs that emerge upon introduction
of modern technology and, second, the impact of new production processes on incentive plans.

HOURLY WAGE STRUCTURES

When advanced technology replaces traditional operating methods, inevitable and often troublesome problems
arise in the resulting modification and evaluation of jobs,
and in the revision of pay structures. New jobs, the altered

content of some existing jobs, and changes in the physical working environment must be taken into account if equitable relationships are to be established between job rates and job content. Of even greater importance are the relationships between the new jobs that emerge, the jobs that change in character, and those that remain unchanged.

For both the union and management, any depression of rates in evaluating new and changed jobs, or of earnings, is detrimental to employee acceptance of change. But, in terms of overall operations, necessary economies planned for by a company leave little room for loose rates or standards—hence the desire of management to evaluate jobs and rationalize the rate structure with dispatch when change occurs.

A union typically looks for rate or earnings increases out of technological change and sees all new jobs as deserving superior rates. By the same token, rate increases are sought when the job content of some traditional classifications is diluted by the substitution of new duties, even though the total value of the job in an evaluation scheme may remain unchanged. Yet, where skill requirements are reduced, the union generally tries to preserve the rate, regardless of change in job content. Union concepts of wage protection are understandable, but inconsistent with the principles underlying wage administration. Thus conflict over rates determined by a job evaluation system typically occurs upon a company's adoption of technological change.

Nature of Adjustments

Where modern technology is introduced in production operations, some new jobs are instituted; and usually a proportion of them require skills of a higher order than those demanded in existing jobs. These jobs therefore merit higher rate classifications than those previously found in a company's normal wage structure. But many new jobs are comparable to existing classifications and thus deserve only equivalent rates. Some existing jobs may take on a new mix of job factors, without increasing in overall value, thus meriting no increase in rates. In other cases, certain characteristics of jobs are nullified by the new technology, and two or more jobs must therefore be merged in order to be full assignments; these consolidated jobs may or may not be worth any higher rate than one or another of the jobs that are merged. Also some jobs no longer demand former skill requirements and have to be removed to lower classifications, and down-rated accordingly.

Under all of these circumstances, equitable pay rates must obviously be determined on the basis of a careful and critical process of job evaluation. Such a process can reveal the best possible picture of the relative value of jobs or groups of jobs in a much-altered work environment. If the evaluation is successful, it is possible to maintain an orderly wage system, to provide pay commensurate with the work performed, and to avoid the inequities that can develop from a random and uncontrolled rate structure. Most of the companies studied had long maintained job evaluation plans, and these plans served, in varying degree, to systematize the task of readjusting wage rates to fit new job requirements.

Well-administered job evaluation processes can also facilitate union-management consideration of wage rates for new jobs. But it must be recognized that job evaluation is not a completely scientific process, since it depends largely on a series of technical refinements and is therefore in a sense arbitrary. For this reason, union-management disagreement over rate-setting cannot always be settled on the basis of the reasonableness of a job evaluation system.

Problems in Job Evaluation

Many problems arise for the job evaluator out of the changing mix of skill requirements for jobs resulting from new technology. But the most basic problems are those concerned with the evaluation of the factor of responsibility. Consider, for example, the operator sitting at a console board. What is his responsibility for the operations controlled by that board? In his job, as in many other new types of jobs, the factor of responsibility may outweigh the requirements of skill and physical effort—factors which have been traditionally ranked high in importance in evaluating jobs. The problem is that "responsibility" in modern technology is rather nebulous and difficult to interpret.

On the surface, the findings of this study would seem to confirm Aronson's prediction, "Physical factors in classifying jobs will probably become less important, but more weight will have to be given to such factors as the value of the equipment, the amount of discretion and initiative required, and background education."[1] While some evaluation systems among the case-study companies were adapted to take account of these new factors, others were not. Interestingly, Killingsworth pointed out that "the most widely used plan in the metalworking trades and electrical manufacturing gives greater emphasis to skill than responsibility factors,"[2] yet this study found no inordinate conflict over job evaluation in plants in these industries.

Among the case-study companies, some wage administrators, taking account of the difficulties involved, bypassed the needed integration of new job factors into job evaluation plans when only a few jobs were affected. In other situations, management people remained wedded to the standards of their existing scheme, with the result that readjustment of the rate structure to accommodate the new job factors became a cumbersome and controversial process, even within the management group.

[1] Robert L. Aronson, "Automation—Challenge to Collective Bargaining?" in *New Dimensions in Collective Bargaining,* Industrial Relations Research Association, Publication No. 21 (New York: Harper & Brothers, 1959), p. 63.
[2] Charles C. Killingsworth, "Industrial Relations and Automation," *The Annals,* Vol. 340, March, 1962, p. 76.

A variety of difficulties can arise when there is rigid adherence to customary interpretation of job values. Noteworthy are those which occur in the evaluation of jobs that entail occasional periods of intense effort interspersed with periods of vigilance to assure proper functioning of a machine.

As an illustration, when a steel mill became highly automated, a controversy developed within the management regarding the evaluation of the jobs on new equipment, particularly with respect to stand-by time. The question was whether or not a man who was tending a larger and more complicated piece of equipment in the automated operations, but who had considerable stand-by time, was doing a job of higher-level skill than one who actually spent a greater percentage of time operating simpler machinery under older production techniques. The wage administrators considered stand-by time to be comparable to idle time and, therefore, not significant in job evaluation. The industrial engineers, on the other hand, believed that stand-by time devoted to tending the larger and more complex piece of machinery called for attentiveness and judgment, which they regarded as important aspects of the man's overall responsibility.

This specific point of controversy never was resolved on its merits. It was disposed of instead by giving physical effort less relative weight. Thus, even when physical effort ceased to be a factor in a job, the overall value of the job was not greatly affected. Moreover, the relatively heavier weight given to responsibility in most cases more than compensated for the subordination of physical effort as a factor.

To avoid adding to the strain that new technology inevitably puts on job evaluation, there is a necessity, revealed by company experience, for taking greater account of such factors as increased responsibility and more frequent handling of product. These factors must be considered in order to compensate for skill dilution and other effects which reduce the value of other factors in jobs as formerly constituted. Where this is done, and jobs are downgraded, a usual recourse, to avoid employee protest, is to maintain the old rates and "red-circle" them as misfits in the wage structure. With accelerated introduction of new machines and resulting changes in classification, however, a company engaging in this practice may soon find itself saddled with a heavy dispersal of "red-circle" rates and a distorted wage structure.

Union Reactions to Job Evaluation Standards

Some union protests against the evaluation of new or changed jobs amount to a suggestion that wage rates should be set in a direct relationship to changes in productivity on individual jobs. This, of course, would be unsound and would produce a chaotic wage structure most difficult to administer. The more sophisticated unions, being aware of the need for job evaluation systems, base their demands for higher rates of pay on allegations that advanced technology produces new job factors which are not given appropriate weight by existing evaluation plans. These unions cite such factors as the operator's unusual responsibility and increased fatigue in working with automated equipment.

Many of the companies studied ran into union distrust of existing job evaluation plans and the claim that these plans were inadequate for rating the jobs resulting from automated equipment. This view was stated quite clearly by the International Association of Machinists:

> Automation has frequently made old job classifications obsolete. In a number of instances, the greater skill and responsibility required to operate complex and expensive machines and the mental fatigue involved justify a demand for reclassification and higher rates of pay. As a matter of fact, wherever collective bargaining is circumscribed by job evaluation systems, fundamental revisions of such systems as a whole may be required to take into account factors (such

as increased responsibility) which are given little or no weight at present.[3]

But, among the companies studied, union representatives too often blurred their argument for greater weighting of the responsibility factor by forwarding the claim of increased responsibility when it did not actually exist. In many cases they obviously attributed "responsibility" to jobs merely in order to press their attempts to secure rate increases wherever possible. Furthermore, some unions were apparently responsible for an undercurrent of specious reasoning, developed from the notions that individual workers should share automatically in the savings which inure to a company from improved technology, and should receive higher pay for operating new expensive machinery, regardless of job content. These considerations obviously had little or nothing to do with proper ranking of jobs and alignment of rates through job evaluation.

Union leaders recognize, of course, that new technology often changes the balance of importance among job factors and that it may, therefore, decrease the value of the traditionally highly-weighted factors of skill and physical effort. But, when the value of these factors is reduced so as to cause a downgrading of existing jobs, union protests against the validity of job evaluation plans are particularly vehement. One observer feels that the objective of unions in urging fundamental revisions in job evaluation systems is not so much to construct "a scientific scheme of payment as it is to prevent earning opportunities from being impaired" during the redefinition of job factors and job standards.[4]

The views of a few company managements cooperating in this study coincided, wholly or partially, with the essence of union complaints about the weighting of new job factors.

[3] International Association of Machinists (Washington), *Meeting the Problems of Automation Through Collective Bargaining*, 1960, p. 33.

[4] Jack Barbash, "The Union Response to Technological Change," *Changing Patterns in Industrial Relations*, Thirteenth Annual Conference (Montreal: Industrial Relations Centre, McGill University, 1961), p. 94.

These managements, having anticipated the disruptive influence of advanced technology on the traditional interpretation of job values, restructured their job evaluation plans to give greater weight to such factors as responsibility and mental strain. As a fundamental principle, however, managements universally disagreed with the union contention that a job merited upgrading when the operator was assigned to more expensive machinery without an increase in duties.

Management Approaches and Experience

In the experience of the companies studied, grave difficulties in adjusting nonmaintenance job classifications to conform to technological improvement were far from the rule. Conflict between management and union representatives was usually resolved in the light of reason or on the basis of compromise. On the whole, managements did not fail to recognize that judgments were involved in the analysis and evaluation of the worth of jobs and, accordingly, dealt with complaints about rate readjustment by listening to and considering seriously all union arguments. When the logic and consistency of management determinations were irrefutable and management refused to retreat from its position, the union concerned usually abandoned such harassing tactics as pressing for arbitration, recognizing that unions have lost arbitration cases in this area when a management's decisions have been supported by sound evidence. In some instances, however, management granted concessions which violated the indicated need for downward revision of the rates of changed jobs and of the proper relative grading of new jobs. Unfortunately, these departures from validity played havoc with the wage structures of the companies and with the future applicability of their job evaluation plans in radically changed operations.

The experience of one company illustrates the need to gauge carefully how new technology will affect jobs before talking about it to employees. In an attempt to gain employee acceptance of automation, top corporate officials had stated boastfully that the new process would greatly increase skill requirements and upgrade jobs. Actually, however, the equipment did not really upgrade jobs. Since the employees' appetites had been whetted, they demanded higher wages, whether justified by job requirements or not, and their union sought to negotiate higher rates across the board for all new jobs. In order to ward off a rash of grievances on the rates it established, management had to be "overgenerous" in evaluating the new jobs.

A few managements admitted to having used a strategy of attempting to outwit the unions with which they dealt, though not always with successful results. Anticipating union demands for higher wage scales, they deliberately undervalued new jobs, instead of rating them properly at the outset, only to concede under union protest to a re-evaluation of the jobs at rates commensurate with their real worth. The managements concerned regarded this tactic as a necessary part of the collective bargaining game, claiming that it suggested a fairness on management's part in being willing to recognize its mistakes and correct them. They held, moreover, that unions liked to play the game in this fashion, for union leadership then had something to "win for the boys."

A variation of this maneuvering was that of overvaluing new jobs. The objective here was to deflect union criticism and thus gain greater acceptance of the technological innovation. But companies found this to be another hazardous course; they were soon faced with grievances filed by other employees who felt that their jobs were underrated in relation to the new ones.

Such policies as those noted above are recognized as having obvious dangers and are therefore eschewed by the large majority of managements. First, they undermine employee reliance on the credibility of management and discredit job evaluation procedures. Second, undervaluing jobs, as a basis for conceding higher rates in negotiations, encourages a presumption on the part of employees that it is always possible to extract a little more, no matter what management sets as the proper rate for new jobs. Third, attaching rates that exceed the real worth of specific jobs offers no guarantee that a union will not seek to have the jobs rated still higher. Fourth, these departures from normal standards can get seriously out of hand, for experience indicates that once a company lends itself to such policies it rarely can abandon them and return to proper job evaluation procedures.

In some of the situations examined, unions pressed for new jobs to be upgraded simply because they were new and involved working with more expensive, labor-saving equipment. In some instances, companies succumbed to such pressures and established higher rates for new jobs than were justified by job evaluation, even though they disagreed with union contentions. Such compromise did ameliorate the immediate problem of rate negotiation, but at the price of creating wage inequities and throwing job evaluation standards out of kilter.

These results also obtained where technological change implied rate cuts and management yielded to union demands that customary wage levels be retained for jobs that had depreciated in content. Under employee pressure, local unions haggled most on this score, through the grievance procedure, and used every possible argument to confuse the issue of changed job content. This problem was most pronounced in a plant in which automation tended to simplify jobs and, therefore, to reduce the points allotted to one or another of the four factors in job evaluation: skill, strenuousness, responsibility, and working conditions. The labor contract stipulated that the evaluation of new jobs resulting from technological change could not be used as a basis for correcting improper rates, that only change in job content could be taken into account, not the looseness of a factor that was not affected by the new machinery. In practice, however, it was difficult to separate change in job content from correction of looseness, and whenever the management acted on the basis that job content had changed, the union contended that an attempt was being made to correct looseness in unaffected job factors.

The company's problems were further compounded by a special "automation" clause in its contract, which stated that rates for new jobs were to reflect the earnings levels of the jobs eliminated by automation. This clause even restricted the company's ability to take account of change in job content where this might reduce rates.

Large-scale introduction of new machinery and processes sometimes had the effect of reducing various jobs to but a fragment of their former requirements. As a consequence, in terms of the residue of duties, the jobs became virtually the same as those having other classifications, and job descriptions were then outmoded. The realistic course would have been to consolidate some classifications which no longer differed in job content. But, among the companies studied, attempts to make such needed adjustments generally encountered bitter union resistance. In one company, when management proposed to amalgamate two classifications which had become comparable on the basis of the actual duties performed, it contributed to a strike at the time of renewal of the union agreement. The issue was over management's right to discontinue or combine job classifications. The union resisted this step toward rationality because it feared that amalgamation of jobs, by enhancing management's ability to utilize the plant labor force more efficiently, would lead to the elimination of jobs and termination of workers.

There were instances, however, in which union representatives accepted the reasonableness of consolidating and reclassifying jobs that were changed radically in content. Upon the automation of a power plant, for example, many jobs encompassed minor elements of the skill requirements of several classifications. This demonstrated that consolidation of numerous jobs under single new titles would be sensible, and the union agreed to this necessary reclassification under the title of "instrument mechanic."

Where technological change was extensive, requiring the establishment of scores of new job classifications and wage rates, collective bargaining at the plant level normally worked to accommodate the interests of labor and management. A case of automation of an automobile plant is illustrative. While undertaking the heavy phase of so-called Detroit automation, management and union officials amicably negotiated higher classifications and rates for those new jobs requiring mental alertness on the part of the worker as a primary factor in reducing "down-time." Under automation, down-time is additive, because all operations along the line, as well as the one directly concerned, are affected.

It was also agreed, in this case, to pay five cents more an hour for jobs requiring operators to set their own machines than on those not entailing this function. There was further agreement that machine-setting as a full-time job would be rated ten cents per hour more than operators' jobs. Contributing to the lack of discord in rate-setting was the fact that management was generous to some degree in its classification and evaluation of new jobs, in order to forestall employee resistance to the new technology. Because so many of the altered jobs were equitably aligned in the evaluation process, the more liberal rates did not upset the internal consistency of the overall wage structure.

Substance of the Experience

It is clear that straightforward handling of the issues in readjusting job grades and rates is the best course. In general, those companies that anticipated the impact of new methods of production, and restructured their job evaluation plans to meet it, were best able to demonstrate the integrity of their plans and to assert the validity of their decisions as to classification and rating of jobs. When a management deferred revision of existing job evaluation standards until a particular difficulty arose, it found that union representatives often seized the initiative and foreclosed management's opportunity to deal with jobs realistically.

Job evaluation techniques are being challenged anew, and have to be strengthened to bear the new strains and to survive to serve effectively in present-day work environments. Outmoded job evaluation plans may have to be drastically changed, or even scrapped in favor of wholly new plans, but the principle of job evaluation cannot be discarded, or rejected in a spirit of frustration, until some better device can be substituted. It would appear that as yet technological change has not caused a change in the techniques of job evaluation, but some adjustments in thinking may be necessary.

Take the factor of responsibility. If this factor is viewed in its traditional sense, the conclusion could be reached that a job tending a major piece of equipment should be upgraded substantially. Unions hold this traditional view. Some job evaluators were also of this opinion, but they were a minority within their own companies. The issue is not so much one of properly weighting the responsibility factor as one of defining responsibility when equipment is largely self-regulating. In such situations, responsibility is clearly confined to the cycles of the equipment and not to responsibility for the entire process.

Perhaps the resolution of the problem of adapting job evaluation to advanced technology requires two bold steps. First, the dilution of the traditional concept of responsibility, as well as other factors, must be recognized in job evaluation systems. Equipment today has a high degree of built-in reliability. Further, vast control systems have been introduced into technically advanced operations, and in many the equipment is self-correcting. Thus new concepts must prevail in establishing meaningful factors for assessing the value of a job, and these will have to build on characteristics that a person must bring to a job—such as diligence and intelligence. Second, employees, even in unionized situations, must be chosen for jobs that they are qualified to perform and which they are able to comprehend. Unions frequently demand job upgrading because employees, unable to comprehend their jobs, overestimate the extent of their responsibility, due largely to a gnawing fear of having to operate a process over which they have but minimal control. This problem would probably not arise if better matches could be made between individuals and jobs, but too often the selection of an individual for a new job is controlled by seniority rather than capability or adaptability.

Looking toward the future, it seems certain that problems with job evaluation will continue to hamper managements involved in introducing technological change, unless the basic difficulties are identified and dealt with. Although the present techniques of job evaluation are not flawless, and administering them is subject to the frailties of human judgment, there is no better tool at hand which companies can use to systematize their wage structures in face of the inroads of modern technology on conventional concepts of relative job values.

Perhaps there is one basic lesson to be learned from the experience of companies, so far, in applying their job evaluation plans to the job structures which modern technology imposes. That lesson is one of preparedness—there should be a natural presumption that any revolutionary change in the technology of production must be accompanied by an equally revolutionary change in existing job evaluation plans. Just as entire plants have to be reconstructed or replaced, or whole work areas dismantled, to accommodate modern machinery, so job evaluation plans have to be examined and regeared early in management reckoning of the upheavals that will be wrought by technological innovation. If, at this early stage, there are indications that the existing job structure will be emasculated by the advent of new technology, it may be necessary to construct a wholly new plan, one which may well reverse conventional concepts. Piecemeal adaptation of job evaluation plans under such circumstances, done on the basis of expediency, will no more serve to erect new and sound wage structures than will the same approach in the installation of new technology.

INCENTIVE WAGE SYSTEMS

Where incentive methods of wage payment exist, the introduction of modern technology also poses problems. At the core of an incentive system is the self-motivation it presumably provides for employees to exert their best efforts without close supervision. Companies that have long used such a system find that their patterns of supervision and management are tied in with the system, and they are loath, or feel unable, to depart from it. By this system of remuneration, the worker's earnings increase proportionately according to increases in the level of output he achieves through voluntary effort.

But some automated operations do not lend themselves to realizing the usual benefits of conventional incentive plans, because the speed of production, being built into the machinery, is outside the worker's control and his individual output cannot be measured. It may require great ingenuity to conceive incentive methods of pay that will correspond with the particular nature of advanced technology and yield the desired results. Further, a change in the method by which an incentive system operates also requires changes in the form and quality of supervision.

Modern technology poses a threat to the viability of incentive methods of compensation as a stimulus for high-level employee productivity. The related problems are not only quite unlike those associated with the impact of such change on the hourly wage structure but are less amenable to immediate solution.

Moreover, the problems are likely to become more pervasive, as modern technology mushrooms into more and more sectors of industry in which the incentive method has been dominant in the compensation systems of companies. The most recent comprehensive survey of the prevalence of wage incentive systems disclosed that in May, 1958, as high a proportion as 27 percent of the nation's 11.5 million production and related workers in manufacturing were paid on an incentive basis.[5]

Incentive systems are widespread throughout the economy, not only because of their intrinsic value in the operations in which they are applied, but also because the principle of wage incentives has been, to a large degree, an essential element of the philosophy of many companies. The managements regard wage incentives as a direct expression of free enterprise and thus look upon this form of compensation as an effective economic stimulus. Some companies also view wage incentives as providing sufficient motivation for the individual employee to enable him to earn the maximum to which he is entitled by his capabilities and industriousness, and without close supervision.

As industry progressively adopted automation and other new technology, dire predictions abounded concerning the fate of incentives under changing technology.[6] Emphasis was given to the inapplicability of conventional piecework and incentive systems, because in the new operations workers

[5] L. Earl Lewis, "Extent of Incentive Pay in Manufacturing," *Monthly Labor Review*, Vol. 83, May, 1960, p. 460.

[6] See, for example, Aronson, *op. cit.*, p. 62; James R. Bright, *Automation and Management* (Boston: Graduate School of Business Administration, Harvard University, 1958), p. 208; Jack Rogers, *Automation: Technology's New Face* (Berkeley: Institute of Industrial Relations, University of California, 1958), p. 83.

would be unable to control output and their input could not be measured. Later it was claimed that technological changes had the effect of expanding incentives, "rather than abandonment of incentive coverage."[7] The findings of this study reject the second contention and highlight incentive problems.

Twelve of the 36 companies participating in this study utilized incentive wage plans in various parts of their operations at the time of introduction of major technological change. The experience of these companies indicates, primarily, that new technology disrupts existing incentive programs in either of two ways:

1. Where automation or other advanced technology is introduced, normal work-group relationships are disturbed, and often the basis of the individual incentive system is destroyed. With enlargement of jobs and machine-pacing of the work flow, the entire production process becomes integrated. Thus it is increasingly difficult to isolate and reward individual effort.

2. In some situations, advanced technology thwarts the basic aim of incentives—that of spurring employees to greater efforts, so as to bring higher earnings for them and increased returns to the company in the form of higher employee productivity and savings in the cost of supervision. Actually, retention of incentive systems in operations with advanced technology sometimes results in payment of high-incentive bonuses for output that is little more than routine and requires minimum effort on the part of employees.

Three recourses are open to companies that find their incentive systems onerous: to retain the incentive system and adapt it to the changes wrought by new technology; to discontinue incentives entirely; or to substitute some new method of incentive that will obviate the difficulty of measuring the degree of output attributable to individual employees. All of these solutions were attempted among the

[7] Garth L. Mangum, "Are Wage Incentives Becoming Obsolete?" *Industrial Relations*, Vol. 2, October, 1962, pp. 87–89.

companies studied. Case illustrations will serve to indicate the typical problems and influencing factors that accompanied company determinations along these lines.

Retention of Individual Incentives

Among the case-study companies having individual incentives as the keystone of their compensation programs, most endeavored to preserve the incentive method of pay, despite technological change. This was particularly true of companies in the steel industry, long devoted to the incentive principle. Considering that in 1958 about 60 percent of the blue-collar labor force in that industry was on incentives,[8] particularly acute problems were involved in so adapting incentives that they would continue to serve their purpose in automated operations. Despite periodic revisions of incentive pay plans by companies in the basic steel industry over a period of time,[9] the steel-producing companies participating in this study found the problems of adjusting to a shift to modern methods of production none the less troublesome. But at no time did these companies contemplate abandoning the incentive method of wage payment, apparently still highly favored not only by the managements, but also by the employees in the industry.

In one steel company studied, thinking within management ranks on the applicability of incentives to jobs in more technologically advanced mills obviously suffered a bias which derived from being long wedded to the concept of individual incentives. The industrial engineers emphasized the importance of keeping the incentive closely related to the work of the individual. Yet it is apparent that the key qualification in the revised incentive system is that, where a small group of employees is engaged in a closely-related operation, the

8 Lewis, *op. cit.*, p. 461.

9 See Jack Steiber, *The Steel Industry Wage Structure* (Cambridge: Harvard University Press, 1959), Chapters X and XI.

incentive must be related to the output of the group, not to the individuals comprising it. Management did not feel that this proviso violated the concept of individual incentives. But as we see it, the company seemed, whether it realized it or not, to be moving toward a sort of group incentive program. More will be said about group incentives at a later point.

In another steel plant, new technology complicated the application of wage incentives precisely because job tasks became less discrete and less under the control of the employee. The company continued to pay incentives; but, because employees had no control over output, incentive payments became simply a form of extra remuneration and were no longer a spur to greater effort on the part of the operator.

Difficulties with pay methods in the steel industry go back to the first days of automation. In an early investigation in this field,[10] Walker cited the troublesome situation that arose at the first continuous seamless pipe mill of the United States Steel Corporation. Employees engaged in a slowdown to force management into paying them either incentives or production bonuses during the difficult transition period, and they also threatened to strike when an incentive plan they disliked was introduced.

In Walker's view, an incentive plan must be psychologically, as well as mathematically, correct—that is, it must be flexible enough to be promptly adjustable to fit changed circumstances, and its coverage must extend to include the indirect labor recognized as necessary to keep production going. Mangum claims that some companies "are explicitly abandoning work measurement as outmoded, and substituting equipment utilization as the basis for incentives on machine-paced operations."[11]

[10] Charles R. Walker, *Toward the Automatic Factory* (New Haven: Yale University Press, 1957), 232 pp.
[11] Mangum, *op. cit.*, p. 88.

The rubber industry is another which makes widespread use of incentives, and rubber companies consequently face both old and new pay problems upon the introduction of new equipment. One problem as old as incentives themselves was found in company experience. In some situations employees used the weapon of holding back on production until new rates were adjusted to their satisfaction. For example, at one plant an old tire-making machine was replaced by a more automatic one. The industrial engineers calculated that the production requirement for an individual to earn the incentive bonus should be raised from 21 tires per day on the old machine to 30 tires daily on the new equipment. But the men turned out only 9 or 10 tires a day. Following discussions on the shop floor, the employees indicated a willingness to settle for an informal quota of 24 tires daily, but management was determined to hold out for production of at least 26 tires each day.

A plant manufacturing electrical components reported another interesting incentive problem resulting from automation. Most, but not all, production jobs were on incentive wage rates, and workers on incentives were able normally to achieve earnings equal to those of hourly-rated jobs evaluated at two grades above theirs. Expanding markets for the firm's products enabled management to place employees whose jobs were eliminated by technological change in other jobs, at the same grade level. But automation decreased the number of jobs to which incentive rates could be feasibly applied, and, as a consequence, there were not always a sufficient number of incentive-paid jobs to which displaced employees could be transferred. Consequently, management was unable, despite its good intentions and efforts, to keep the displaced employees happy, because the nonincentive jobs to which they were transferred, even though of equal grade, meant declines in take-home pay.

Not in all cases, however, were the problems of maintaining incentive wage plans in a new technology particularly difficult. In a flooring products manufacturing operation, the management continued to believe in wage incentives, for it was able to maintain the integrity of its program despite technological change. The company's industrial engineers held that they found no inconsistency between individual incentives and automation, but did admit that it took some hard work on their part to fashion an incentive system tailored to new technology. They argued, further, that other companies could also work out successful programs by putting forth the needed effort in identifying the individual's share of credit within the total performance of a group. The management of a metal fabricating plant concurred with this view. It also found no undue problems in running its incentive plan following the introduction of new technology, which included such innovations as multipurpose and in-line transfer machinery.

For one company, the introduction of new technology provided the occasion for a correction of looseness in its incentive plan. Following the installation of various types of automated machinery, management came to partial grips with the problem of paying average earnings for off-standard time under its incentive system. The company wanted to pay only base rates for off-standard work. But it compromised the issue with the union by agreeing that all such time would be paid for at a 75-unit hour, whereas the company had been previously paying, on the average, on the basis of a 95-unit hour. In this way, management hoped to reduce money outlays for nonproductive time, decrease the amount of idle time, and get fuller use of the new, expensive machine tools.

Discontinuance of the Incentive Method

In only a few of the cases studied, the anticipated or actual difficulties of maintaining incentive systems proved so intolerable in a new technology that the companies simply decided to abandon them. A company in the stone, clay, and glass industry avoided the use of incentives in a new plant, and used technological change as the vehicle for ridding itself of a very loose incentive wage system in an old operation. When automation became feasible in one of its product lines, the company built a plant at a new location, partly to escape from possible pressure for use of the old high-cost incentive wage schemes that were in effect at its other plants.

Another problem in a second product line of this company was that highly-skilled hand operators, who received very high individual piece rates, were able to thwart management efforts to mechanize the work, under the terms of their labor contract. Loss of business because of non-competitive prices, to which high labor costs contributed significantly, led the management to be determined to take corrective action. The company's willingness to face a long strike, if necessary in order to end the intolerable situation, finally brought the small craft union around to withdrawing its opposition to the more economic production method of utilizing automatic machinery. Upon the introduction of the new technology, with machine-pacing of work, paying piece rates for machine-cutting became an inane method of compensation, and the operation was put on an hourly-paid basis.

Abandoning wage incentives cannot always be accomplished, even though a management may desire to do so. In a machinery manufacturing plant, for example, new technology built production speed into the equipment, and the resulting tasks of establishing incentive rates and measuring individual performance were fraught with difficulties. The incentive plan was so inconsistent with automated operations that the management thought it sensible to abandon incentives entirely and put all jobs on hourly rates. This course was not followed, however, because of the management's fear of the likely union demands in negotiating wage rates to compensate employees for the loss of incentive earnings.

Substitute Approaches

Merit Increases in Lieu of Incentives. A nonunionized plant manufacturing home drugs adopted a noteworthly solution to the problems of tying in individual incentives with highly technological operations. This case was an anomaly among the cases analyzed. As the management saw it, automation of the operations, together with the problem of preserving quality control, made incentive wage plans impractical for the company. As a means of rewarding employees for diligence in keeping production rolling, the management adopted a program of merit wage increases, based on the capacity of employees to master, and be willing to do, more than one kind of job. In most unionized plants, however, the managements would undoubtedly find such a course of action barred to them, for unions are generally hostile toward merit wage increases as a method of compensation in production operations.

Group Incentives. The more usual course followed by the companies studied to resolve the problems associated with individual incentives was a gradual movement, often without premeditation, away from the individual incentive basis toward group incentives of one sort or another. As in the case of the steel company discussed earlier, a shift to calculating incentive earnings on the basis of group performance may occur by force of the realities of advanced technology, despite a management's original intent to retain individual incentives as the best motivation to greater effort. In automated operations, group incentives might be a significant means of motivation for greater output. They might integrate an entire plant more easily into the type of social unit needed to achieve high levels of efficiency, and, at the same time, be a means of allaying worker concern over the impact of technological change.

The compensation program of a company in the food-processing industry was historically one of base rates plus incentives (a modified Bedeaux system). But there, also, the management met an irreconcilable problem in attempting to measure individual worker output in the continuous operations of an automated plant. Management tried various approaches in seeking a means of calculating employee incentive bonuses. In some departments, group incentives were substituted for individual incentives. In others, a system of job rotation was introduced, whereby all workers could take turns in working in occupations in which the work could be measured. A third approach tied in the incentive earnings of the employees in indirect production jobs with those of the workers whose production could be measured; in essence, this too was a form of group incentive. Plant management was not satisfied with the results of any of these solutions, but, still viewing incentives as essential for the reduction of supervisory requirements, it continued experimentation with them.

Scanlon-Plan Adaptation.[12] Other observers of the impact of advanced technology suggest adoption of a Scanlon-type plan,[13] which ties earnings to the output of an entire plant or department and encourages worker participation in solving production problems. From his study of the problems of introducing automated operations into the steel industry, Walker concludes that such a plan might fulfill the need in continuous-flow operations to associate worker interest more closely with that of management. He holds that a willingness can thus be induced among employees to bear the financial deprivations and frustrations of long break-in or experimental periods, when the financial reward is the lowest and the men are working their hardest.

A recent survey of management views revealed, how-

12 For an analysis of the Scanlon Plan, see Industrial Relations Counselors, Inc. (New York), *Group Wage Incentives: Experience With the Scanlon Plan,* 1962 (Industrial Relations Memo No. 141), 48 pp.

13 Walker, *op. cit.,* pp. 161–175; Louis E. Davis, "The Effects of Automation on Job Design," *Industrial Relations,* Vol. 2, October, 1962, p. 62; Mangum, *op. cit.,* p. 92.

ever, that only one out of every three of the 210 respondents believed that automation increased managerial interest in Scanlon-type plans, that very few favored profit-sharing, which is integrated in such schemes, and that there was considerable doubt about the effectiveness of all group incentives.[14] This reaction to profit-sharing and the Scanlon plan was also broadly true of the companies participating in this study, with but one exception. The financial situation of this company was being adversely affected by the high cost of the individual incentive system, which had become, over a period of years, extremely loose and difficult to administer. The union refused, however, to renegotiate the plan to put it on a sounder basis. Consequently, as automated technology became operationally feasible, the parent company began searching for a new location for the plant. At this point, the union became interested in saving the jobs of its members, and the company expressed willingness to introduce the new technology in the old plant if it could be relieved of the runaway incentive rates.

Finding a solution to the incentives problem proved far from simple, until management hit upon the idea of adopting a modified Scanlon-type group incentive plan. The company sought by this means to tie incentives directly to the new technology, which would serve also to gain employee acceptance of the approaching change. Accordingly, management proposed a group incentive plan which would permit a sharing of the gains of automation. Through conferences with union leaders and addresses by company executives to union meetings, worker and union compliance was achieved, except that management had to accede to "star rates," designed to protect normal earnings during the period of transition.

After two years of operating under this modified Scanlon-type group incentive plan (no inclusion of indirect labor in

14 Otis Lipstreu, "Personnel Management in the Automated Company," *Personnel*, Vol. 38, March–April 1961, p. 41.

the bonus formula), there was general acceptance of the plan and agreement that it was working to mutual advantage. The plan gave employees a feeling of participation in the development of automated equipment and of sharing in its benefits. The employees liked working with the equipment, and the suggestions offered by them (a feature of the Scanlon Plan), though not major, proved helpful to management in many instances, and, after a long period of working out the bugs in the new technology, the employees began to receive monthly bonuses.

Inferences From Experience With Incentives

It is clear from this study that automation has drastic effects upon incentive wage systems because such technology, by its very nature, eliminates opportunities for individual employees to improve the quantity and quality of their production by their own competence. Appraisal of the experience of companies that retained individual incentive systems in automated plants leads to the conclusion that no universally applicable formula has yet been developed for making such incentives meaningful under automated conditions. However, certain generalizations may be made, based on the approaches taken by companies, about the experience with and the future of incentive pay methods.

1. There seems to be a deep reluctance to relinquish incentive systems on the part of the large majority of companies that have traditionally maintained them, regardless of the tortuous problems of relating incentive pay to the vagaries of revolutionary technology. The problems stem from the basic incongruity of adapting the incentive principle to machine-regulated output. In automated operations, individual endeavor is linked in with the chain effort of numerous employees engaged in assuring uninterrupted functioning of continuous-flow machinery. Even the specific contri-

bution made to production by groups of employees is often difficult to circumscribe.

2. The approaches taken in adapting individual incentive plans to automation and other forms of highly developed technology have been largely experimental, and the companies continue to seek means of operating such plans successfully. Difficulty in administering incentive systems is greatest during the period of transition to new technology, when the machinery itself is still experimental and work groups are in flux. Once the new conditions of production are fully established, however, the applicability of incentives does become somewhat more manageable and meaningful.

3. Where an incentive system has been characterized by loose standards, it is undoubtedly best discontinued in the face of the additional problems of new technology, as a few of the companies have done. It may be necessary then to offer employees some compensatory gain, related to the operation of the new technology.

4. If a management concludes that its system of individual incentives is no longer applicable, two alternatives are possible: abandoning the incentive pay method entirely in favor of a system of straight hourly rates for all employees or shifting to a system of group incentives. Some companies are moving in the latter direction, albeit slowly and without design.

Substituting a system of overall hourly rates involves a problem attendant on negotiating the change. If an incentive system has customarily yielded high earnings for employees, negotiation of hourly rates throughout the operation might bring arbitrary demands for rate levels equivalent to former incentive earnings. And yet the new job requirements may not be at all comparable to those for which the incentives were earned. This consideration has at times been a deterrent to discontinuation of incentives, for it only poses a choice between two evils—coping with the incentive plan or undertaking the perils of rate negotiation.

Group incentives appear to have greater kinship with the work environment created by advanced technology than do individual incentives. Keeping automated machinery operating at maximum capacity requires diligence and effort on the part of the workforce, as a group, in order to maintain uninterrupted production—a most important factor in automated operations. This ascendancy in the importance of group effort also tends to bring about extension of group incentive coverage to include indirect labor, since the efforts of all employees are necessary to prevent down-time, which is extremely costly under automation. A budding trend toward basing incentives—individual or group—on equipment utilization rather than on work measurement also is related to this concept of group responsibility for total machinery performance.

5. Although major technological change has not prevented companies from profitably employing incentives, complete automation may force plants—if and as they progressively reach this extreme stage—to abandon incentives entirely. Moreover, ever-changing technology, at any stage, calls for a degree of flexibility to be built into the incentive plan to permit its adaptation to altering needs. Such a flexible plan must be administered with utmost alertness and vigilance, or its value will inevitably deteriorate under the impact of any further change in plant technology.

Beyond the foregoing generalizations, advanced on the basis of company experience, lie certain long-range implications for management. These relate to changes with regard to supervision of work, selection of employees, and the viability of incentives over the long run. Because automated technology reduces the importance of incentives, it is incumbent upon management to direct work more effectively through sharpened supervision. With speed built into machinery and with individuals no longer engaged in discrete tasks, there is a reversal of the premises whereby incentives have been seen as valuable.

In automated operations, the workforce operating as an integrated unit determines the efficiency of operations. The resulting need for effective intergroup relations places significantly greater responsibility on the supervisory role. Sayles has expressed this quite explicitly:

> ... The modern factory ... consists of a number of closely interrelated, interdependent groups. .... It is the recognition of the problems associated with these specialized groups that is really the essence of what has come to be called the "second industrial revolution." The important element here is not the hardware (the computers, the servomechanisms) but the implicit recognition that the problem of the manager is maintaining *continuity, coordination, sequence*—of the interrelationships between his own employees and even between them and the employees of other managers. Getting the group to work "harder" or "faster" is rarely the answer; rather, the manager's objective is coordinating the efforts of people so that something approximating a smooth, continuous flow of work results.[15]

Old standards of employee selection are becoming obsolete and will have to be replaced. Employees on automated operations need not be "fast" or "hard" workers, being no longer engaged in discrete tasks. A strong back ceases to be a job necessity once advanced technology enters into production. Rather, the employee has to be resourceful, intelligent, and capable of coordinating his efforts with those of his fellow workers. As Mann and Hoffman pointed out in their study of an automated power plant: "The extreme interconnectedness of automated processes means that the crippling of any part incapacitates the entire system. The worker must be able, then, to react to deviations in the operation by immediately identifying the difficulty, diagnosing its cause, and taking appropriate measures."[16] As yet, few companies have

15 Leonard R. Sayles, "New Concepts in Work Group Theory," in *Behavioral Science Research in Industrial Relations* (New York: Industrial Relations Counselors, Inc., 1962), pp. 79–80.

16 Floyd C. Mann and L. Richard Hoffman, *Automation and the Worker* (New York: Henry Holt and Company, 1960), p. 210.

sufficiently revised their methods of selection to recruit employees with such abilities.

Finally—even though at this stage of the current technological revolution individual incentives may still be capable of motivating employees to greater effort and output—it is apparent that as automation becomes more widespread the value of individual incentives will decline precipitously, and the problems of using them will multiply. Steps can be taken to prepare for this eventuality by viewing objectively the implications of the changes that have already occurred in terms of their impact on the traditional values attributed to individual incentives. An important factor is to recognize the growing need to provide group motivation and to promote cooperative intergroup relationships. Pertinent to any such deliberations are the findings of the newer research in the behavioral sciences relative to the behavior of work groups.

CHAPTER VII

Benefits and the
Employment Security Issue

In relating the influence of modern technology to developments in the field of employee benefits, consideration must first be given to the evolutionary aspects of the benefits picture in recent decades. Benefit programs today are certainly a far cry from those of earlier times, when they depended on employer good will and the benefits provided were actually employer expressions of concern for the welfare of employees. The cost of benefits was then justified not only in terms of the security provided for employees but also on the basis of the gains achieved by employers in attracting and holding competent personnel, thus reducing employee turnover and its incidental costs.

In 1949, however, a decision of the United States Supreme Court, in the noted case against the Inland Steel Company, abrogated the privilege of voluntary unilateral employer action in the benefits field and made it compulsory for companies to bargain with employee representatives on benefit provisions. Since then, unions have sought benefit gains in collective bargaining as zealously as they have demanded wage gains. From a practical point of view, benefits have actually become an adjunct to wages, as we find that more and more wage settlements are calculated in "package" form, with benefits of various kinds constituting one element of the package. Moreover, the scope of employee benefit programs in many industries has been changing in the years since benefits became subject to collective bargaining. The changes have been manifest not only in the emphasis on benefit improvement and extension but in the emergence of benefit demands and provisions in response to economic or other pressures at given times.

The exigencies of the employment situation in recent years have brought about a pronounced emphasis in collective bargaining on securing benefits and a lessened pressure for substantial wage increases. The business recessions of 1957–1958 and 1960–1961, together with reductions in the blue-collar workforce in the mass production industries and declining union membership, have turned the attention of many influential unions to securing various forms of job and income protection for their membership against the contingencies of layoffs. Moreover, employees have seemed to lay great store by collective bargaining gains that promise job and/or income security. It has not been difficult, therefore, for union leaders to impress on employees the greater long-term importance and benefit to them of forgoing liberal increases in hourly wage rates in favor of security measures.

This is the setting in which advanced technology has reared into prominence on the industrial scene. Its rise and spread have brought new anxieties concerning job security, and these have heightened union interest in negotiating protective measures within the framework of, or supplementary to, existing benefit programs. It seems reasonable to say, then, that one effect of the introduction of modern technology has been to intensify this previously evident tendency. As technological change becomes more widespread, unions increasingly press more vigorously for benefit provisions to assure for employees some degree of continuity of income, against possible displacement, and they may even tone down wage demands, in order to improve the security package.

Technological change has led to new roles for benefit plans which can be useful in dealing with workforce dislocations. Modern technology has also induced new kinds of protective arrangements in certain industries and has prompted broad proposals for offsetting its impact on employee jobs and income. This chapter gives an overall review of these developments, illustrated with relevant experience from among the companies studied.

EXTENDING THE FEATURES OF BENEFIT PROGRAMS

Where the introduction of modern technology has severely reduced customary manpower requirements, the problem of excess personnel often has had to be resolved, in the last analysis, by effecting permanent layoffs. As described in earlier chapters, companies have endeavored to keep actual employee displacement at the irreducible minimum—by speeding up normal attrition in the workforce, arranging intra- and interplant transfers, and retraining employees for new or changed jobs.

Employees have, however, been terminated, for managements have generally resisted union pressures to force an excess quota of workers on changed operations. Yet, judging by the companies studied, managements have given the utmost attention to the human problems of employees who have had to be terminated. On their part, union leaders have sought extra income in one form or another for members who are displaced.

The focus of unions on job or income security, together with the desire of companies to ease the impact of technological change on the situation of employees, has led to the liberalization of benefit plans during recent years. Benefit plans were originally conceived by companies as an aid in the recruitment and retention of employees, but they are now being used as an aid in handling the dislocations incidental to technological change. This new function of benefit plans has brought the liberalization of early retirement, vesting, and disability provisions of pension plans; extension to laid-off employees of health and other benefits; and revision or adoption of severance pay plans.

Special Pension Adjustments for Early Retirement

It has been found that younger employees tend to have greater learning ability, adaptability, and generally more advanced educational backgrounds than older employees (see Chapter V). Therefore, in effecting permanent layoffs, if a choice must be made between older and younger employees, it is often to the advantage of a changed operation to retain the latter. Moreover, because the investment in training younger persons has a potentially longer payoff for the company, management attempts to make retirement attractive for older workers in advance of the normal age specified in the pension plan.

The wide prevalence in industry of pension plans that provide for early retirement or disability retirement facilitates this approach. Nearly 90 percent of 300 bargained pension plans studied by the Bureau of Labor Statistics in 1959 permitted early retirement under either early or disability retirement provisions, and 75 percent of them had no age specification for disability retirement. The age requirements for early retirement were usually from five to fifteen years lower than for normal retirement. Among the 224 plans that provided for early retirement, 75 percent permitted qualified workers to retire early on their own volition, and the remaining plans either required the employer's consent or permitted the employer to initiate early retirement.[1]

Pension plans in the automobile and rubber industries have special features attuned to making early retirement more palatable in an economic sense. These plans combine elements of early retirement, a severance pay arrangement, and modified disability retirement related to the employee's capacity to perform his job rather than to total permanent disability.[2] In the automobile industry, early retirement benefits for workers under age sixty-two are supplemented until they become eligible for social security, at which time benefits revert to the level actually earned under the plan.

This study found that the pension plans of all but 2 of the 36 cooperating companies had some provision for early retirement; many had liberalized their pension policies considerably, not only to permit early retirement but to encourage it, in anticipation of employee displacements due to technological and economic changes. Typically, liberalization reduced the usual actuarial discount for early retirement, as based on the pension payable at the normal retirement date, and/or provided some supplementary income for retirees until they could qualify for federal social security benefits.

When a surplus of manpower occurs, companies favor early retirement of older workers for several reasons. First, retirement on an adjusted pension is a security measure for older employees since it gives them a lifetime basic income, whether or not they continue to work elsewhere. Second, managements regard early retirement of employees of advanced age as being quite equitable, for it allocates the risks

[1] U.S. Bureau of Labor Statistics, *Pension Plans Under Collective Bargaining: Normal Retirement, Early and Disability Retirement*, Bulletin No. 1284 (Washington: Government Printing Office, 1961), pp. 29, 31.
[2] *Ibid.*, p. 29.

of displacement to those employees best able to sustain them. Particularly in periods when jobs are scarce, the availability of even modest pensions for older workers is seen as vastly more advantageous than unemployment for younger ones with greater family obligations.

Balanced against the costliness of early retirement, managements hold, is the factor of plant operating efficiency. Productiveness, adaptability, and potential years on the job are seen as weighing more heavily on the side of retaining the younger rather than the older employees. Other cost considerations are also involved, particularly in companies that provide displaced employees with liberal severance allowances. In the last analysis, it is a choice of costs—the cost of severance payments to displaced employees or the expense of liberalizing early retirement benefits under an already-established pension liability.

The case of a chemical company participating in this study is broadly representative of trends in this area. In dealing with technological displacement, the company exercised extensively its privilege under the pension plan to retire employees who were incapable of adapting to new job requirements. At some of its plants there were considerable numbers of older, marginal employees whose jobs were eliminated by the new technology. The limitations of many of these employees prohibited their transfer to other jobs and, in the management's judgment, rendered them unemployable in production operations. It was considered best for them, therefore, to be given the income protection afforded under the early retirement provisions of the pension plan. In fact, the company now provides for full pension payments— no actuarial discount—to employees having 30 or more years of service who voluntarily retire after reaching age sixty.

A petroleum company takes another approach in encouraging early retirement. A special limited-period offer of early retirement allows employees accepting it to avoid significant reduction of normal retirement income. A sixty-year old worker receives about 91 percent, instead of the normal 77–78 percent, of his age-sixty-five benefit. The plan also incorporates a special "Social Security Allowance": from age sixty to age sixty-two, the early retiree receives additional monthly payments of $90; and from age sixty-two to age sixty-three, he receives, whether or not he applies for social security benefits, $50 monthly. Under certain conditions, employees between age fifty and age sixty may also be eligible for early retirement under the plan.

A second petroleum company permits retirement of employees who are subject to termination and are age fifty-five or over if the combination of their age and years of service equals at least 80. Employees with only 10 years of service are also eligible for early retirement, subject to company approval. The displaced employees receive severance pay in addition to their pensions.

A number of companies allow displaced employees with 10 or more years of service to retire at age sixty, with a temporarily increased benefit to compensate for the social security benefits for which they are not yet eligible. In some cases of plant shutdown or transfer of operations to another location, early retirement benefits are double the amount they would be normally under the pension plan, and are continued until social security benefits are payable; then the employee's retirement income is reduced to the normal level.

The drive for liberalized early retirement has been advanced by unions as well as management. In the maritime industry, for instance, members of the National Maritime Union recently voted to pass up two 2¼ percent increases in wages due them under existing contracts with the American Merchant Marine Institute in hope of removing the sixty-five-year age requirement, and of permitting seamen to retire at any age after 20 years of service in the industry.

The extent to which employees voluntarily seek early retirement varies among companies. The management of a chemical company reported that relatively few eligible employees elected voluntary retirement when threatened with displacement, unless they were actually designated for termination. In other companies, however, high percentages of older employees applied for early retirement, even though they were not to be displaced. Some managements indicated that very often older workers volunteered for retirement reluctantly, largely because fellow employees pressed them to do so in order to preserve jobs for younger workers.

As discussed in Chapter III, companies employ two basic approaches with respect to early retirement. Either they have a fixed policy of early retirement, or they establish for a special limited period a pension for those accepting retirement that is higher than it would normally be. The advantage of the limited-period approach is that it can be timed to achieve a higher rate of acceptances of early retirement when such an increase is most urgently needed—during the period of heavy technological displacement. On the other hand, one disadvantage is that it penalizes the older employee who refuses retirement at that time because he is still capable of performing well on the job, for should he wish subsequently to retire early he may find that the special inducements have been withdrawn. Another disadvantage is that some older employees, who opt for early retirement during a special limited-period offer, may be those whom the management wishes to retain because of their skills and ability.

Vested Pension Rights

Among other developments in the benefits field that have been attributed to the spread of modern technology, there is an accelerating movement in industry toward vesting of pension credits accrued during service with a company. Although the principle of vesting is not new, it had not been widely applied until recent years because of the costliness of vesting such benefits. A recent survey of 1,213 pension plans, however, reports that approximately two-thirds of the 950 plans in manufacturing and the 99 plans in public utilities have vesting provisions, and that vesting generally is more common among contributory than noncontributory plans, whether the plan is negotiated or unilaterally established.[3] Eligibility for vested benefits is usually based upon the employee's age or years of service (or participation in the pension plan), or some combination of age and service.

The logic of "vested rights" has been propounded from more than one standpoint. Theoretically, if a company has not obligated itself to provide employees with pension coverage, it would have to grant some pay equivalent over the years. Pension vesting, therefore, protects the terminated employee against the loss of the income he might have received earlier.

A further argument in favor of vesting is that it responds to a dynamic economy by encouraging labor mobility. The presumption is that a worker who knows he can accumulate pension credits, as he changes from one place of employment to another, feels that on this score he makes no sacrifice in moving from one location to another having greater work opportunities. This concept is, of course, embodied in the federal social security system.

The President's Advisory Committee on Labor-Management Policy, in its report on automation, noted that the nontransferability of pension rights complicates the adjustment to technological change because it reduces the mobility of workers.[4] Professor Haber also has suggested that a rapid spread of the practice of vesting pensions at age forty, after 10 years' employment, would be economically desirable, as

3 Harland Fox, "Pension Plan Vesting," *Business Management Record*, October, 1963, pp. 41–42.

4 The President's Advisory Committee on Labor-Management Policy (Washington), *The Benefits and Problems Incident to Automation and Other Technological Advances*, 1962, p. 3.

it would encourage the more settled workers to relocate as industry shifts from one area to another.[5]

The rising interest in "portable pensions" as a means of increasing labor mobility, easing unemployment, and meeting the "threat" of automation, led to formation, in 1962, of the President's Committee on Corporate Pension Funds and Other Private Retirement and Welfare Programs. A study prepared for the Committee held it unlikely, however, "that even liberal vesting provisions . . . would do much to increase the total amount of job changing of workers with vested pensions." Interestingly, the study suggested that early retirement "may make an important contribution to decreasing the immobilizing effects of pensions, since early retirement makes it possible for the worker who is only a few years away from normal retirement age to leave his job without forfeiting his pension."[6]

The absence of both early retirement and vesting provisions can work serious hardship on older employees who must be terminated. This was precisely the situation at a machinery plant that closed down. The retirement plan at this plant provided neither vesting nor early retirement benefits. Upon the final closing of the plant, many workers between fifty and sixty years of age, who had up to 40 years of service with the company, were left with only a few hundred dollars of severance pay to face competition in a highly unfavorable labor market.

Arguments in favor of pension vesting should be viewed cautiously in particular company situations. The burden of liberal vesting provisions can be great, and it would be foolhardy for a company to undertake pension vesting without carefully projecting costs. The importance of adequate fund-

5 William Haber, in a speech before the 15th Annual Conference on Aging at Ann Arbor, Michigan, reported in Bureau of National Affairs (Washington), *Daily Labor Report*, No. 122, June 22, 1962, p. A–7.

6 U.S. Bureau of Labor Statistics, *Private Pension Plans and Manpower Policy*, Bulletin No. 1359 (Washington: Government Printing Office, 1963), p. 17.

ing of all pension liability is fully appreciated by industrial management, and advisers on pension financing have stressed this point.[7] Under professional guidance and with sound actuarial advice, gradual vesting of pension benefits, with parallel funding of the costs, may be feasible. Actually, 30 of the cooperating companies provided some form of vesting of pensions.

Continuation of Health and Life Insurance to Employees on Lay-off

Another route being taken to ease worker adjustment to technological displacement is that of extending health and other benefits to laid-off employees for specified periods of time. Studies of benefit plans made by the Bureau of Labor Statistics in 1959–1960 disclosed that about half of the 293 plans providing surgical benefits continued such coverage to workers during layoff; the ratio of plans extending medical benefits was about the same. The duration of such coverage was most frequently for a month; significantly, approximately one-third of the plans permitted laid-off employees to continue under coverage for another six months, but at their own expense. Similar coverage was provided with respect to hospitalization benefits. Continuation of life insurance coverage during layoff was found in almost 60 percent of such plans, usually for six months; many plans permitted employees to undertake the cost of coverage for additional periods—for as much as eighteen months in some cases.[8]

Among case-study companies, the provisions for extension of benefits to laid-off employees were much in line with

[7] Walter J. Couper and Roger Vaughan, *Pension Planning: Experience and Trends* (New York: Industrial Relations Counselors, Inc., 1954), pp. 27–28.

[8] U.S. Bureau of Labor Statistics, *Health and Insurance Plans Under Collective Bargaining* (Washington: Government Printing Office), Bulletin No. 1280, Surgical and Medical Benefits (1960), p. 12; Bulletin No. 1274, Hospital Benefits (1960), pp. 23, 25; Bulletin No. 1296, Life Insurance and Accidental Death and Dismemberment Benefits (1961), p. 8.

the findings of the Bureau of Labor Statistics. A typical contract clause reads as follows:

> All hospitalization, surgical, and maternity benefits will be continued for laid-off employees (including dependents) with 2 or more years of continuous service at the date of layoff for up to six months following date of layoff, provided such continued coverage shall cease if and when seniority is terminated.

Sentiment in favor of extending health benefits to displaced employees was prevalent even in companies that had no such provision, but the managements were deliberating the matter of cost. Taking the judicious course in the benefits field avoids about-face action when experience proves that liberality was ill-advised. Witness the experience of the United Mine Workers' Welfare and Retirement Fund, which provided hospital and medical benefits not only to employed but to unemployed miners, regardless of the length of their unemployment and with eligibility terminating only if the worker accepted employment outside the industry. When the fund continued to operate at a deficit, however, the trustees were forced to limit the period of eligibility to one year following termination of employment. Although this sparked a revolt of unemployed miners, the limitation remained; and John L. Lewis, then United Mine Workers' president, defended the reduction in aid to the displaced as a matter of "simple arithmetic."[9] Should a company find it necessary to withhold negotiated benefits, the matter certainly could not be disposed of by such elementary reasoning.

Severance Pay Plans

The Trends. Definitely attributable to the influence of technological change is the trend during the last few years

[9] Thomas Kennedy, *Automation Funds and Displaced Workers* (Boston: Graduate School of Business Administration, Division of Research, Harvard University, 1962), pp. 32–42.

toward expansion or adoption of formalized severance pay plans for both organized and unorganized production workers. Severance payments upon permanent termination of employment are being related to the validity of the concept that employees have a property right to a job. The question at issue is whether or not a company has a responsibility to compensate workers whom it has employed when it no longer can provide them with jobs. Some academicians have revived the Commons-Perlman concept, holding that recognition of the job as a property right requires severance pay—the buying back of the property right that has become obsolete.[10]

American management has never accepted the concept of the job as a property right; yet, in its typically pragmatic approach to resolving industrial relations problems as they arise, it has responded to the reasonableness of providing severance pay to ease adjustments to technological change. Thus, companies that have, or are considering adoption of, severance payment plans are motivated neither by recognition of a property right to the job, nor by the necessity to "bribe" workers, as one writer has suggested.[11] Moreover, most theoreticians reject the property-rights concept.[12]

In considering severance pay plans, companies are motivated by three desires: (1) to assure employees of some economic security against the dislocations of technological change and thus forestall exaggerated fears and resistance to the introduction of new technology; (2) to alleviate the hardship of displacement where it occurs, particularly for older, long-service employees, who generally have the toughest problems of readjustment; and (3) to demonstrate to employees

10 See William Gomberg, "Featherbedding: An Assertion of Property Rights," *The Annals,* Vol. 333, January, 1961, p. 129; Gomberg, "The Job as Property," *The Nation,* Vol. 191, November 26, 1960, pp. 410–412.

11 Gomberg, "Featherbedding: An Assertion of Property Rights," *op. cit.,* p. 129.

12 See, for example, Simon Rottenberg, "Discussion—Property in Work," *Industrial and Labor Relations Review,* Vol. 15, April, 1962, pp. 402–405.

and the community the company's genuine sense of responsibility for the immediate welfare of those of its employees who may become the victims of technological change within its operations.

This study found a distinct trend in management thinking generally toward the payment of severance benefits as a mitigant factor in dealing with problems of technological displacement. Severance pay is seen as offering partial compensation to an employee for loss of the income he expected from continuing employment with the company. Based on such income expectations, the individual may have made future financial commitments, such as home-mortgage payments, which he might not have undertaken had he been able to foresee the termination of his employment.

A majority of 23 of the 36 cooperating companies provided severance payments. A number had long-established severance pay plans, some of which had been broadened to take account of technological change. Others began to provide such benefits more recently, either unilaterally or through collective bargaining. Among the minority of companies that had no form of severance pay were some which had not needed such plans, having never found it necessary to deal with the problem of permanent separation of employees. In a few instances, however, displaced employees were badly disadvantaged because they received no severance pay. Most severance pay plans provided graduated benefits, related to seniority, age, or a combination of the two.

The action of a leading food-processing company illustrates how existing severance policies have been extended to meet the problem of technological displacements. The company had a long-standing policy of paying termination allowances to blue-collar employees, if they were disabled or if their jobs were eliminated by the closing of a plant or department or by the sale of the business. Then the pace of technological change quickened at the same time that growth in the volume of company sales slackened. The management proceeded to amend the plan to grant eligibility for termination pay to all employees who had three or more years of continuous service and were laid off permanently or were not recalled for twelve consecutive months because of the introduction of new production equipment or processes. The amount of payment was determined according to a schedule that took into account the employee's earnings, age, and years of continuous service and provided for a maximum of 52 weeks of pay. To attain the maximum, an employee had to be at least fifty-seven years of age and to have had 32 years of service; a forty-five-year-old employee with 10 years of service received ten weeks of severance pay.

Provisions for severance benefits underwent an interesting evolution at a machinery plant that was being phased out of existence over a period of years. In this case, the company provided no severance allowance when the shutdown of various departments started in 1952. The condition of the local job market at that time was very good, permitting most employees terminated to get other jobs quickly and without much difficulty, and there was little union or employee concern over a threat to security. As the buoyancy dropped out of the labor market, however, management ran into union opposition, which led to the establishment in 1958 of a modest severance allowance. Concern with security grew when the more senior employees faced termination, and the severance allowance was raised twice before the plant was completely closed in 1961.

For several reasons, companies are inclined to the adoption or liberalization of severance pay plans in this period of technological innovation. The individual employee is understandably prone to view the introduction of new technology as a threat to his job security, whether or not he is likely to be displaced. This individual reaction could inevitably add up to concerted employee resistance to technological change. Managements reason, therefore, that such resistance will be reduced if each employee, in facing the eventuality of displacement, can look forward to receiving severance pay. With financial resources thus assured to tide him over, he can take the necessary time to find another job, or to relocate, or to retrain himself for other employment. In the absence of any other form of unemployment benefit in a company, a severance pay plan is regarded as a realistic and just method of smoothing the adjustments necessitated by technological change.

Dealing with resistance to change by an organized group of employees, however, is far different from giving assurances to individual employees. Representatives of organized groups may try to obstruct any change reducing the number of jobs and to advance "make work" proposals to save jobs. In such situations, negotiation of a severance pay plan is not only better for the company, it also brings credit to the union in the eyes of its membership, being evidence that it "struck a good deal" for employees to offset the threat of technological displacement.

The heightened interest of unions in negotiating severance pay has been sparked by other factors than the aid granted their displaced members. Knowledgeable union leaders are well aware that modern technology gives companies competitive advantages and that it therefore serves not only the best long-term interests of a company but those of union members also. They recognize that it is the economic soundness of the enterprise which will enable them to protect the jobs of those union members who remain in the company's employ. It may be assumed, therefore, that union pressure for severance pay plans will mount, and that companies which have none, or are deliberating the introduction of such a plan, may be pushed into adopting one.

Some Reasoning on Severance Benefits. In common with other employee benefits, severance pay is one form of security companies provide for employees against the contingencies of an uncertain economic future. It is held in some quarters that employee security is particularly enhanced by severance pay plans because the accompanying liability deters management from effecting "frivolous" layoffs. There was no evidence in this study that companies engage in frivolous layoffs. Nevertheless, the severance pay liability can be a stimulus for all managers within a company to try to achieve more effective manpower planning, along the lines discussed in Chapter X. Moreover, progressive companies, recognizing their responsibilities as corporate citizens of the communities in which they operate, see the liability, in some circumstances, as embracing more than the cost factor. When a primary employer in a labor-market area reduces the size of its labor force, there are serious economic implications for the community; and this is one of the considerations that led to voluntary institution of the early severance pay plans.

The cost of severance pay can be a deterrent, however, to the adoption of such a plan by a company. This is particularly true for the company that faces substantial employee terminations within a short period of time as the result of technological change. In some instances, the outlay needed to provide meaningful benefits could be so great as to obliterate the cost of the savings expected to result from the new technology. But if there is no provision for severance pay, employees and their bargaining representatives may block the introduction of any new technology that would cause widespread displacements. In that case, the price of not providing termination allowances might turn out to be the inability of the company to carry out its modernization program.

On the other hand, if the company establishes a severance pay plan on the basis of the costs it can afford, it might find it can provide meaningful benefits only for very long-service employees or only token benefits for all displaced employees. If it makes such compromises, however, the company would probably not fulfill any of the three objectives in adopting a severance pay plan—alleviating the hardships of unemployment; assuaging employee anxiety over, and consequent resistance to, technological change; and strengthening the regard of employees and the community for the company.

A dramatic experience with this very dilemma occurred in one of the companies studied. The management was contemplating negotiation of a severance pay plan in order to deal with the problem of occasional employee terminations because of technological innovation. Even before negotiations with the union got under way, however, the company lost a large defense contract. Thus it faced the necessity of effecting immediate layoffs of extensive proportions, which the projected severance plan was not designed to accommodate. The union, however, insisted all the more strongly on substantial severance payments, and a strike took place. The compromise settlement was to no one's liking, for the severance plan adopted obligated the company, which was already in financial difficulties, to a more expensive plan than it could afford and, at the same time, provided the displaced employees with much smaller benefits than those of other severance plans.

Providing overgenerous levels of severance benefits may also be an ill-advised action, particularly if this benefit is paid in a lump sum. For one thing, in some states severance payments make the recipients ineligible for unemployment insurance benefits. Second, they often discourage the displaced employee from immediately pursuing new employment. Third, workers may consider such payments as windfalls and use them for major purchases—as, for example, a new automobile—or creditors may take advantage of employees who have received severance payments to collect bills due; either way the displaced employee cannot use the money to tide him over a period of unemployment.

The dubious kindness of granting payments that are excessively magnanimous, in terms of amount and duration, is illustrated by the experience of the petroleum refinery which also undertook a program to assist displaced employees in finding other employment. As described in Chapter III, the majority of displaced employees either ignored the program entirely or did not avail themselves of the work opportunities it afforded. Being armed, in an economic sense, with generous severance benefits, many were disinclined to enter new jobs, and found what they thought to be reasonable excuses for turning down job offers. Further, some did not seek jobs on their own initiative.

The aftermath in this case took an ironic turn. At the end of six months, severance benefits ended, and some displaced employees were faced with no income and no jobs. Many of them then returned to the refinery with pleas for help. The very generous benefits proved to be a disservice to some workers, by discouraging early and active pursuit of other work, which in very many cases was available. The dual role of income provider and placement medium assumed by the management brought about an unanticipated dependence upon the company on the part of the displaced workers, even after their employment had been terminated.

Not all companies need to adopt a severance pay plan. Benefits would be superfluous in a company that has no separation problem or that has some other type of program protecting employees against the loss of income due to unemployment. The program of one of the case-study companies is illustrative. Some years ago, the company negotiated a form of supplementary unemployment benefits based on individual employee accounts, rather than a common fund. Employees may draw against their accounts benefits of up to $30 a week for either prolonged sickness or layoff. When a group of workers was actually displaced by new machinery, each collected $600 ($30 for each of 20 weeks of unemployment) in security benefits.

Company experience indicates that a company, before adopting severance pay, should carefully appraise its existing benefits program to see if there is need for such a plan. If there is, then the plan adopted should be tailored with due regard to the current and prospective manpower situation of the company. It should also be integrated with other benefit programs and with all applicable provisions of collective bargaining contracts.

INNOVATIONS IN THE BENEFITS FIELD

The anticipation that advanced technology would induce employee relations problems of unparalleled dimensions has caused new institutional arrangements to be produced through collective bargaining. These new arrangements, designed to cope with the new problems and to smooth the course of current technological progress, are of two major types: (1) special so-called "automation" funds to provide benefits and other safeguards for employees, often in exchange for express recognition of the employer's right to introduce advanced methods of operation; and (2) bonus formulas through which employees share in the monetary gains resulting from increased employee productivity or improved company performance. As nascent developments, these programs were surrounded with much publicity, but attention, even if no more than cursory, must be given to them here, so as to round out the benefits picture in relation to technological change.

Automation Funds

The highly publicized technique of setting up special automation funds has not been pursued beyond the initial push for such funds, indicating the limited applicability of this device in dealing with problems of technological change. It is clear from the findings of this study that for most American industry the establishment of special automation funds has been unnecessary in adjusting to the introduction of advanced technology. Furthermore, the value of these funds as aids to displaced employees is highly questionable.

Detailed analysis of existing funds by one researcher led him to conclude that they have provided little or nothing in the way of benefits for the workers displaced by automation.[13]

The primary aim of most automation funds is, in fact, not so much to provide aid for the displaced as to blunt opposition to technological change. Thus they are designed either to give those employees who are retained a share in the resultant savings or to provide a medium for better communication between management and labor through the joint committee that administers the fund. In these respects they appear to have been successful in most instances. But, in the experience of companies cooperating in this study, even the accomplishment of these aims has not necessarily required the establishment of special funds. Kennedy has pointed out the factors that influenced their adoption in particular types of industries:

> . . . it is significant that all of the funds except . . . one (the Armour Fund) are in industries where: (1) labor and management engage in multi-employer or industry-wide bargaining; (2) there are numerous employers, some of whom lack financial stability; (3) some employees are likely to work for more than one employer over the years or even during a particular year. In industries of this nature it has long been recognized by labor and management that the soundest and most practical way of allocating the costs of and insuring the payment of certain employee benefits is through the operation of a fund or funds. . . . It was natural, therefore, that labor and management in these industries should turn to a fund as one of the means of achieving their goals with respect to the industrial relations aspects of automation.[14]

It is not the purpose of this study to examine the workings of these special funds, as Kennedy has done that most thoroughly in his analysis of the subject. However, this study

13 Kennedy, op. cit., p. 340.
14 Ibid., pp. 350–351.

permitted examination of experience with such a fund in the longshore industry on the West Coast, in which one of the case-study companies participates. The findings are of interest here.

West Coast Longshore Fund. The "Mechanization and Modernization Fund" in West Coast longshoring came into being in 1960, when a six-year agreement relating to automation of dock work in West Coast ports was reached between the Pacific Maritime Association and the International Longshoremen's and Warehousemen's Union. The pact has had major significance because it has enabled the companies involved to buy out restrictive work rules with a substantial benefit package. The fund to finance the benefits has been derived from employer contributions aggregating $5 million a year for about five and one-half years.

With respect to advantages gained by management, the agreement guaranteed to the employers the right to introduce any labor-saving equipment and machinery deemed necessary for efficient operations. It also gave them freedom to decide how to run the docks—to determine the number and size of longshore gangs needed, the weight of sling-loads in loading and unloading ships, and the number of times cargo would be handled. Further, the agreement provided for elimination of a long list of union "make-work" practices and restrictive work rules, many of which had been in effect for twenty years or more.

On the labor side, the agreement provided for benefits and safeguards to longshoremen and other employees represented by the union. In it were guarantees of no layoffs stemming from mechanization for regular longshoremen and a minimum of 35 hours' pay per week if, as a result of mechanization, earnings from available work fell below that amount. These provisions served largely to eliminate the use of casual workers. Also included were guarantees against "individual speed-up" and infringement of safety rules. The agreement provided for increased death and disability benefits. It also permitted early retirement or, alternatively, a lump-sum benefit at normal retirement. This encouragement of early retirement speeded up the attrition rate in the industry. Historically the rate had been 4 percent per year, but after 1960 it rose to 9 percent per year.

An attempt was made in this study to discover, from the experience of the case-study company participating in the ILWU-PMA automation fund agreement, the extent to which the management has been free to introduce work changes in its operations since the agreement went into effect. In general, the management was pleased with the results of the agreement. However, its full operation was inhibited by a union jurisdictional dispute and by the wait, up to the time of interview, for an Internal Revenue Service ruling with respect to the tax treatment to be accorded to the funds paid by the employers.[15]

According to the 1960 agreement, the company is free to introduce changes in work methods, and the union is free to file grievances when it considers treatment to be unfair, or regards a modification as inappropriate or unsafe. Some members of the management feared at first that the union would so clog the grievance procedure as to preclude effectuation by the company of new methods of operation. Actually, however, although a considerable number of grievances were filed, procedures were developed which permitted rapid handling of grievances at shipside. As recognized by management, the grievance procedure has a further value, from the standpoint of intra-union relationships. This extra value is that it provides an escape valve for use when union leadership recognizes the need for, and agrees to, work changes that may not please the union rank and file.

Procedures under the agreement, as well as various forms of technological change, are still evolving. But under

15 After one year, the Internal Revenue Service did permit the deduction of employer contributions to the Fund as business expense, thus allowing the payment of benefits to employees.

the plan, whenever the company tries out a new method of operation, the union may file a grievance. If it does, the arbitrator then goes to the waterfront and issues a temporary order. Generally the order permits the employer to make the modification, but subjects it to further review and appraisal.

In many instances, it proved necessary in introducing a change to negotiate supplementary agreements providing additional safeguards for employees, in terms of their health and safety. The procedures, however, did not hamper the management in effecting methods of improvement, technological change, or new operating techniques. An important factor of flexibility was the availability of immediate arbitration in cases of disagreement between the parties. This prevented long delays in settling issues. Moreover, the arbitrators were men with a close knowledge of waterfront operations and a deep understanding of the implications of proposed technological improvements and of the necessary human adjustments that are entailed. They, therefore, have enjoyed high standing with both parties, and their awards have been mutually respected.

The agreement permitted extensive improvements in operations in the company studied. The management noted that in loading one type of ship it was able to save almost 20 percent of labor costs. This company was optimistic enough to expect that, during the life of the contract, total cost savings from the improved processes would more than offset the amount of money contributed to the fund.

East Coast Longshore Fund. None of the companies studied were participants in the "automation" fund agreement relative to containerized cargo in East Coast longshoring. Consequently, no case experience can be reported, but the known experience with the agreement in that branch of longshore operations stands in sharp contrast to the situation on the West Coast. The East Coast automation fund was established following a 1959 coastwide dock strike, in protest against the innovation of containerized cargo. Under the automation fund agreement, shippers pay royalties for the privilege of using prepacked containers. The royalties range from 35 cents a ton for loading containers aboard a conventional freighter to $1 a ton for loading them onto ships fitted especially for containers. This arrangement represents a forward step, as formerly the union insisted that prepacked containers be stripped and then reloaded by dock workers.

The major fault of the agreement, however, is that it covers only one aspect of the entire question of port-loading efficiency. It resolves nothing concerning normal gang size, sling-loads, the use of lift-on-lift-off vessels, and the introduction of mechanized equipment in general. As it turns out, this piecemeal attempt is simply postponing the broader solution needed to resolve the problem of securing efficient operations. In 1962–1963, union-management differences over technological change, particularly size of work gangs, were an issue in a long strike.

In contrast with the East Coast situation, the West Coast settlement derived from careful definition of the overall waterfront problem, and recognition that the problem was far broader than one of containerization alone. The agreement takes account of the need for more efficient practices in all waterfront operations, ranging from methods improvements to the introduction of new equipment. So broad a concept establishes a common interest or stake among all employers, for it provides a basis for improvement of operations for all companies involved in the settlement, whether or not they handle containerized cargo. This offers the opportunity for far more significant progress in achieving efficiency in waterfront operation than does the East Coast settlement. Furthermore, the West Coast pact gives workers greater protection against layoffs and short workweeks due to mechanization. In fact, on the East Coast the employers and the International Longshoremen's Association have yet to agree on the benefits that are to flow to employees from the employer contributions, but it is predicted that they will not be designed to aid employees who are displaced.[16]

Sharing the Gains of Automation

Within the last two years, two unique collective bargaining agreements have emerged on the American industrial scene—at the American Motors Corporation and at the Kaiser Steel Corporation. Both involve the concept of sharing with employees the gains of increased efficiency and economic performance.

Under the "Progress-Sharing Plan" negotiated in 1961 by American Motors and the United Automobile Workers, employees share in the company's profits. In the first year of plan operation, the profits generated were more than adequate to pay for all 1963 improvements in employee benefits and to permit distribution to some 27,000 hourly-paid workers of an average of 7.3 shares of AMC stock each. The value of the average stock package was $128.70. The progress-sharing plan has been hailed by both company and union representatives, but so far there has been a noticeable lack of imitation of this device.

Another type of sharing arrangement was that negotiated early in 1963 by the Kaiser Steel Corporation and the United Steelworkers of America. Unlike the American Motors-UAW "progress-sharing" arrangement, the Kaiser plan is linked to production costs of finished steel, not to company profits. Under the Kaiser Steel plan, employees receive monthly, in supplementary wages and fringe benefits, 32½ percent of any savings that result from increased labor productivity and more efficient use of materials.

The arrangement was developed by a tripartite Long-Range Committee, over a two-year period of study and negotiations. According to Professor George W. Taylor, chairman of the committee, the aims of the plan are to

16 Kennedy, *op. cit.*, p. 125.

protect workers against unemployment caused by technological change and to give them an opportunity to share in the gains resulting from increased efficiency. In addition to the monthly bonuses, the plan includes various devices for maintaining wage rates. It also provides for protection of workers' jobs and incomes, by establishing a plant-wide employment pool for the displaced, through which they can be retrained and reassigned to other jobs. The cost of these provisions is to be deducted from the cost savings generated by the plan.

The employment reserve pool is expected to remain small, because the rate of attrition in the workforce at Kaiser Steel has historically exceeded that of employee displacements due to technological change and other causes related to improved productivity.[17] Although the company cannot lay off employees displaced by technological improvements, it may continue to lay off workers because of a lack of business.

The plan also seeks to eliminate incentive pay scales, which now apply to about 60 percent of the company's workers, by providing a variety of ways for them to transfer to the "Long-Range Sharing Plan." The Kaiser Plan appears to be a modified version of the Scanlon Plan (see Chapter VI), and employees have already received substantial monthly bonuses under the plan, which went into effect on March 1, 1963.

It is still too early to evaluate the long-run effectiveness of either the American Motors or Kaiser Steel experiments, and it cannot yet be determined whether or not they are significant developments in American industrial relations. In any event, for a fuller understanding of these plans, both must be viewed in the light of the specific situations in which they emerged.

In the case of American Motors, the United Automobile

17 "The Labor Month in Review," *Monthly Labor Review,* Vol. 86, January, 1963, p. iii.

Workers was looking for some new collective bargaining breakthrough, and the company was seeking a means of tightening work rules at its plants. Although the profit-sharing arrangement is not necessarily tied to technological change, it does provide a device through which union members share in the company's good fortunes. It may, therefore, be an incentive for the union and its members to cooperate more actively with the management in achieving economies and efficiency that will improve profit position and the growth of the company.

The Kaiser Steel settlement grew out of the deliberations of the tripartite Long-Range Committee that was appointed following the long steel strike of 1960 and Kaiser's withdrawal from the industry's joint bargaining front. The Committee sought some formula for averting similar collective bargaining breakdowns. Paving the way for the novel agreement were union fears that automation was wiping out blue-collar jobs and company dissatisfaction with its individual wage incentive program. Through the new sharing formula, the company has secured a mechanism for abandoning individual incentives, and the employees have gained protection against unemployment caused by technological change. Since the agreement seems to be tailored to fit the particular Kaiser situation, there appears to be little broader union or management interest in it.

OTHER SAFEGUARDS FOR JOBS AND EMPLOYEE INCOME

Various proposals have been advanced for spreading available work and for prolonging employee pay into periods of unemployment, to meet the problem of shrinking employment opportunities—a presumed dire consequence of progressive technological improvements in industry. Shorter weekly working hours and higher penalties for overtime work have been advanced as essential means of spreading available work among all members of the regular workforce of companies. Guarantees of pay continuation upon layoff for lack of work have also been espoused as a necessary vehicle for maintaining employee income. Though these proposals have not materialized on a sweeping basis, one or another of them has been adopted to some extent in particular industries, through collective bargaining.

Spreading the Work

During the past year, public statements by union officials have echoed the theme that the nation needs a shorter workweek, in order to reduce "technological unemployment." The AFL-CIO and numerous individual unions have officially endorsed reductions in weekly hours of work as both collective bargaining and legislative goals. Labor representatives on the Armour Automation Committee and on the President's Labor-Management Advisory Committee have also gone on record as favoring a reduced workweek. This goal has actually been recently achieved in sections of the building trades.

Despite all these pronouncements, this study uncovered only one instance of a specific union request to a company for reduction of normal hours of work, and it amounted to little more than a share-the-work proposal. In an attempt to prevent the layoff of a group of employees, an independent local union proposed to the management of a petroleum refinery that a 36-hour week, at existing hourly pay scales, be substituted for the prevailing 40-hour week. Management resisted this course of action, however, for a number of reasons:

1. Abandonment of the 40-hour week would have created serious scheduling problems.

2. Reduction in the workweek without compensating increases in wage rates would have decreased employee income and, hence, led to dissatisfaction in the workforce.

3. Such dissatisfaction would have inevitably induced a union demand for raising of wage rates in order to restore weekly income; this would have increased operating costs, which were already burdensome and from which the company sought relief through the modernization program.

4. Reducing the workweek would have been pointless, as the layoff was not an interim action but part of the long-run process of adapting to product and technological change; the resulting reduction in manpower requirements had to be viewed, therefore, as permanent, unless increased sales should later necessitate an expansion of operations.

The device of reducing normal working hours as a way of preserving jobs was not found to be very popular generally. Where working hours were shortened it was usually to meet temporary fluctuations in manpower requirements due to, say, seasonal factors. In the case of technological improvements or shifts in consumer tastes, manpower adjustments tended to be permanent. In nine plants among the cases studied, some form of work-sharing was provided to spread the burden of temporary cutbacks in production. It took the form either of reduction in weekly hours with retention of prevailing hourly wage rates, or of rotation of work periods. Typically, the maximum period for operating on reduced schedules was fixed, and was usually four weeks. The number of hours constituting a reduced workweek was also specific; the common standards were 36 or 32 hours. Beyond these limitations, employees were laid off.

In some cases, there were no contractual obligations with respect to work-sharing, except a commitment on the part of management to discuss the issue with the union whenever temporary cutbacks in production were in the offing. Under these circumstances, unions turned down work-sharing just as often as they favored it. In one company, an electrical machinery producer, the labor contract specifically ruled out any work-sharing, stating: "It is mutually recognized that less than a full week of work is unsatisfactory to both employees and company. When there is a definite reduction in the production schedule for a group or section, employees will be laid off to maintain a full workweek."

The newest idea for spreading the work is to increase the penalty payment for overtime work. Many unions are threatening to make this a demand in their future collective bargaining negotiations. Furthermore, bills have been introduced in Congress that would require companies to pay double normal rates, instead of the present time and one-half for overtime work. President Johnson has proposed higher overtime penalty rates to be applied in those businesses or industries which consistently work their employees overtime, with special management-union-government commissions to determine those segments of the industrial economy to come under such regulation.

Attempts to restrict use of overtime run counter to management efforts to stabilize employment. As shown in Chapter III, overtime work is one device used by management to minimize separations when technological change is in the offing. A good part of the present overtime problem stems, moreover, from demands reflected in union agreements. Some contract terms have made the cost of hiring and laying off workers so expensive that many companies prefer to pay overtime wage rates to currently employed workers. Now to increase the costliness of overtime, in addition, might only serve to discourage any temporary expansion of production as consumer response may dictate.

In fact, proponents of double-time pay for overtime are working on a false assumption. To them, it seems to hold the promise that overtime work will automatically be converted into new jobs. But given the uncertainties of production scheduling needs, it is doubtful that the procedure would produce a substantial number of new jobs. The total employment cost of new workers, moreover, is not limited to their straight-time wage rates. Thus, it is naive to assume that an employer who cannot afford double rates for overtime will somehow be able to pay for significant numbers of new workers. The point at which additional hiring for temporary situations is preferable to paying overtime rates for increased production is best determined by the overall economic situation of a given company. To attempt to make this determination by law, or by labor contract, can only further cramp national economic growth by making the cost of increasing production prohibitively high for many employers.

Spreading the Pay

Where the drawbacks of spreading the work are recognized, the alternative route seems to be an attempt to spread pay for workers over periods of employment and unemployment. This has been, in fact, the more usual route followed in recent years, with many unions setting as their ultimate goal a guaranteed annual wage.

The leading innovator of this approach is the United Automobile Workers, which has been an aggressive union, but also one that has been realistic about technological change. Instead of attempting to block new production techniques, the union, as change has come, has continually put forth demands designed to increase the job security of its members. Early retirement, vested pension rights, and transfer rights in cases of plant relocation or shutdown have all been secured by the UAW in its major contracts. The most important breakthrough, in terms of income stability for blue-collar workers, occurred in 1955, when supplementary unemployment benefits (SUB) were secured in the automobile industry.

In that industry, the maximum supplementary unemployment benefit now stands at $40 per week. In combination with state unemployment compensation, the yield for an unemployed worker is 62 percent of his gross pay, or nearly 80 percent of his normal take-home pay, with an extra allowance of $1.50 per week for each dependent for a maximum of four dependents. The maximum benefit period is 52 weeks.

Supplementary unemployment benefits in the basic steel, can, and rubber industries are similar. Other industries have their own variations of SUB. In meatpacking, the Armour Company provides "technological adjustment pay" of $65 per week, less unemployment compensation and wages earned elsewhere, which is payable for up to 26 weeks to employees with 25 years of service. Other industries provide a form of SUB based on an individual employee savings account, rather than through a common fund.

The goal of income stability for production workers was further advanced in the automobile industry in 1961, when short workweek benefits were established. These are equivalent to 65 percent of a worker's wage for any hours by which a workweek falls short of 40 hours. Indeed, the short workweek guarantees now in effect in the automobile, basic steel, rubber, farm equipment, and cement industries come close to guaranteeing income for extensive periods to production workers.

* * *

This discussion of the relationship between benefit programs and technological change makes it apparent that managements have applied a very pragmatic test in extending benefits. Is the added cost of the new or liberalized benefit justified in terms of gaining employee acceptance of change? Added cost is more easily accepted where longer-service employees are concerned because management feels a greater sense of responsibility to them than to those who have been with a company for but a short period of time. Unions, on their part, have also been rather practical. Though they may initially resist the inroads of technological change on jobs and employment, they usually come to recognize the futility of such a course and are then willing to negotiate improved benefits for their members.

CHAPTER VIII

Changes in the Nature of Work and Jobs

Many observers of the industrial scene term the automation age the "Second Industrial Revolution." With
respect to the industrial relations matters discussed in the
preceding chapters, the impact of advanced technology is
proving more evolutionary than revolutionary. But the
impact of automation on the nature of work and jobs does
assume revolutionary proportions, for it requires of employees new approaches to work and a changed perspective
with respect to their work situation and their relationships
on the job. That automation has manifold effects on the
nature of work is not surprising, for it embodies totally new
and unique operational methods. According to one fitting
definition, it is "a concept of the organization of work."[1]

Generally, but far from universally, modern technology

1 Peter Drucker, *The Practice of Management* (New York: Harper &
Brothers, 1954), p. 21.

tends to reduce physical effort and to increase mental effort in the performance of work. It also demands greater versatility on the part of those who do the work—a man who has been long accustomed to working steadily on a given operation may be called upon to move from one type of assignment to another. Each member of the workforce now has to relate his performance to the entire operation, rather than to a specific task, and this necessitates change in the employee's perception of work. Along with these changes have usually come lighter, airier, cleaner, and safer working conditions. Thus today's industrial plants offer a more pleasant job environment, except that the noise of machinery in operation has not been noticeably reduced—in fact, it is more pronounced in some situations.

Evidences of change in the nature of work and jobs are far more conspicuous, of course, where the more advanced forms of technology have been installed. For this reason, the case experiences discussed here are drawn from company situations in which two such types of technological change have been introduced: continuous-process operations, which are controlled by automatic self-correcting devices, and so-called Detroit automation, which encompasses the automatic handling and transfer of parts between progressive production stages.

CASE ILLUSTRATIONS OF WORK AND JOB CHANGES

Continuous-Process Operations

The effect of the introduction of a continuous-process operation on work and jobs is highly evident in the case of a chemical plant that converted from batch-producing to continuous-flow production. A signal result of the change was a tremendous reduction in the kind of "dirty" work formerly characteristic of the old operation; there is no need now for men to go outside in inclement weather to check the various gauges and to change pressures, speeds of flow, and the like, by manually turning valves and making other adjustments on the equipment. A further result was great reduction in sheer physical effort. Bags of chemicals are no longer unloaded and fed manually into the batch, since these functions are now handled by automatic unloading and feeding devices. Another notable effect, moreover, was a striking change in the nature of the jobs, as the once discrete tasks of batching are now merged into a wholly integrated process of production. No longer is each employee concerned with but one phase of the total operation; in the continuous operation the individual employee's job is related to the entire process and is essential to the sequential flow of production.

In this continuous-flow operation, a computer-controlled console board guides the entire process, and the board is monitored by one operator and one supervisor. The operator sits at a desk in the building housing the console board, and his functions are to watch the board's various dials and gauges, make needed changes in pressures and speeds of flow by turning dials and pressing buttons, keep accurate records, and fill out reports. He is responsible for judging the proper functioning of the process and for quickly manipulating the equipment to correct divergencies from the norm. He must also alert those concerned when there is need for other remedial action. Only if something goes wrong is any physical labor involved, and even then the repairs are made by a special maintenance crew, not by the operator.

Actually, the operator now resembles a white-collar employee. He could sit at his desk in a suit, white shirt, and tie, but he continues to wear the green coveralls of the production and maintenance workforce. Since he remains an hourly-rated employee and a member of the bargaining unit, management feels that it is best not to distinguish him from his co-workers by manner of dress.

In another continuous-flow operation—a plant manufacturing proprietary drugs—there are almost no remaining distinctions between blue- and white-collar work. No segment of the workforce of this plant is unionized; hence, the management is unfettered by rigid skill or departmental demarcations in the flexible use of manpower. This circumstance permits broadened use of a program of job rotation originally designed to give individual operators periodic relief from the tedium of concentration on a single task. Production workers can now be transferred to office assignments when they are needed there. Today, therefore, plant employees are no longer clearly identifiable as members of either the production or the office force, because they can be moved back and forth between the two as conditions warrant.

A third case in point is a gas pipeline operation which converted to centralized computer control of the entire line. The resultant changes in the nature of work and jobs are similar to those experienced in the chemical plant discussed earlier. An important factor in this case is that employees in the new jobs are required to operate at more sophisticated levels of skill and responsibility than before. For example, a station man no longer issues necessary work directions to a lineman by telephone; instead, the operator himself controls the entire system and the processes from his central console board, by pressing the proper buttons. Such employees now have functions which are, in essence, more like those of salaried technicians than those of hourly-rated production workers in the traditional sense, but these men remain in the latter category.

Experience in a food-processing plant further confirms the trends of change in the nature of work and jobs in continuous-process operations. Three distinct changes in jobs are recognized as having resulted from the automating of operations: some new jobs created, such as console-board operator, are at a higher skill level than those replaced; working conditions are much more pleasing than before; and jobs are much less arduous physically, although greater attentiveness and resourcefulness are required of the employee.

The definite effect of the continuous-flow process is also illustrated in the changed nature of jobs at the electric power-generating stations of a public utility company. The findings in this case are largely in accord with the findings of other studies.[2] The new power plants are cleaner, safer, and better lighted. Almost no back-breaking types of work remain. Instead, the new tasks impose on operators the responsibility for maintaining the flow of production, largely through watchfulness. Thus the jobs involve new stresses and pressures. The employee must remain alert, exercise careful judgment, and react quickly to changed circumstances. He is, moreover, subject to pressure for accuracy.

In automated power plants the content of jobs is also altered. No longer do jobs utilize a single skill, as in the classifications of electrician or pipefitter at the old generating stations, for these demarcations are now outmoded. A new classification, "instrument mechanic," is used, and that job encompasses elements of work that utilize a variety of craft skills. This consolidation of skills within the content of jobs makes for the flexibility that is needed in automated operations. It is not universal practice, however, because in case after case unions insist on preserving the old craft demarcations.

"Detroit Automation"

The so-called Detroit automation, adopted first in the automobile industry, utilizes multipurpose transfer machines and tape-controlled equipment which affect the nature of work and jobs in much the same ways that other forms of automation do. A report by Faunce on his study of an auto-

---

[2] Floyd C. Mann and L. Richard Hoffman, *Automation and the Worker* (New York: Henry Holt and Company, 1960), pp. 73–77; Charles Walker, *Toward the Automatic Factory* (New Haven: Yale University Press, 1957), pp. 55–59.

mated automobile engine plant sets forth his observations of the impact of work and job changes on employees. He regards the reduction in the amount of materials-handling required of the operator as a positive benefit, for the job is less strenuous, but he also sees negative effects. He points out that the employee no longer actually operates the machine and, therefore, no longer has any control over the work pace; that greater attentiveness is required of the employee; and that normal work groups are destroyed. Faunce concludes that employee dissatisfaction with the new work situation is induced by the lessened opportunity for social interaction, the increased extent of supervision, the rise of feelings of "alienation" from work, and the heightened tension and anxiety associated with the jobs in automated operations.[3]

Fortuitously, one of the plants embraced by this study is the very plant covered by Faunce's research. Although there was no intensive survey of employee opinions about their new working conditions, some views were gathered from discussions on the plant floor with industrial relations staff people, operating management and engineering personnel, as well as with production workers themselves. Those interviewed acknowledged that there is some truth in Faunce's conclusions, but there was a strong indication that the vast majority of workers would not wish to exchange their present jobs for those in the old nonautomated operations. Interestingly, this very fact, affirmed by Faunce himself,[4] raises a question about the degree of dissatisfaction employees really feel or the significance of the reported dissatisfaction.

The study findings in another automobile engine plant confirm the general experience elsewhere with the effects of automation on the nature of work and jobs: on the one hand,

---

[3] William A. Faunce, "Automation and the Automobile Worker," *Social Problems,* Vol. 6, No. 1, Summer 1958, pp. 68–78.
[4] *Ibid.,* p. 76.

an elimination of many simple repetitive tasks and relief from exhausting physical effort; on the other, a greater demand for mental application and greater responsibility in operating the more complex and expensive equipment. Work is, in essence, less manual and more visual. For instance, the positioning of an engine block into place is now done automatically, and the operator is relieved of doing so manually. But he has to be continually alert to the signal lights that warn of any malfunction and be ready to make quick adjustments. Many of the new jobs actually hold an intellectual challenge greater than any found before in mass production jobs. At this plant, too, employees evidence preference for their new jobs over those of the pre-automation era.

As to group relationships, the management also disputes the contention that automation causes a loss of social contact. Even though old work groups are now broken up, new group relationships are evident, deriving from the nature of teamwork that takes place. Not only does each crew member have to understand his own responsibilities and tasks, he also has to coordinate his efforts with those of his co-workers, particularly in diagnosing and correcting machinery breakdowns. Work groups are smaller, and employees are not in as close proximity to each other; but they have more time and energy to move about and socialize within the plant.

In fact, in the overwhelming majority of cases, no matter what the form of technological change, the managements report an increase, rather than a decrease, in employee job satisfaction. This is the view, whether the change was simple mechanization that turned an unskilled laborer into a machine-tender, or the application of electronic computers that converted a machine-tender into a console board monitor.[5]

[5] Similarly, in reporting on the automation experience of the Inland Steel Company, its vice president, industrial relations, stated that few workers were dissatisfied with new jobs. See William G. Caples, "Automation in Theory and Practice," *Business Topics*, Vol. 8, No. 4, Autumn 1960, pp. 7–19, 16.

NEGATIVE FACTORS IN AUTOMATED WORK

Perhaps some of the disagreement concerning employee job satisfaction is related to the timing of the various studies of worker attitudes in situations of technological change. There is undoubtedly an adjustment period after a change in operations when reactions are negative because of change itself rather than the nature of the change. In Walker's study of an automated steel mill, he finds that in the initial transition period the employees are unhappy. But he also finds that once the mill is fully in operation employees lose their fears, as they gain on-the-job knowledge and come to recognize the opportunity for teamwork and for getting acquainted with one another.[6]

Although employee dissatisfaction with the effects of automation is demonstrated most when it is first introduced, some aspects of automated work continue to be viewed negatively. For some employees the very automaticity of the machinery establishes their working routine: short periods of intense effort in the diagnosis and correction of malfunctions, interspersed with long periods in which there is little or nothing for them to "do." Their role during these latter periods is simply to watch the operation to assure that it is functioning smoothly.

Adjustment to a situation in which work no longer means "doing" something is most difficult for people long conditioned to action, not perception, in their prior working lives. Because little actual physical effort or movement is required of them, boredom emerges as a problem. At an automated glass plant, where the preponderant amount of the employees' working time is spent watching a ribbon of molten glass flow by continuously, employees file hosts of grievances over very minor matters. Probably, they simply have to find something to do.

At a food-processing plant, workers are no longer pena-

[6] Walker, *op. cit.*, pp. 84–86.

lized for dozing on the job when watching a console board for eight hours a day. Management recognizes the boredom involved in a job of this kind and therefore considers it unfair to discipline workers for occasionally napping under such conditions. There is hardly any risk to operating efficiency when an operator naps, since he would be awakened by the built-in alarms which go off automatically upon any breakdown or malfunction in the system.

The management of an automated instruments plant takes a different approach to the same problem. It requires console board operators to check their readings and file reports every 15 minutes—much more often than is necessary to assure efficient control of the operation—in order to give employees something to "do" and thus keep them from becoming bored.

At a chemical works the problem of isolation of console-board operators, and the attendant boredom they suffer, has been met by bringing together in one room several console boards, even though each of them controls different processes. Because several operators now share one large control room, social interaction is possible which offsets the tedious routine of watching their panels.

In some plants, the mixture of brief periods of intense activity and long spells of inactivity is even more pronounced with trouble-shooting maintenance crews than with operating personnel. In some of these situations, crew members spend idle time during "working" hours in reading or playing cards. Some plant managers, believing that such pursuits are detrimental to plant discipline, try to provide maintenance work, whether needed or not, to keep the employees occupied. Other managers, however, view their maintenance forces as "fire brigades"—men who "put out the fires" of equipment breakdown or damage. These plant managers therefore feel that as long as each man fulfills his assigned function with promptness and efficiency there is no reason to be particularly concerned about how he spends the time in which he is not needed. Actually, idleness among maintenance crews is tantamount to good news, for it signifies that the operation is functioning perfectly.

In some cases, automation obviates the need for employees to exercise the capacity for judgment which they may have developed through years of experience. In a food plant, operators of coffee roasters no longer have to judge and control the quality of the roast by comparing the color of the beans with standard specifications. Now an automatic color-scanner controls quality, while the operators are required merely to push the right buttons on the electronically-controlled roasters.

That automation brings about an increase of shift operations may be regarded also as a negative effect, since it intensifies the problem of employee dissatisfaction over having to work on the undesirable shifts. Normal home life and social relationships are disrupted by work-leisure schedules that operate contrary to those of wives, children, friends, and neighbors.[7] Shift work is unavoidable, however, since it is not technologically feasible in many situations to shut down and start up operations daily. From an economic standpoint, also, an expansion of shift operations is often necessary to achieve maximum utilization of the automated equipment, in order to secure an equitable return on the high capital investment it entails.

THE NEW WORK SETTING

In considering changes in work and jobs, it is important to contemplate not only the effects on the individual's wages, hours and working conditions, but also the implications for selection, training, and future advancement of indi-

[7] Other research findings indicate that shift workers often develop into fairly tight social groups, cut off from their area of society by their odd hours of work. See, for example, Seymour Martin Lipset, "The Political Process in Trade Unions: A Theoretical Statement," in Walter Galenson and Seymour Martin Lipset, editors, *Labor and Trade Unionism: An Interdisciplinary Reader* (New York: John Wiley & Sons, 1960), p. 226.

viduals, and for employee motivation. An understanding of the implications of technological change for the individual carries with it the possibility of gaining from the current technological revolution more than the material benefits of increased output, for the nature of the new work setting presents opportunities to capture the benefits that can accrue from high levels of job satisfaction.

Typical Manifestations of Change

It is worthwhile to review the highlights of the research findings that indicate how modern technology changes the nature of work.

First, in some production operations there is a higher degree of machine-pacing of work. Moreover, in many machine-paced jobs, the employee on the production line is performing only a portion of the range of his former tasks, as he now engages in a lesser number of repetitive tasks than before. These factors serve to dilute the value of individual incentive plans as a motivator of worker effort. But machine-paced work introduces a core of new jobs concerned with planning and scheduling, as well as maintenance work, and such jobs are frequently far removed from production activities on the factory floor.

Second, there is a trend toward combining and upgrading jobs, particularly where operating and maintenance functions are merged, and this requires of employees a greater degree of versatility. The trend is usually stronger in operations where a process is easily adapted to a more or less continuous flow—as in gas, petroleum, chemical, and food-producing industries. On the other hand, job enlargement along these lines is inhibited by opposition from some unions which resist the combination of functions both among and between operating and maintenance jobs. This resistance flows from employee fear of a consequent reduction in the number of jobs and, in some cases, an apparent union fear of jobs slipping out of its jurisdiction. Moreover, industrial unions regard the mingling of craft skills in operating jobs as creating a risk of craft identification which could threaten the cohesiveness of their organizations.

Third, some forms of technological change can induce a polarization of jobs toward the higher and lower ends of the skill ladder, and this creates a series of problems. Polarization tends to identify a new worker elite—the highest skilled. It puts a strain on relationships within a union, for seniority applications may have to be more circumscribed in order to get trainable or capable people in the right jobs. It also disturbs existing and traditionally accepted job hierarchies in the plant, and thus may lead to a depression in the pay rates of many employees. These effects tend to have an unsettling effect on management's relations with employees, requiring new emphasis in communicating and new accommodations in supervisory and subordinate relationships.

In addition to these problem areas, yet related to them, is the obvious one: effective selection and placement of employees in production work will become more important as use of the new technology spreads into more and more operations. Unions and management both are accustomed to relying on the more or less automatic working of seniority rules to govern the assignment of work. In a period of restructuring of work, however, it may no longer be feasible to abide by seniority as the mechanical determinant in job placement. The challenge faced by unions is not whether they can resist the inroads of change on seniority practices, but whether they are able to face up to the realities of change and slough off the traditional importance they have attached to more or less mechanical seniority systems. For management, the challenge is to find ways to bring about union acceptance of the need to modify seniority applications so as to permit the use of more sophisticated techniques in selecting and placing employees and determining their "trainability" for new assignments.

Perhaps the barriers being encountered in placement and work assignment will be overcome gradually, as better tools are developed for matching men and jobs. In the interim, however, seniority rules will continue to have an important bearing on assignment of the workforce. In any event, some current seniority clauses are more flexible than others. Illustrative of both types are the two cited below— one being most restrictive by tying the promotion of men entirely to length of service, the other having enough flexibility to permit the selection of men with needed skills in specific job areas.

> *Example:* Promotions from one classification to another within a department shall be made on the basis of seniority as vacancies occur within that department, as provided herein.
> *Example:* The Company agrees to recognize the principle of seniority in upgrading employees with consideration given to ability and aptitude. When an opening occurs in the permanent organization that may in turn lead to a more responsible position, any employee in that department shall be given an opportunity to bid for the job and will be considered. However, the final choice shall rest with the Company.

The wording of a particular seniority clause does not, of course, preclude reasonable adaptation of its terms to a given situation. Much depends on the manner in which a clause is actually applied. Nevertheless, it is important to both management and unions that seniority clauses be rid of their "strait jacket" features and transformed into instruments designed to permit the assignment of each worker to a job in which he has a reasonable chance for success.

The Employees' Situation

Work itself is a great organizer of man's effort. The accumulation of raw materials, the shaping of them into a product, the distribution of the product, all bring about specialization in the organization and direction of human effort. Historically, some perform the tasks, and others plan, correct, adjust, and direct them. And this system is not altered today, even in an automated work environment. It is the actual work setting which is refashioned by automation of production operations. Technological innovation changes the nature of jobs and alters the relationships of employees with fellow workers and supervisors. Some jobs become more boring; others become more exciting. Some jobs are dead-end assignments; others offer possibilities for advancement. Where employees see a possibility of advancing, they are more likely to develop a clear perception of their role in the scheme of work. Otherwise, employees may find it difficult to identify and appreciate the importance of their functions.

Employee reaction to change in work is, of course, a wholly personal matter, and it is beyond the scope of this study to report firsthand on how employees do react. Despite this limitation, it is possible from observations made to categorize the salient features of change to which employees are likely to react.

Boredom is nothing new in production jobs, having long been recognized as a curse of assembly-line operations. But the nature of boredom in automated work is different. In assembly-line operations, boring work requires the operator to repeat a particular task incessantly. Under automation, the tedium derives from the fact that the worker must observe something over which he can exercise little control, but which calls for his constant alertness. In many of the companies studied, significant differences are evident between these two types of work.

Significantly, managers reported that both boredom and tediousness are less important as negative factors among younger workers than among their seniors. It is interesting to speculate over the reasons for this difference. The older worker has been conditioned by a work environment that stressed the actual doing of tasks and handling of work materials and tools. And, frequently, he has come from a rural background in which active work was considered most commendable and satisfying, both culturally and socially. He has therefore remained action-oriented in his work. The younger worker has not been employed long enough to have become as steeped in these concepts of work as his father. Moreover, he has had greater opportunities to develop a capacity for participating passively in events around him, through observing various spectator forms of entertainment and sports.

Further, where companies have been able to select younger people for assignments in an automated operation—in an instrument room, for example—the employees selected have been found to be more compatible with the job demands than those selected on the basis of seniority alone. As compared with older workers, younger workers appeared to be better qualified in terms of temperament and background.

In some of the recent literature, much is made of the factor of boredom in work caused by the lack of opportunity for workers to engage in friendly relationships at the workbench. These studies of individual reaction to technological change cite the loss of opportunity for personal interaction as one of the more significant developments in today's industrial work setting. It is true that in some circumstances employee "A" is no longer able to lean two inches to his right and talk to employee "B" about yesterday's baseball game, but he also is not as tied to the workbench. He has greater freedom to move about and interact with a larger number of co-workers. It is evident from study observations that work group horizons are now broader in many instances, because any one segment of work is no longer limited to a group of men doing similar jobs. The "group" today is an assembly of men working relatedly on a complex of jobs in a department or on a shift, and new and different types of individual interaction occur. Thus, in many situations, greater group homogeneity emerges when new methods of operations are introduced.

It appears that modernization or automation of operations sets up a sequence of reactions among employees. Individual workers at first often feel isolated from their fellow workers, and this factor holds the strong implication that employees react at the outset by feeling a nebulous sort of dissatisfaction. Their discontent then leads to complaints, grievances, and, possibly, demands leading to strike action over issues which may or may not be related to technological change. In time, both workers and supervisors begin to adjust to the changed circumstances of individual separateness combined with intragroup dependence. They then begin to recognize the importance of group effort in achieving the goals of the operation.

Where the physical adjustment to new methods is swift (and that appears to turn on the quality of supervision and the abilities of the workers), the personal difficulties tend to dissipate quickly. The employees in an operation then develop a strong group identification. They become absorbed in the new job demands and begin to join with their supervisors in setting group-oriented goals. At first, these goals may be to avoid a breakdown of the equipment, minimize waste, or speed up the time taken in setting up or adjusting equipment. Later there may be an attempt to set new records of output. Eventually, a further evolution seems to take place because of the changed attitudes of both workers and supervisors: there emerges an interpersonal bond which is stronger than had existed before technological change, and which may even extend beyond the work situation. Perhaps this bond derives from a form of work-group cohesiveness, built on respect for each person's role in the work group, or in some instances, from a degree of economic leveling between the supervisor and the supervised.

The stages of interaction into which employees apparently move, after their initial reaction of feeling isolated, may be charted as follows:

Progression of Group Relationships

Out-of-Plant Association with Co-workers

Personal Interaction Within the Group

Homogeneity of Purpose with Others in the Group

Identification with the Group

Employee Alliance with His Supervisor

Feeling of Isolation by Individual Employee

Whatever the reasons for the cohesiveness that develops, it is still too early to speculate on the long-term implications of this development. It is clear, however, that group cohesiveness is encouraged both by the ability of individuals to conceptualize the entire work process embraced by the new technology, and by the ability of some individuals to relate their roles to the goals of the organization in terms of output or keeping equipment at maximum efficiency.

In giving due regard to these changes in the work environment, it appears that a modification of our ideas of motivation are in order. Whereas traditional production processes give scope to, and permit identification of, individual action on the job, the continuous work flow inherent in many automated operations merges individual performance into the teamwork of groups of individuals. In the advanced stages of technological change, the person who is motivated toward work is the person who can comprehend the objectives of the organization and work in unison with others to accomplish them, even though he may not touch, lift, shape, or otherwise come into contact with the product of the plant. Experience in the case-study companies indicates that where the individual is so motivated, it is not always necessary to find ways to combat the boredom frequently associated with watching instrument panels in modern plants. Some company psychologists report that the differences among employees may be explained by the ability or lack of ability to conceptualize an automated process. This observation is an interesting one, and explains the almost universal use of flow charts in automated operations. Wherever an advanced application of modern control and processing equipment is in effect, a flow chart describing the process is prominently displayed. These flow charts translate the mass of wires, pipes, tubes, and their function into simple pictures and often relate the innovations to the pre-automation process. The flow chart is not only important in training but is felt to be valuable even after operations are in full swing.

Training specialists report that the ability to comprehend and follow the graphic presentations varies greatly among both workers and supervisors. Here perhaps is one of the real challenges in realigning the workforce and developing constructive employee attitudes toward change. The use of flow charts is a step in the right direction, but other ingenious devices may be needed to foster in employees the ability to conceptualize.

An even more vital factor today in the conversion of operations is the need to staff them effectively. Only if men and jobs can be matched so as to be in harmony will it be possible for those who can work effectively to function at their best in modern plants. To bring about effective staffing, refined judgments come into play, and the difficulty of defending them in the face of union resistance to restructuring of work is an additional barrier to successfully adapting the workforce to new methods of production.

Underlying much of this discussion is the idea that technological change leads to a separation of production employees from the actual *doing* of a job. The individual's former tasks are now handled by automated machinery, and his new function is to monitor some phase of the automatic process through visual rather than physical contact. His consequent loss of identification with the doing of work often creates a novel situation—as observed in the case-study plants, many "production" workers, seated at consoles or stationed before panel boards, now wear white laboratory coats on the job. The suggestion here is that they be called the "white-coat workers" since their skills and tasks may be more like those of the typical white-collar worker than those of the production worker.

The existence of this new group may be cause for uneasiness on the part of management over the unionized status of the group relative to nonorganized white-collar personnel. Also worrisome is the changed man-boss relationship. There is a more direct interdependency between the supervisor and the supervised, and the associations are closer and more personal because work units are small. In fact, some supervisors direct the work of only one man, and in many instances, the functions involved could be handled equally well by one or the other singlehandedly. Thus it is not surprising that fractious issues frequently arise between the white-coat worker and his supervisor. Still, it may be that the man-boss relationship has not yet adjusted to this one-over-one form of supervision. In these circumstances, how does the supervisor evaluate the performance of the white-coat worker? How does he share the job while still retaining the "boss" status?

One other problem for management derives from the deafening noise of many modern plants. Aside from its physiological impact on people, there is the effect of noise on communication among individual workers and between supervisors and employees. In some companies, there is today greater reliance on meetings away from the workplace, and in others, on written communications. But day-to-day oral communications are essential in any work group, and thus the noise factor poses an interesting challenge for the supervisor in maintaining effective communications.

These are but some of the questions and problems which are evident from the field study. Clearly, what is occurring is an individual adjustment to new types of work situations, as well as an adjustment of management thinking on the organization and direction of work. It is difficult to predict how smoothly the problems will be overcome, from the individual's point of view. For the company, the significance of the changes is their eventual influence on traditional patterns of accommodation within the plant society.

CHAPTER IX

Changes Affecting Salaried Plant Personnel

Inasmuch as technological innovation brings about deep changes in direct-production and maintenance jobs, it can be expected also to alter the work and status of some salaried employees, and their relationships with production employees. The discussion in this chapter takes us only a step over the threshold in identifying some of the accompanying problems and in relating some of the actions taken to meet them. In many cases, the problems and adjustments are similar to those applicable to the blue-collar workforce, but they hold some unique challenges for management, especially in the case of supervisory and technical personnel.

Stated briefly, company experience indicates that the impact of change on salaried groups is felt in three ways:

1. The restructuring of the workforce brought about by advanced technology sometimes blurs the lines of demarcation between production and first-line supervisory jobs, as

well as clerical and technical jobs, and thus causes conflict over the allocation of work or assignment of new jobs to salaried personnel.

2. The role of supervision changes to require a higher level of competence in such assignments, from both the technical and human relations standpoints; thus, in turn, the qualifications for first-line supervisory jobs are also altered.

3. Engineering staffs expand, and new categories of salaried technicians come into existence upon the adoption of advanced technological processes; both the size and importance of these groups lead to problems concerning their standing and treatment relative to other personnel.

SALARIED VERSUS HOURLY-RATED STATUS OF NEW JOBS

As more and more operations are modernized, unions increasingly charge that work "belonging" to union members is being given to employees outside the bargaining unit as a consequence of automation. Such charges arise usually where new technology eliminates the jobs of a former group of supervised operators and the new tasks entailed are assigned to a supervisor. In some cases, moreover, work falls into a "gray area," because it is incidental to the main duties of a supervisor, and, realistically, may well be performed by him rather than by a production worker. It is easy to understand that in such situations union-management conflict may arise over whether such jobs should be assigned to supervisory personnel or to hourly-paid operators.

Unions are, of course, most zealous about seeking to preserve all available work for their members, to the exclusion of salaried employees—whether supervisory or technical. Some also endeavor to offset any decline that technological change may bring about in the number of production workers by trying to extend the scope of their bargaining units to embrace technical occupations.

One of the most dramatic disputes over work allocation occurred in a rubber factory, and this case illustrates well the nature of the problem. The issue arose over the control and operation of a new tire-making machine. The new machine, a more advanced model of the one formerly operated mechanically by a member of the bargaining unit, had an automatic control system that eliminated the repetitive routine of the operator. The management assigned to a supervisor the duty of monitoring the machine from a nearby control booth, reasoning that the operator's functions had been eliminated, leaving only the continuing supervisory responsibility of overseeing the work being performed.

The union contended, however, that pushing the buttons to activate the machine was an operator's function, which should have been assigned to a bargaining-unit employee. Having failed to win its point with management, the union filed a grievance. The case was then carried to arbitration, and the management's assignment of the work was upheld. The arbitrator held that the operator's former duties had been built into the machine rather than assumed by the supervisor, that control-room monitoring was more comparable to the normal functions of supervision than to production-line duties, and that the occasional pushing of buttons by a supervisor was of the same nature as issuing instructions to employees.

More generally, however, union leaders who feel that work has been improperly assigned argue their complaints unofficially with plant management, rather than file formal grievances. In a plant using tape-controlled machinery quite extensively, union officials had been harping to the management for some time about the assignment of set-up work with tapes, claiming that this work, which was being done by salaried personnel, properly belonged to its members. Yet the union had not filed a formal grievance up to the time the plant was visited. Apparently, the unions are unsure of their ground in this area and are fearful of arbitration awards.

Unfavorable awards would set precedents that would relegate to the realm of lost causes any further attempts to influence the allocation of new jobs. They see a safer approach in continuing to harass plant managements with informal complaints in the hope that their claims will be recognized favorably at least some of the time. This study did not, however, turn up any case in which a plant management, having once decided on the propriety of an assignment of work to salaried personnel, had withdrawn from its position in the face of union protest.

THE SUPERVISORY FORCE

The role and status of the first-line supervisor have gone through a number of metamorphoses within this century. The deportment required of a supervisor in the present industrial environment bears little resemblance to that of a foreman of yore, who often acted as an industrial despot, albeit sometimes a benevolent one. The chief concern of the oldtime foreman was assuring adequate output from the employees in his charge. To that end he hired and fired at will, and his word was law within his work group. With the evolution of modern management and personnel practices, the scope of the supervisor's independent influence was gradually narrowed, though he gained new responsibilities. Moreover, with passage of the Wagner Act, management was required to assume new obligations toward employees. Thus foremen, in turn, became involved in the requirements of law, which made their responsibilities more complex and further restricted their freedom to take independent action in matters affecting employees. The old image and authority of the foreman soon faded so drastically that his role had to be redefined and more closely aligned with overall management functions.

Today there is a coalescing of views about supervisory responsibility. Despite differences among companies—in management organization, in the history of company-union relationships, and in the nature of the particular industrial environment—the importance of the role of the first-line supervisor as a *human engineer* is being more universally recognized. Typically, foreman training courses now emphasize leadership—aptly described by one writer as "consisting not only of command, but of instruction, help, understanding, and the winning over of personnel."[1] Social scientists, in their studies of work-group behavior in industrial settings, emphasize the need for supervisors of all ranks to be leaders, not bosses, of men, so as to achieve group endeavor toward common aims.[2] In some situations, first-line supervisors were only beginning to absorb the meaning of their human relations functions when technological change intervened and further compounded their adjustment problems.

The latest types of technology obviously demand of the supervisor a much higher level of technical knowledge. He must be able to understand the equipment with which he is working so that he can properly supervise its operation, and sometimes, its maintenance also. In addition, advanced technology requires him to think in terms of overall management objectives, as well as to exercise the human relations skills necessary in maintaining the teamwork that is not merely desirable but vital in modern operations.

Emphasis on Technical Skills

The supervisory function is once again facing a challenge more dynamic than is yet fully recognized. It is no exaggeration, as many executives hold, that the impact of automation on supervisors is far more critical than its impact on

[1] Georges Friedmann, *Industrial Society* (Glencoe: The Free Press, 1955), p. 298.
[2] For expositions on this subject, see Industrial Relations Counselors, Inc. (New York), *Behavioral Science Research in Industrial Relations*, 1962 (Industrial Relations Monograph, No. 21), 177 pp.

workers.[3] Yet, the challenge holds great promise for the future role of supervisors. On this point, Lipstreu concludes:

> . . . the supervisor will regain some of his lost discretionary authority. Automaticity of work requires that he make decisions at the work level quickly, decisions which formerly were made at higher levels in the hierarchy. His work will increasingly resemble that of present middle management— he will supervise fewer workers; he will be required to co- ordinate his functions more closely with his colleagues at the same management level; and he will probably be called upon to supervise and coordinate the work of a maintenance staff.
>
> With the number of his supervisees reduced, the super- visor should be able to do a better "human relations job. . . ."

There will be no reduction in the amount of direct verbal interaction required between supervisors and workers.[4]

Experience in the case-study companies clearly supports these conclusions, for, without a doubt, new technology has endowed the first-line supervisory function with new oppor- tunities for both responsibility and prestige. In plant after plant, it was apparent that the "boss-workman" role of the old-line foreman has become obsolete. Companies are seeking younger, more technically-competent supervisors to handle the work. A background of about two years of college-level engineering courses is now considered a prerequisite for the job of foreman in automated operations.

This demand for technical competence on the part of supervisors stems, to a degree, from the need for precise advance scheduling of production activities, which must be based on full comprehension of the ramifications of advanced technology. Inept production planning can nullify the capa- bility of modern machinery to increase productivity and lower costs. In a plant manufacturing abrasive wheels of

3 James R. Bright, *Automation and Management* (Boston: Graduate School of Business Administration, Harvard University, 1958), p. 209.

4 Otis Lipstreu, "Organizational Implications of Automation," *The Journal of the Academy of Management*, Vol. 3, August, 1960, p. 123.

various sizes, it did not matter, formerly, if the operation constantly alternated between making a six-inch wheel and a ten-inch wheel. The sequential handling of like orders was unimportant in a day's production, so long as quotas were met. Today, however, the costliness of shifting automated machinery necessitates careful scheduling of production to assure that the desired output of each type of product is accomplished in uninterrupted sequence.

In terms of direct supervision, the requirements are just as exacting. In plants using complex machinery, the supervisor must be able to surpass the high degree of technical competence required of blue-collar employees working under him. And although the individual supervisor generally has fewer people to supervise, he often has broader areas of activity to control. Where the foreman lacks technical skill, he finds himself besieged on two fronts. First, if he is unable to give members of his crew the aid they seek on production problems, he compromises his position of leadership. Second, if he compensates for his own inadequacies by seeking help from staff engineers and technicians, he undermines his role within the managerial hierarchy.

One prognosticator, in viewing the supervisor's increased need for heightened technical skill, and the need for greater managerial prowess on the part of the technician, suggests that "such an evolution will deal a serious blow . . . to traditional line-staff relations and will bolster the forces making for plural leadership in industry."[5] Another believes that the line-and-staff principle may have to be re-examined in the light of automation, because "it may impede the kind of rapid communication needed between machine tenders, technicians, and maintenance men . . . in case of breakdowns."[6] The machine tender may short-circuit the foreman and call

[5] Joseph A. Raffaele, "Automation and the Coming Diffusion of Power in Industry," *Personnel*, Vol. 39, May–June, 1962, pp. 32–33.

[6] John A. Bekker, "Automation: Its Impact on Management," *Advanced Management*, Vol. 24, December, 1959, p. 22.

upon the right technician directly, leaving the foreman more "concerned with record-keeping than production." This has not happened, however, in the plants studied; instead, foremen have either become more technically competent or fallen by the wayside.

Even those foremen who adjust to new technology and exercise their supervisory role competently may find that the complex nature of automated operations prevents them from rising within the managerial hierarchy. Few of the older supervisors now have the essential qualifications to move up the ladder to department head, plant manager, and beyond. It is interesting to note an omission in the current discussion about retraining under governmental programs and in the training proposals within industry as well. Almost all have been concerned with the problem of the production worker whose skills have become outmoded, or the engineer or scientist whose professional knowledge has suffered obsolescence in the period since he acquired his college training. But what about the foreman or supervisor in industry? Is he a forgotten man?

In recent years, supervisory jobs have often been filled by promoting technically-trained men from staff positions, rather than lower-level supervisors; or such positions have been filled through external recruiting.[7] But the situation is likely to change as younger and better educated men move into first-line supervisory positions. Their opportunities for advancement will be greater, as they will be better able to measure up to the new requirements of a supervisory position.

Older supervisors are finding themselves in the same situation as older production workers. The more complex the technology, the greater the probability that they are on dead-end assignments, because their educational background

---

[7] Experience on this score in a British steel works is interesting. See W. H. Scott, et al., *Technical Change and Industrial Relations* (Liverpool: Liverpool University Press, 1956), pp. 91–93.

is inadequate to equip them for promotion. The situation of the older foremen is even more unfavorable when technological change wipes out their particular jobs. Companies have found they can successfully transfer younger foremen and other salaried employees to other departments or plants. But they have had little success, in most of the situations studied, with transferring "career" foremen, few of whom have proved adaptable to new production processes.

Importance of Group Relationships

Conjoined with the technical proficiency required of a supervisor is his ability to function successfully in matters of human relations. The supervisor has to uphold his prestige as leader of his group and yet maintain an atmosphere of camaraderie among the members of the group, between them and himself, and, to some extent, with other supervisors. As never before, the attitude of a supervisor toward his subordinates must reflect both respect and appreciation for the contribution each makes to the production effort, particularly where technological change has brought the skill level required of operating personnel close to that of their supervisors. Further, although the supervisor may be given helpful training in the principles of supervision, he has to improvise, on his own, the ways in which he will daily forge satisfactory relationships. According to Mann and Hoffman, reporting on their study of old-line and automated power plants, in both situations "the human relations competence of the foreman was found to be more highly correlated with employee satisfaction with his foreman than was the foreman's technical or administrative competence."[8]

The changed requirements of supervision were most dramatically illustrated at an automated engine plant of an automobile company. Technological improvement at this

8 Floyd C. Mann and L. Richard Hoffman, *Automation and the Worker* (New York: Henry Holt and Company, 1960), p. 188.

plant embraced the use of the most modern pieces of transfer and other equipment for handling and shaping engine blocks. At the time the plant was visited, all bugs in the process had not been eliminated. Upon being told that engine blocks periodically jammed at a particular machine, we watched that machine in the hope of observing a typical breakdown situation. There was only one man in the vicinity of the machine, and he was engaged in adjusting equipment and checking readings. Soon a breakdown did occur. Immediately, this man moved to the affected machine, and seemingly from out of nowhere he was joined by his supervisor and another worker. With the smoothness and precision of a *corps de ballet* each man moved confidently into an expected role, guided by unspoken cues from the supervisor, and together they speedily diagnosed the trouble and corrected it.

For a work group to function with such coordination and aplomb obviously demands of a supervisor a high order of leadership characteristics. The supervisor himself has to have a thorough knowledge of the machinery in his charge. He also has to develop in the members of his work group an understanding of their respective responsibilities as individuals entrusted with a specific task and as interdependent co-workers in a problem-solving situation. In emergencies, the supervisor has to coordinate the efforts of the group into cohesive and effective teamwork, in which knowledge is important and speed essential. It is clear that supervision in an automated operation, where a breakdown in any part of the line halts the entire process, assumes a new kind of significance in comparison with older production processes, where supervision meant overseeing such segmented activities as, for example, the work of a group of drill-press operators.

Some younger foremen in the plants studied have demonstrated the technical competence and adaptability required to retain their supervisory status, as well as the ability to maintain effective relationships with their subordinates and to provide them with the necessary guidance and leadership.

Crossman points out that if the foreman has the technical skill he can become a roving technical adviser to men who largely self-supervise their work, and that if he has the personal qualities he can become the leader of the integrated team.[9] Furthermore, because each foreman supervises a relatively small group of employees, there can be greater interaction within the group. Another researcher, in reporting his observations in an automated steel mill, notes that "the degree of 'friendliness' between crew members and supervision appears to have varied in fairly direct proportion to the amount of interaction between them."[10] Other observers contend that just the opposite results—closer supervision in automated plants is viewed negatively by those supervised, and is a source of worker job dissatisfaction,[11] but no substantiation of this contention was found in the plants covered by this study.

Perhaps part of the disagreement in the literature stems from confusing foreman-employee interaction with the fact of closeness of supervision, for the two are not necessarily correlated. According to one study, "high-rated foremen spent more time communicating information to their employees . . . whereas the low-rated foremen gave a great many more specific and direct orders."[12] This suggested the conclusion that the general supervisory and training methods utilized by the most effective foremen made for more efficient and self-sufficient workers who, in turn, needed less close supervision.

Supervisor-employee tension may derive, however, from

[9] E. R. F. W. Crossman, *Automation and Skill*, Problems of Progress in Industry, No. 9 (London: Her Majesty's Stationery Office, 1960), p. 51.

[10] Charles R. Walker, *Toward the Automatic Factory* (New Haven: Yale University Press, 1957), pp. 143–144.

[11] William A. Faunce, "The Automobile Industry: A Case Study in Automation," in Howard Boone Jacobson and Joseph S. Roucek, editors, *Automation and Society* (New York: Philosophical Library, 1959), p. 49.

[12] "The Effective Manufacturing Foreman—An Observational Study of the Job Activities of Effective and Ineffective Foremen," Study conducted by the Public and Employee Relations Research Service, General Electric, 1957, p. 17.

the greater integration of operations brought about by advanced technology and the resulting interdependency among the component units for smooth operating results. A mishap at any one point induces a breakdown of the entire line, thus enlarging the costliness of individual error. Supervisors therefore have a pressing responsibility for accuracy; their every decision is of great moment, and their instructions to work crews must be precise and clearly understood. On the other hand, once each employee has been given the proper direction, he has to carry out his assignment independently, and too close supervision at this point may be more hindrance than help. Some old-line supervisory personnel find it difficult to allow their subordinates this greater degree of freedom.

In the view of the top management of a printing and publishing plant, the advent of more advanced technology had a salutary effect on the performance of the first-line supervisors. According to the traditions of the industry, the foremen were members of the same union to which production employees belonged, and they often regarded their domains as private fiefs over which they ruled. Typically, they would argue about personnel problems within their jurisdictions with union leaders, but top management had little to say about the proceedings. With the shift to automated operations, however, the foremen, recognizing their technical limitations, became more dependent upon the industrial relations department for training and guidance. This gave the management an opportunity to instill in these supervisors some principles of good management and personnel relations, and thus led them to discard their feudal behavior.

Aids to Supervisors

Preparation of supervisors for the more complex requirements of a new technology is a feature of advance planning in the companies studied. As noted earlier, supervisors are usually acquainted with the new machinery in the debugging period, during which they receive instruction from staff development engineers in its operation and maintenance. In plants where fairly standardized equipment is purchased, supervisors learn about the new processes either at the plant that manufactured the machinery, or from instructors sent by the manufacturer after the equipment is installed. In some cases, special classroom instruction in the basic engineering principles of the new technology is also given. Some companies also step up their emphasis on the human relationships side of supervisory training, particularly where supervisors are required to instruct their crew members in the operation of new machinery.

These attempts to broaden the knowledge of supervisors are not always successful, for many foremen lack the basic qualifications to benefit from the training offered. Supervisors sometimes recognize their own ineptitude and, therefore, react negatively to technological innovation. One company reported that middle and lower management exhibited greater resistance to such change than did the employees on the production line. This company instituted training programs for supervisors at these levels and, in the training process, rooted out those who were not competent, or were unwilling, to keep up with the changing times.

A chemical company attempted to compensate for the inability of first-line supervisors to cope with the more complex technology by adding another level of supervision staffed with more technically-competent people. Another management took the approach of assigning to each operating department a technical man whose function was to assist and advise the general foreman and the line foremen on technical matters.

The job security of supervisors is affected not only by inadequate qualifications but also by severe reductions in overall employment. Cases of surplus foremen are handled in various ways. In some instances the men facing displacement are assigned to supervise simple types of operations, even though the supervisory function may be somewhat extraneous to the needs of the operations. Management often prefers this rather costly procedure to the dismissal of supervisors, which would be detrimental to the morale of supervisory and middle-management groups.

Another approach to the problem is simply to transfer displaced or excess foremen back to direct production. Many companies shun this course, however, because they feel that shifting men from management ranks to the bargaining unit undervalues the management role of first-line supervision. A second drawback to returning foremen to the bargaining unit is that usually their years as supervisors are not credited toward bargaining-unit seniority; long-service former foremen are, therefore, at a distinct disadvantage in case of subsequent layoffs of production workers.

Some companies attempt to prevent displacement of supervisory personnel through transfer to other operations or plants having appropriate openings. As indicated with respect to bargaining-unit personnel, this approach proves largely unsuccessful and for similar reasons. Limited potential, deep ties to home communities, and relatively advanced age stand in the way of fruitful application of an interplant transfer policy among old-line supervisors.

A more successful means of dealing with the problem of displacement in the supervisory force is to encourage acceptance of early retirement by those for whom it is feasible. This is a practicable route because a high percentage of foremen who are not equipped to deal with modern technology are of relatively advanced age and generally are eligible to retire with a pension, or are approaching the age when they will be able to do so. In these cases, companies usually either encourage early retirement or find some way to keep the men employed until they reach the early retirement age. A company that had to close down one of its larger plants faced a very difficult problem respecting long-service supervisors who were below age sixty, and not eligible for early retirement benefits, and for whom there were no transfer opportunities. The management felt that terminating them with severance pay would have been inadequate recognition for practically a lifetime of faithful service, which most of them had given. The dilemma was resolved by providing a special retirement income for displaced supervisors who had 25 or more years of service.

A less humane solution to the displacement problem is that of simply dismissing supervisors who are no longer needed. While most of the companies studied refrain from such action, at whatever cost, a few resort to effecting terminations summarily. In a machinery plant, for example, supervisors who do not have the qualifications to meet the new requirements of their jobs are, in management's discretion, either transferred to other operations, allowed to re-enter the bargaining unit, or are dismissed. The right of this management to return supervisors to the bargaining unit was won by management in recent contract negotiations; but the right is seldom exercised, for the plant manager prefers to terminate the service of foremen who are no longer competent.

More often than not, however, supervisors are given special consideration in periods of change. Where they receive such special treatment, there are generally good reasons for it. First, not being fettered by the restrictions of a collective bargaining agreement, management is free to effect transfers and changes in assignments. Second, the size of the group is such that liberalizing various layoff provisions is simply not as costly as would be the case with bargaining-unit personnel. Also, the supervisor who would otherwise be surplus may be particularly useful during the period of installation and testing of new equipment.

PROFESSIONALS AND TECHNICIANS

The expansion of salaried classifications in plants that have been automated or have undergone other technological change is attributable primarily to an increase in the number of engineers employed and to the rise of new categories of technicians. This enlargement of the technical force varies among industries, being related to the extent to which advanced automatic machinery is utilized and the degree to which research and development are integral to manufacturing operations. For example, the number of technical employees in a plant may nearly equal the blue-collar force in such continuous-process industries as petroleum refining and chemicals, and in those segments of the electrical machinery industry that manufacture new electronic devices directly from the laboratory and drawing board.

Rise of New Technical Groups

The new categories of technical employees that emerge as a result of technological change and the development of new products vary from plant to plant. In a case-study plant manufacturing advanced electronic equipment, it was found that in addition to graduate engineers, there were classifications of "Engineering Associate" and "Technical Assistant." These titles were affixed to jobs filled by high school graduates, whether or not they had engaged in some college studies, if they had had special training in physics, chemistry, and mathematics. The first-mentioned classification connoted requisite training and experience of a higher order than for the other title and, therefore, a capability for carrying out more complex assignments. Although there was no automatic progression upward, the employee could advance from the role of Technical Assistant to that of Engineering Associate by virtue of his work in the plant and/or outside studies. Incumbents were also able to pursue certified college studies toward an engineering degree and then seek employment with the plant as an engineer.

In some cases, new technical groups come into being by a sort of evolutionary process and without any preconceived designations. A good example of this is the experience in a machinery manufacturing plant that progressively introduced more advanced technology over recent years. Since the break-in period on the new machinery was crucial, the employees having the widest knowledge of machinery and proven operating skills were assigned to work out the bugs before the new processes were made fully operative. This procedure proved most valuable in accomplishing the difficult transition. But as operations became routine, the skill and abilities of these men were being wasted; and they were the highest-rated hourly employees in the plant. To utilize them more effectively, the plant management created a special group of "machine developers," comprising 37 of these highly skilled bargaining-unit employees. It assigned these men the continuing function of operating and debugging all new machinery until it was in shape to be turned over to regular operators. Upon each such accomplishment, the machine developers moved on to working with other new technology.

Another interesting example of the conversion of a group of production workers into specialized technical personnel was found in a public utility company. To improve the efficiency of its transmission of natural gas, this company introduced highly advanced applications of automation, one of which involved centralized computer control of all the generating stations along more than a thousand miles of pipeline. The machinery of the new central station also was advanced and complex. These innovations required much more sophisticated skills and much higher degrees of responsibility on operating jobs. Formerly, a station man had issued instructions by telephone about the adjustments to be made on the line. Under the new system, he exercised complete control over the line from a central console board, and had to make the adjustments himself by pressing the right buttons. Thus, in essence, the assignments called for specialized technicians rather than production workers. The company was able to staff these new technical jobs from within, because the production workers had educational backgrounds that made them trainable for new assignments. The management had adopted a policy of hiring only high school graduates some five years earlier, having foreseen the future staffing needs.

In some cases new technical groups are brought into existence because of the shortage of professionally trained people and the resulting need to so break up work loads that lower-level employees can be assigned to some aspects of the work. To that end, a steel-producing company has been giving much attention to redesigning its technical assignments in order to free engineers and other highly trained technical personnel from those aspects of the work which might be considered routine. If this program is successful, it will result in the emergence of a large group of fairly low-level technical assistants. In time, however, there will probably be a general upgrading of the group as the employees gain the competence to engage in more difficult tasks.

The increasing complexity of new technology also raises job requirements at the lower salaried levels, and thus creates new types of technical-supervisory assignments. A food-processing company now has the classification of "Junior Engineer," comprising young college graduates with science or engineering degrees, who are placed in management development programs and trained specifically to run new types of operations.

In factories where there is extensive computer-control of operations, the whole gamut of new occupations associated with information technology comes into play. In a plant that began to use numerically controlled machinery for milling and drilling operations, programming and similar occupations involved in preparing tapes became important. Moreover, the functions connected with preparing the tapes were interlocked with the actual process of manufacture, and this blurred the distinctions between the office group of technicians and technicians operating on the plant floor.

Inherent Policy Problems

Myriad industrial relations problems accompany the rise of new and often large categories of technical personnel, and the shortage of such personnel in most areas is a contributing factor. The problems with respect to such employees revolve around matters of salary, opportunities for advancement, job status, relationships with other employee groups, and the impact of these factors on morale.

With professional personnel, a rather typical problem in the salary area is the compression of pay scales, ascribable to the competitive struggle among companies to secure needed talents in the face of manpower shortages, particularly as to engineering occupations. Each company seeks to gain an advantage in recruiting by offering higher entrance salaries than would be warranted, were the situation less competitive. Thus, a young man may go directly from school into employment that pays a starting salary of $600 a month. He may then work alongside a man in his mid-thirties who has been with the company for 10 years or so, but whose salary has progressed from a more conservative starting salary to only $750 per month. It is not surprising to find that long-service employees feel discriminated against in such situations and that problems of morale and interpersonal relationships arise. Moreover, such reactions lead to turnover, which compounds the problem of recruitment.

Tied in with the problem of relative salaries is the matter of promotional opportunities for college recruits within a plant (this discussion is focused on the plant, not the research and development laboratory). Because these young technical men start with comparatively high salaries, they often enter employment with inflated ideas about progressing upward in the company—ideas that are sometimes stimulated by company recruiters in their zeal to make employment with a particular company most attractive. Once a college recruit is in the plant, however, he may find that the work is less challenging than he had imagined and that advancement within an industrial plant is, by the very nature of a factory operation, fairly restricted.

Subtle status considerations also arise to plague managements. Engineers and scientists wish to be recognized as professionals with unquestioned standing, and they are therefore prone to resent direction by plant managers who are not themselves professional engineers or scientists. On the other hand, the college-trained technicians are often jealous of the status accorded the professional engineers and scientists, feeling that there should be some special form of recognition to differentiate their own positions within the plant hierarchy. The problem of status considerations occurs most often where nonprofessional technicians are assigned to an engineering department. The professional engineers, observing that some technicians are doing work identical or similar to their own, begin to fret about their relative status as engineers.

Of course, a management's aim in bringing technicians into an engineering unit usually is to upgrade the work of the engineers by freeing them from some of the more routine tasks. This is not always possible to accomplish, however, because some engineers have been doing routine work for so long that they have lost touch with the latest developments in their fields and are not capable of immediately switching to more complex assignments. Managements sometimes attempt to ameliorate these situations by giving engineers special consideration, including time off to attend professional meetings, so that they can keep abreast of technological progress. This practice, however, can often foment resentment among the technicians because they are not given similar opportunities—even though their work may be comparable to that of the engineers. Working out a solution to this dilemma is far from simple, and it continues to plague managements.

There is apparently a desire for autonomy with respect to work assignments on the part of the professional or technical group within the plant as well as the individual within the group. But this desire causes them to run afoul of what is practical for achieving efficiency and harmony in the operations. Illustrative of this problem is the case of a food-processing plant in which technological change had a profound impact on the functions of its major group of technical employees. Originally, this had been mainly a time-study group, composed of men who were knowledgeable but were not trained engineers. As more advanced machinery and production methods were introduced, the unit was converted into a full-fledged industrial engineering department. It was staffed with professional engineers and charged with the responsibility for maintaining the efficiency of existing equipment and for conceiving further refinements in the technology.

The engineers' perception of their responsibilities made them more machinery-minded than people-conscious. Thus, in the effectuation of methods changes, altercations developed between the industrial engineers and the personnel department when the latter sought to work out with the engineers how best to introduce the changes without damage to employee morale and without creating industrial relations problems. But the engineers, whose experience was limited to handling technical matters, refused to take into account the personnel implications of their actions. In several instances, they accomplished the engineering objectives only to fail on the human relations front. Only through these failures did they learn the importance of coordinated activity between staff groups in adapting the organization to the impact of technological change.

Experience With Union Organization

The findings of this study suggest that it is the general dissatisfaction felt by professional and technical personnel, together with their inability to bring management attention to bear on their interests, that makes some groups vulnerable to unionization. It is not the purpose here to probe for cause or effect, or for solution of the problems; these matters deserve more exhaustive study. The case studies do present, however, some interesting illustrations of company experience with the organization of professional and technical personnel, which are suggestive of trends.

An electrical machinery company's experience with unionization of engineers and technicians is noteworthy, in terms of the kinds of issues involved. At one of its plants manufacturing advanced electronic equipment, a local independent union was organized by the unusually large number of scientists, engineers, and technicians employed. A critical issue then arose over the matter of salary progression for these professionals. In negotiations, the union successfully opposed an attempt by the management to restrict the application of annual increases to a specified maximum salary level. In the absence of any such ceiling, salaries soared year after year. Moreover, since the company's quite liberal contributions toward pensions and other fringe benefits were based on total earnings, the combined cost of salaries and benefits approached prohibitive limits.

A compromise was reached eventually, whereby earnings remained unrestricted, but a limit was placed on the salary base to which benefit contributions would apply. This outcome later appeared to be a dubious victory for plant management. To strengthen its position in negotiation of the issue, the union surrendered its independence and affiliated with the national union that already had two locals in the plant. Today, every nonsupervisory employee in the plant, from sweeper to scientist, is a member of the same national union (though in different locals). In collective bargaining with plant management the three locals cooperate to advance both their common and separate interests. At this plant a strike threat poses a multiple problem. Should a strike materialize, not only would current production be halted; future expansion would also be jeopardized, as all research and development work on new products would also cease.

In a plant of another electrical machinery company, the technical personnel also turned to unionization as an outlet for their general discontent over matters affecting them. The group organized as a local of the short-lived American Society of Engineers, but it disbanded when the Society collapsed, largely because of indecision as to whether it would function as a professional association or a full-fledged employees' union. During the period of the local's existence, the plant management endeavored to identify and resolve some of the major problems of these professional employees. The most tangible evidence of the management's concern over the problems felt by the employees was the provision of a formal grievance procedure for channeling their protests up to the plant manager.

There were only three plants among those studied in which engineering and scientific units organized to bargain collectively with management. In some other situations, a minority of such personnel were definitely pro-union, but they failed to influence the majority into organizing. In a plant manufacturing construction machinery, enough of its employees signed pledge cards in favor of a national union of technical employees to warrant a National Labor Relations Board election, in which the union lost. In line with the Board's practice, the ballots of the engineers were counted separately from those of the nonprofessionals. It is interesting that the engineers voted unanimously against union representation, though some prounion sentiment was evidenced in the voting of the technicians.

In some plants, various groups of nonprofessional technicians, either hourly-rated or salaried, were absorbed into the bargaining units of production employees. Where such employees desired union representation, managements regarded that course as preferable to their possibly becoming the nucleus of a union of all technical personnel. There were also instances in which operators' jobs were upgraded by new technology to the technician level, but management refrained from reclassifying them out of the bargaining unit.

Clearly, it is the semiprofessional technician who is having the greatest difficulty in defining his role and determining his status within the industrial plant. The engineers will not permit him to don the mantle of a "professional," and he feels removed from both the management and the production workers. In this survey of plant situations, the indications are that so far technicians consider themselves more estranged from production workers than from management. But no group of employees will be satisfied to float for long without being identified with some source of influence in the plant. Given the unique and important contribution that the technician can make as plant technology becomes more complex, the dimension of the management problem is underscored. Here is an area in which the use of something more than stereotyped personnel approaches is vital.

Some Approaches to the Problems of Specialized Personnel

In many situations, plant managements are accustomed neither to dealing with large numbers of engineers and technicians nor to handling the salary, status, and morale problems of these personnel groups. Perhaps a period of uncertainty and difficulty must be experienced, out of which may develop the clues to needed management action. In any event, anticipating and planning will help. For example, one company's experience with unionization of professional employees made for greater attentiveness to the problems of an expanded professional group at another plant. There the company clearly identified engineering personnel as members of management and treated them accordingly. The result was the emergence of a generally satisfied group of employees, posing a healthy number of problems but showing absolutely no concern with unionization.

At the previously mentioned electrical machinery plant, where the experience of its sizable group of professional and technical personnel with unionization had proved abortive, the management demonstrated its concern for their interests by setting up a separate personnel department to handle matters affecting them. This department was charged with maintaining regular communication with these employees, and with establishing a grievance procedure to assure them of a medium for voicing their complaints.

A chemical company recognized that its technicians had to be accorded some special treatment which would differentiate their positions from production assignments. Thus, when displacements occurred, intensive efforts were made to prevent the layoff or dismissal of technical employees. To that end, a particularly liberal policy of interplant transfers was adopted for technicians—to keep them within the company and thus assure the greatest return on the company's investment in their training. This transfer policy worked well, as young technicians were normally more willing than production workers to relocate for job opportunities. The course followed in a machinery plant to prevent layoff of its engineers and technicians was (1) to use them elsewhere in the plant when their jobs became surplus, and (2) to transfer them to the research and development laboratory of the parent company when they could no longer be absorbed in plant employment.

Some companies reported that, in their experience, due attention to the professional concerns of engineers and technicians not only improved overall personnel relations, but promoted better performance. The managements stressed the need to guard against obsolescence of skills among engineers by aiding them to keep up with advances in their fields. Apparently, the fear of falling behind new developments in their profession is a pervasive one among engineers and college-trained technicians, and it leads to an undermining of their morale and professional pride.

* * *

Throughout the preceding discussion we have shown how subtle changes taking place in the structure of work have manifested themselves with respect to supervisory, professional, and technical employees. These changes arise out of a general reorganization of work within the plant as well as between the plant workforce and others in the company or elsewhere in the economy.

An illustration within one company is pertinent. In this company, electrical wiring of panel boards was always a job of high skill. But the job lost its high-skill qualities as a result of advances made in design and engineering, color coding, and greater machine capability to precision-cut and code panel-wiring parts. On the other hand, the design and engineering jobs employed much higher skills. This study could not trace, either in the company or throughout the economy, this type of job restructuring, or perhaps it is more precise to call it a reallocation of responsibility and skill. During a period of such reallocation of work, the demand is, apparently, for more people who can both design and install the changes. Typically, the reliance is on the supervisory and professional and technical workforces. Here, in common with other areas of work, management will be faced with complex problems of selection, placement, and training.

Company experience with plant salaried personnel points to the need for and significance of training in both the human relations and professional areas. It is well to stress the significance of such training and developmental activities. The problem felt by the engineer of having only a "half-life" in his profession after he has been out of school for from five to ten years, because he has fallen behind the times, is not the only problem among plant salaried groups. All people in salaried jobs must have an opportunity to articulate their reactions to their work experiences, for this gives them the insight to understand and cope with their problems. It is in this area of dealing with salaried employees that the industrial relations staff can be most constructive by helping them to see realistically and to rise above the difficulties they find in work and work relationships.

CHAPTER X

The Management Process
and Technological Change

Throughout the earlier chapters, the reactions of management, employees, and unions to technological change have been presented and discussed, and the interactions among the three have been described. Little attention has been given to the coordination of management effort in anticipation of change. In this chapter, therefore, consideration turns to certain essential steps in managing change.

These steps are identified here in terms of three major questions. First, how can manpower planning be made most effective by managements in anticipating technological change? Second, when and how should communications and advance notice be given to employees, informing them of the imminence of a planned change? Third, how can the industrial relations staff responsibility be best organized to aid in achieving a smooth transition to the application of new methods and equipment?

MANPOWER PLANNING

The literature on the art or science of management abounds with references to planning as an essential part of the management process—and indeed it is. But planning takes many forms. It may contemplate a single occurrence or crisis, or it may be a continuous process, completely integrated into the practice of management. There has been a trend toward sales forecasting and, in recent years, attempts to plan for corporate growth. In many of the programs of long-range planning there have been efforts also to forecast the manpower needs of a company. Initially, such manpower planning gave particular attention to shortage occupations, especially in the professional and scientific fields, and, more recently, to management positions. Today, many companies —including some cooperating in this study—are attempting to forecast manpower requirements for all occupational levels, and they are making realistic attempts to key industrial relations programs to the manpower needs of the future.

Within the study group, companies were far from unanimous in their acceptance of the value of manpower planning as a predictive tool for future overall manpower requirements. One of the leading industrial relations men contacted in the course of this study considered the planning process in these terms: "Manpower planning? It is a phrase that holds great promise, but can do so little considering our inability to predict the advances emerging from our laboratories and engineering studies." Even though all of the cooperating companies attempted to plan their manpower needs, only a small proportion had a program designated as manpower planning or an approach to their manpower situation that could be categorized as a formal method of projecting manpower needs over the long term. Nevertheless, based on an amalgam of the experience of the companies engaging in some form of manpower planning, a series of steps is apparent in typical manpower planning programs.

Projecting Manpower Needs

First, corporate projections of production are made, based on sales forecasts, which, in turn, are based on a series of management assumptions regarding company objectives, desired growth patterns, and the company's anticipated performance in the product market. Consideration is given throughout to the current and projected levels of national economic activity. Building on reasonable sales forecasts and production estimates, manpower needs are established for occupations that are directly related to production and, subsequently, for all indirect labor activities. The raw estimates of manpower needed to meet the projected production levels are further adjusted for anticipated attrition of the workforce.

Once a fairly realistic picture of manpower needs is established, industrial relations programs are planned accordingly. These programs must reflect accommodation to the immediate, as well as the anticipated, impact of accomplished and contemplated changes in technology, product lines, plant locations, and the like. Staffing must be adjusted to consider the assumed future needs of the organization. Further adjustments must be made to take into account the assumed changes in labor productivity, stemming from the

---

Steps in Manpower Planning

1. Corporate projections of sales and production.
2. Estimates of gross manpower needs to meet projections.
3. Adjustment of estimates of manpower needs, for attrition through deaths, retirements, turnover, and the like.
4. Personnel programs designed to assemble and maintain a workforce with the necessary skills to meet production and marketing requirements.

use of more advanced machinery, as well as from the change in the skill composition of the labor force.

In one company in the study group, a comprehensive planning program was meticulously carried out at the corporate level by a special task force. It carefully surveyed future possibilities and plans and constructed three series of estimates of company performance for the future, based on a set of conservative, average, and high growth assumptions. When the findings were translated into manpower needs, they both startled and perplexed the management. Its five-year projection resulted in an estimated requirement for additional engineers which was greater than the company could reasonably expect to recruit. Because of this planning exercise, the company was forced to review its current use of engineering personnel. It has now embarked on a study designed to determine if it is possible to separate the duties of existing engineering jobs into professional and non-professional categories. It is hoped that this research will enable the company to increase its utilization of engineers, both now and in the future, by training nonprofessionals to provide supportive services for the engineers. Equally as important, future staffing will make certain that engineers will not be underutilized.

Whereas the planning of this company uncovered a problem in current staffing patterns and suggested a solution for what might be a future problem, the manpower plans in other companies were not so broadly developed. In attempting to anticipate needs and requirements for only one or two years in the future, they were generally tied to a plant or to a particular operating situation. In these more limited applications, manpower planning might be judged to have been effective, provided too much was not expected, because actual experience can never precisely meet anticipated targets. Those managers engaged in manpower planning acknowledged the divergence between projected and actual personnel needs. And consequently they were generally in agreement that such planning has merit only if it is clearly recognized as, at best, a rough art.

Assigning Responsibility for Planning

Designating a clear responsibility for planning is essential in making it a reasonably valuable tool for management. The general dimensions of the planning process are shaped by the skills and talents of many individuals in many parts of the business. Before a company plunges into the intricacies of a planning program, therefore, its logical approach is to make some one person responsible for the direction of the program. But there is no pronounced pattern in the assignment of this responsibility. In some cases, a special task force group or a staff department outside the industrial relations area was responsible for planning—perhaps a corporate, business, or economic planning department. In a number of cases, planning was the responsibility of the financial department. In almost all cases, however, the final estimate of the impact of anticipated future events on the personnel situation was a task assigned to the corporate industrial relations department. The ability to cope with the multifaceted employee relations implications of future developments appeared to be enhanced where both industrial relations and organizational responsibilities were delegated to a single staff department.

Considerable planning to handle changes in methods and work was discovered also at the plant operating level. Rarely, however, was it viewed as a formal program of manpower planning; instead, it was generally regarded as the "application of common sense to operations." The difficulty in many of the companies was in getting communications to flow from the line departments to industrial relations long enough in advance to make possible positive personnel approaches to employee dislocation on a plant- or company-wide basis. In the smaller plants, management communications at the operating level were considerably more effective than in the larger plants. And far more could be accomplished in the smaller plants, because of the flexibility inherent in the situation and in the plans for handling change. In the experience of the companies with planning programs, a significant difficulty, at the corporate level, has been tying together the many elements of the enterprise into a consistent future plan.

Based on the record of past plans and accomplishments, many companies have achieved reasonable success in planning for the future. Generally, success appears most achievable in situations where a company has learned that forecasts and plans can only be targets, and where operating managers and their staffs have achieved a high degree of coordinated effort. Further, planning has been relatively accurate where a company's growth rate is tied closely to population growth trends, which themselves are relatively predictable, and where the rate of technological innovation and productivity change has been fairly consistent over time. Thus, public utilities, in the main, have done a better planning job than many other enterprises because they are not so quickly affected by slight changes in consumer preferences, sources of supply, and foreign competition.

Many company people feel that manpower planning at the corporate level can be made to work in a period of reasonably steady growth, especially where the effect of both domestic and foreign competition on operations is minimal —as was the case for many companies in the first postwar decade. But, given keener competition, a management may have to adjust the company's product line, output patterns, methods of production, and perhaps even the locus of particular operations. In such circumstances, in the view of many managements, long-term planning becomes almost impossible.

Another problem experienced in companies is that it is extremely difficult, regardless of where the responsibility for planning is lodged, to pull together all the information necessary for a comprehensive plan. This is not a matter of any department's unwillingness to cooperate, but is, rather, a problem of how to isolate the information needed for a special planning project from the management process itself. An engineering department, or a production-planning department, frequently will not realize the employee relations implications of what might seem to be a trivial change. But such a change, or series of changes, may have deep implications with respect to either or both the number and quality of men required in the future.

Reviewing the observations made in the companies, it may be said that effective overall manpower planning is most difficult, except in periods of economic growth, when expansionary trends are predictable. Pressure for manpower planning is greatest, however, between growth periods. And yet it is at just that time that managements begin to question the practicality of estimating future manpower needs. Would it not be better, they argue, to work toward an understanding of actual operations and the specific individual problems which may arise as operations change? Such direct efforts on behalf of employees, it is contended, would be of real value, in contrast to the sometimes futile efforts of trying to predict the long-term future manpower situation for the entire corporation.

Planning Experience

In the light of the above discussion, it might be valuable to examine briefly the planning experience of three companies. In one of these companies, although there was no actual formal program of manpower planning, there was much advance preparation within the line management organization in anticipation of technological change. Overall corporate planning for change was attempted in the second company on the basis of budget information, and tended, generally, to be effective. The third company engaged in a program designed to deal with a problem of management morale, and out of it came dividends in the manpower area.

1. *Planning Within the Line Management Process.* During the first interview with this company, one of the industrial relations men said, "To understand how and why we handled employee problems in periods of technological change as we did, you must understand how our management thinks." In reciting the experience of his company with planning for technological change—with particular reference to the number of people required for the future, as well as the quality and educational background they had to have to fill the future jobs—the point made, and it was reinforced in plant visits, was that operating management saw as its job, and not the job of the staff man, the anticipation of change and its impact on people.

Because of the sophistication of the line managers, it was possible for the company to put into action far in advance of any other company studied, industrial relations programs and practices which were attuned to technological change. Indeed, one radical change affecting an entire plant was anticipated eight years before the change was activated in that plant. Management thus had more than ample lead time to develop programs that made it possible to retain employees who might otherwise have been terminated.

There was no formal manpower-planning program in this company but management was sensitive to upcoming problems and willing to accept the responsibility for making reasonable adjustments to meet future developments. The pattern of management action in this company over the years has had the beneficial effect of creating an environment within which change is not viewed as a threat; this has made possible accommodation to technological change at all levels of the organization.

This company's experience is an illustration of what might be referred to as management action that embraces planning and comprehends industrial relations needs. The case illustrates the need to view planning for technological change within the context of, and as part of, the total management process.

2. *Overall Corporate Planning.* In considering the formulation of its planning program, this management was aware of the typical problems of manpower planning encountered in other companies. It was believed that manpower planning could succeed, if a method could be found to integrate the many aspects of planning into a comprehensive plan that would be of value to all managers—engineers, sales, production, financial, employee relations, and the like. The management in this company found that the corporate budget and financial control system could be used as the integrative process for management planning.

The main elements of the company's program are as follows: Every department and operation is required to obtain from top management approval for its budget in advance of each fiscal period. The corporate budget is so arranged that appropriations for research and capital improvements are identified on a departmental basis. The industrial relations department has the responsibility for preparing a report based on the budget; let us call it the "appropriations affecting manpower report." The report shows the implications for manpower requirements of each appropriation for capital improvement and also the anticipated effects on manpower of current developmental research. It further provides an opportunity for the industrial relations staff to consult with the research and engineering departments and with line managers on the manpower implications of each appropriation, and to thereby plan for possible dislocations.

A quarterly review is made of any new projects, the anticipated completion dates of current projects, plus their implications for the organization in terms of manpower needs. Based on the form used by the company, the following listing suggests the type of information extracted from the budget and collected and maintained by the industrial relations department with respect to new and current projects.

Budget Information
1. Budget appropriation number,
2. Date approved,
3. Date work started,
4. Date originally set for completion,
5. Revised completion date,

Manpower Data
6. Surplus, categorized by type of work and level of skill,
7. Shortages, categorized by type of work and level of skill.

Each new budget approval or revision is followed by a comprehensive survey by the industrial relations department, which reviews the changed manpower implications of each proposed appropriation. Revisions are made as necessary and translated into manpower implications. These implications, in turn, are related to current hiring and termination patterns. Thus, new hires can be made in anticipation of the changes within the corporation, and appropriate preparations can be made for layoffs. In some cases, interplant transfers can be effected, depending on what changes are taking place at other plant locations and the availability of special skills and know-how.

The value of the "appropriations affecting manpower report" is that it can aid in anticipating changes in the operations and the subsequent effect of these on manpower, so there is no need to engage in an elaborate forecasting or planning process. Every request for an appropriation, whether for capital improvement and research expenditures or for staff time, must be reported on the "appropriations affecting manpower report." These reports serve to trigger employee relations considerations with respect to the jobs affected for both long-term and short-term projects. The procedure establishes a clear responsibility for the industrial relations department to review plans and consult with those whose job it is to innovate. The procedure focuses management's attention on the manpower implications of its action. Finally, it gives the industrial relations department a reasonably accurate projection of emerging developments, thus enabling it to adapt programs to technological and methodological change.

3. *Effective Stimulus for Management Planning.* The experience of the third company is unusual but significant for the discussion. In this company, the management was convinced, upon analysis of its operational methods, that vast improvements were necessary within the management organization if the financial performance of the company was ever to be improved. As seen by top management, one of the most serious deterrents to effecting a series of needed changes in operations was the attitude of the supervisory and management group, which had grown accustomed to what was reported to be a "loose" way of running the business. Top management decided that it was essential to develop attitudes within management conducive to establishing more efficient methods. The company undertook to shape attitudes through a program which came to be known as a "profitability improvement program." Through this program, the message of the urgency for needed improvements and increased profits was carried to all levels of the management organization, including the first level of supervision. The improvement program was talked and written about until it became understood that modernization was a part of the job of every supervisor and manager, and that each could directly contribute to improving profits. The success of the program could be measured in terms of how well the organization responded to the idea of profit improvement for the company.

The "profitability improvement program" appeared to have a bonus value for management in presenting and handling technological change; it tended to weld all management thinking into a consistently positive approach. The desire for modernization had become so strong that ways of improving operations were viewed as an opportunity and not as a challenge. Indeed, new technology would not have been introduced nor profits improved had it not been for the change in supervisory and management attitudes and motivations. Through the meetings and communications growing out of the program, management was stimulated, and there developed a cohesiveness in its thinking, planning, and action for dealing with change and its employee dislocations. In many cases, the company was able to shape programs and actions—which formerly might have been impossible. There was far greater sensitivity to the implications of change for employee relations, with the result that imaginative approaches—including transfers, training, and outside job placement—were taken in handling problems of employees who were dislocated. In addition, more thought was given to these programs in anticipation of technological change.

The programs and actions taken by these three companies are not out of line with practices cited throughout earlier portions of this book. Still, these cases do call attention to the importance of viewing planning as part of the overall management process. Planning is integrated with the operational aspects of running an enterprise. In the first case discussed above, a *philosophy* was revealed that recognized line management's responsibility for manpower planning. It the second illustration, a *system* of management coordination of manpower control was achieved through a budgetary technique. In the third case, a special *program* effectively provoked managers into taking forward-looking actions with respect to areas of their responsibility, suggesting that manpower problems can also be attended to as a part of the normal management process.

The implications of company experience with manpower planning are twofold. First, manpower planning as a "management program" will take on little meaning unless some method is found to blend management's normal planning of operations with a manpower planning program. Second, some method of anticipating manpower requirements is essential if the complicated problems emerging out of technological change are to be dealt with. Comparative experience in companies suggests that instead of seeking a procedure for manpower planning, what should be sought is a form of *integrated management planning* which pulls together the capabilities of the staff and line organizations so that future problems, needs and requirements can be realistically anticipated and evaluated.

COMMUNICATIONS AND ADVANCE NOTICE

Integrated management planning would reinforce the mutual recognition by line and staff departments of the importance of communications during technological change. But even in the absence of such planning, as this study has stressed, employee communications play a significant role in adjustment to change. The way in which notice of impending change is handled within an organization has a vital influence on that organization, for any abrupt change disturbs the *status quo*. In those few instances where line management introduced new technology without sufficient notice, unfavorable employee reactions developed and special efforts were required to overcome the resultant employee relations problems.

Intramanagement Communications

If industrial relations departments are to plan communications programs in anticipation of impending change, these departments obviously must be keyed into the operational decisions at an early stage. Frequently the industrial relations departments of the case-study companies were asked to decide upon the most auspicious timing and tone of the communications that served notice of planned management action. In many companies such intramanagement communications are achieved through formal meetings where there is a clear recognition of the importance of keeping staff groups informed of line management's plans and objectives. Regular management meetings to discuss plant operations make it possible for industrial relations men to be aware of, and alerted to, future developments. Regardless of the specific form of the communications, these meetings are just as important as the recognition by both line and staff people of the value of communications to the overall management process and to the achievement of the management's goals.

The Communications Process

The lead-time in giving advance notice of change among the companies studied varied, depending upon the particular circumstances—including such considerations as the scope of the technology, the pace at which it would become operational, and the climate of labor-management relations. Some companies went well beyond simply giving advance notice; they designed elaborate communications programs to give employees an understanding of the need for technological improvements. The experience with such programs provides some useful guides:

1. A climate of opinion favorable to the introduction of new technology is important. Generally it can be achieved through sustained communications with employees which explain the long-run benefits that prospective changes have for the enterprise and, hence, for the employees. As the timing of a change becomes known, frank explanations of the reasons for it are given, and information is provided on the

nature of prospective dislocations. Periodic briefing of first-line supervisors as part of the communications process enables them to clarify questions raised by their subordinates arising from the overall communications effort. In developing the "climate of opinion," all communications media can have value for publicizing management's thinking and the facts about change. Among the media used by the companies are plant bulletin boards, periodic informational letters to employees' homes, and company or plant newspapers. One special communications device found was the issuance of employee notebooks detailing the proposed changes.

2. Advance notice of an impending technological change is an indispensable feature of an informational program. It is essential for accomplishing a smooth adjustment to new methods of operation and often promotes positive employee attitudes toward change. In the experience of the case-study companies, such notice seldom resulted in employee efforts to thwart management action despite the prior fears of management that this would be the case.

Early notice permits employees to evaluate alternatives open to them, such as accepting job transfer, taking severance pay, or seeking early retirement. It also gives employees time to adjust their lives to the consequences of change, whether by altering family living patterns to conform with new shift schedules or, for those who face layoff, by undertaking to retrain themselves and to seek other jobs.

From management's point of view, a primary purpose of advance notice is to insure that employees receive accurate information concerning proposed changes, thus compressing the time during which false rumors might circulate. The truth, no matter how harsh, engenders less fear and is less damaging to morale than the uncertainties of speculation based on gossip, which, as has happened, may transform a leak about tentative company plans into a certainty of imminent plant shutdown and permanent layoffs. When this occurs, the resulting anxiety lowers morale and may drastically affect current production schedules.[1]

3. Advance notice of technological change to the union or unions concerned can also be a realistic procedure, as they too have a stake in the consequences of technological change, not only as representatives of employees, but as institutions. Informing a union of impending changes in production processes is essential from a practical standpoint as well, since in most instances there are contractual matters involved in effectuating change, and it is best to work these out together as long before the installation of new equipment as is feasible. Whether union representatives are informed before or at the same time that employees are notified would depend upon the prior history of management-union relations. Where union leaders have always been reasonable and cooperative, no harm can come of their knowing ahead of employees about a management's forthcoming action, and planning together may benefit all concerned. On the other hand, there would hardly be any gain in giving early notice to union leaders who are known to have a bent for obstructionist tactics. In any case, notification needs to be based on firm decisions rather than on tentative plans, for should the latter fail to materialize, anxieties are unnecessarily aroused. Moreover, if the plans should materialize at some later time, both employees and unions might not take the notification seriously.

4. In communicating to employees about the introduction of new technology, exaggeratedly optimistic statements and generalizations are to be avoided. It is best to be entirely frank and factual, in order that employees will know the true score at the outset. Meaningful communications set

---

[1] While visiting a plant, the authors witnessed a dramatic illustration of how unfounded rumors spread. The personnel manager had to terminate the interview and rush to the plant floor to scotch a rumor that the company had decided to shut down the plant. The rumor got started because someone had seen a memorandum dealing with the location of company facilities, though no plans were under way for relocation of any of them.

forth the nature of dislocations to be expected and the company's proposed program for meeting the attendant problems. By reaffirming for employees the rights and benefits to which they are entitled, and explaining any supplementary measures being planned on their behalf, management shows it has not been unmindful of the impact of change on them.

Communications Techniques

Some highly imaginative communications techniques have been employed to show realistically the need for change. Particularly effective was the accumulation of instances of business failure, plant shutdowns, or declines in production and employment where companies and plants had not kept abreast of the latest technology. (In one company these presentations were colorfully referred to as a "chamber of horrors.") A chemical plant in which employment had expanded after technological improvements were made pointed to a similar plant within its own company that had lost production and cut employment because of its failure to modernize continually. Another successful approach was to enlighten employees about the workings of the advanced technology, causing their anxieties to give way to their enthusiasm over the new machinery. This was done through charts and diagrams explaining the operation of the new technology, visits to the manufacturers of the equipment, and especially-built display models of the machinery to be introduced.

The industrial relations departments of companies which have adopted new production processes have had to exercise ingenuity in shaping their communications efforts to the climate of the particular situation. Increasingly, in company after company, the communications function has been found to be far more important today than the mere publication of the house organ. Perhaps this is but the beginning of a trend that will lead to a more general recognition of the importance of communications in the total practice of management.

Company experience has established the importance of effective communications with employees and their representatives in paving the way for the introduction of advanced technology. This experience suggests that communicating about impending change is a continuing process that goes well beyond giving advance notice. It is necessary to report periodically on the progress of innovations and on the course of management's program to cushion the impact of change on employees.

IMPLICATIONS FOR INDUSTRIAL RELATIONS

Both planning and advance notice by management in anticipation of technological change create a set of interesting challenges for the practice of industrial relations within a company. Structurally, there is the matter of identifying and establishing responsibility for dealing with the "people problems" during a period of change. Functionally, there is the problem of adjusting programs and practices to bring them into conformance with the needs of the organization. Changes in the staffing requirements of an operation call for a consideration of the number and type of people who will be required for the operations. Training, recruitment, and separation problems may be involved for future staffing. Questions of pay, union relations, and the like may be raised. How the problems in these functional areas are considered, and solutions found and integrated so as to provide for smooth adjustment to changed conditions, becomes a major task in the practice of industrial relations today.

Because of the nature of the evolution of the industrial relations function, most departments have been built by identifying clear areas of functional responsibility and charging staffs to work in their respective areas of specialization. Drawing the various functions together at this juncture to present the best possible approaches to dealing with technological dislocation has not always been easy.

In some cases, the structure of the industrial relations department magnifies the functional problem. This is the situation particularly where the department is highly compartmentalized, with relations with production workers handled by one staff group and relations with white-collar and professional employees handled by another. In many companies where such compartmentalization has been in effect, there is little coordination with respect to ways of handling "corporate-wide" employee relations problems. Moreover, a technique found effective with white-collar employees may not be recognized as having possible application among production workers, and vice versa.

In other cases, the problem has been a derivative of over-specialization of individuals within the staff groups. The earlier discussion of job evaluation illustrates the problem of viewing the rules of job evaluation as being of more importance than the achievement of solutions to the human and management problems inherent in technological change.

Despite these observations, the experience of the companies studied would suggest that internal and structural problems have been overcome. There has been signal success among the companies studied in dealing with technological change. Such success, however, should not make management sanguine. The need to separate a large number of employees, or to retrain many workers, presents a very clear problem. Typically, staff departments can focus on how to deal with that type of problem. Any relatively dramatic adjustments will spark total management effort to deal with employee dislocation. When, however, subtle changes take place in operations, day by day and week by week, without adjustments in staffing being made, because no one change alone makes a man or his skills superfluous, the staff job may be extremely difficult. The cumulative impact of change can have a tremendous influence within a company. Thus it is not surprising to find in many companies, such as those in the railroad industry, major struggles as they attempt to adjust to the cumulative impact of change, over time, on people and jobs.

These observations have significance for management. First, the responsibility of the industrial relations staff to work alongside line management in long-term planning is manifest. Such planning will highlight the future operating needs of the corporation and should trigger specific plans for dealing with the human problems which may result.

Second, consideration should be given in corporate industrial relations departments to identifying the responsibility to plan for handling emerging personnel problems on a multifunctional basis. By this we mean that within a corporate personnel department someone or some group, other than the chief industrial relations executive, must have the authority to plan for dealing with the "people problems" which arise because of change.

What is contemplated is an all-embracing function that can first view emerging and developing situations and identify the scope of the actions that will be required. This group must then be in a position to draw on all skills and talents available within and outside of the organization, in order to be able to develop necessary plans, policies, and practices.

In some organizations the task described above has been reserved to the chief personnel officer or his deputy. In others, a particular person, because of his abilities or his acceptance throughout the organization, has assumed the job of handling the planning for employee dislocation. In some cases, where a major problem of dislocation has been anticipated, a special *ad hoc* task force has been established to cope with the problem.

The authors believe that, in the future, technological change will not disappear as a problem, for change is a constant, and it will continue to have a subtle effect on day-to-day work situations. Therefore, the industrial relations responsibility will have to be refocused and organizational arrangements made within the industrial relations department which will establish a planning, problem-solving, and advisory staff available to line management. This staff will have to be adequately identified—and line management made aware that it is available—and its position will have to be such that it will be able to coordinate the special functions already existing within traditional industrial relations departments.

To the extent that an industrial relations department operates on the basis suggested above, close liaison with operating management should be achievable. The basis for such a conclusion is that both line and staff departments would have a clear and specific understanding of the respective roles to be played in facilitating management plans at the time of technological change. Moreover, the interlocking of staff effort with line management would create the possibility of achieving more effective, integrated management planning for change. It would also arm the industrial relations staff with the information necessary to create or at least assist in the creation of a climate of employee opinion conducive to the acceptance of change.

CHAPTER XI

The Broader Institutional Setting

The impact of technological change reaches well beyond the immediate plant setting. The community in which a plant is situated is deeply affected when employment opportunities are reduced by drastic modernization of plant operations, the closing down of a plant that is obsolete, or the relocation of a particular operation as the economic situation of a company may dictate. The structure of unions is being disturbed as automation progressively restructures the workforce of companies. Public concern over the impact of automation on people exerts a pressure on companies to act in the public interest and on government to become involved in labor-management relations, directly or indirectly, by shaping the workings of the economy.

These groups—unions, the public, and government—are important in conditioning the environment within which management action takes place. Therefore, in this chapter we consider these external forces and relate them to the management practices and problems discussed in this study.

286

UNION CONSIDERATIONS

Membership Shifts

New technology is having an influence on the size, structure, and policies of American unions. Traditionally, union strength has been concentrated among production and maintenance workers in manufacturing, construction, and transportation, while the great mass of white-collar workers has remained unorganized. Automation and other technological change have been curtailing the number of blue-collar jobs and, therefore, have retarded the growth of some unions. Indeed, union membership of 15,539,000 in 1960 represented a decline of almost a million from the peak of 16,404,000 in 1953.[1] The drop in membership as a percent of the nation's nonagricultural labor force was even greater: from 32.7 percent in 1953 to only 28.6 percent in 1960. To some extent these membership figures reflect the recession in the economy in 1960, but mainly they mirror the changing composition of the labor force.

Not all unions, however, have suffered from labor-force restructuring; in fact, some have benefited from it. As described in Chapter II, the number of operative-type jobs has declined relative to maintenance jobs. Since maintenance groups have separate bargaining units in many plants, even some organized by industrial unions, a number of craft unions have been able to take advantage of workforce restructuring to add to their memberships at the same time that the industrial unions have been losing members. Three prominent former CIO industrial unions (Automobile Workers, Steelworkers, and Electrical Workers), for instance, lost a total of about 400,000 members between 1956 and 1960. In the same period, three former AFL craft unions

---

[1] Leo Troy, "Trade Union Membership," in *Tested Knowledge of Business Cycles*, Forty-second Annual Report (New York: National Bureau of Economic Research, Inc., 1962), pp. 52–53.

(Operating Engineers, Sheet Metal Workers and the Brotherhood of Electrical Workers) added close to 240,000 members, because of growth of employment in their jurisdictions.[2]

Internal Restructuring

New technology has also had its impact on the internal structure of industrial unions. The changing composition of the plant labor force—the decline of operative jobs and the growth in the number of maintenance jobs—is causing a shift in the locus of power within many local unions toward the skilled craftsmen. As a result, industrial unions have become more conscious of skill demarcations among the various maintenance crafts, at precisely the same time that new technology has been blurring the traditional distinctions. This, as already noted, is creating a new area of labor-management controversy.

As yet, the relative swell of highly skilled maintenance employees in the ranks of the industrial unions has not had an impact on their wage policies, which over the years have narrowed skill differentials in pay. But there is a question for conjecture. With the semiskilled becoming less dominant in these unions as restructuring of plant labor forces become more pronounced, perhaps union leaders will shift toward a wage policy that gives greater recognition to the element of skill.

Some craft unions also have been adversely affected by automation, as illustrated in the case of a small union of skilled workers in the stone, clay, and glass industry, engaged in a manual cutting operation. When automatic cutting machines were developed, there were fewer jobs for the membership, not only because mechanization had reduced overall manpower requirements for the cutting process but because some of the operator jobs on the new machines were awarded

2 U.S. Bureau of Labor Statistics, *Directory of National and International Labor Unions in the United States* (Washington: U.S. Government Printing Office), Bulletin No. 1222, 1957, p. 11; Bulletin No. 1320, 1961, p. 49.

by the National Labor Relations Board to the industrial union representing the semiskilled production workers. This case demonstrates dramatically how technological change may lead to the obsolescence of an old skill and may, as a result, threaten the continued existence of a craft union. Thus, realistically, the long-run prospect for this small craft union is one of surrendering its separate existence by merging with the dominant industrial union in the plant.

Another factor in the internal union situation is the power relationship between a national union and its constituent locals. Several of the case-study companies which conduct collective bargaining on a national basis found that this factor had emerged with the onset of advanced technological change. The ability of the national unions to control the behavior of their locals, either at the time of company-wide bargaining or during the life of the agreement, is being severely challenged.

Interestingly, some management representatives ascribed the problem to the widening of a gulf between the thinking of top union leadership and that of the membership in the plants. Being further removed from the plant scene, the national leaders are no longer able to identify easily those matters which are of primary concern to the local membership. Moreover, as a result of the changing composition of the plant workforce, as well as other socio-economic changes, the local membership is itself no longer as cohesive a group as it was a decade ago, and divergent interests within the group cannot always be reconciled to the satisfaction of all.

If these impressions are correct, then further technological change will cause a still deeper rift within unions that bargain on a company- or industry-wide basis, as the locals intensify pressure for either more autonomy or a stronger voice in bargaining. There will be a need to forge a new relationship between the two levels, designed to accommodate the locals' desire for greater recognition and, at the same time, to maintain the internal union discipline that will make for responsible labor-management relations. If the national unions accomplish this reconstruction of relationships with the locals, unionism will emerge materially strengthened. The important yield may be greater satisfaction among the rank-and-file membership, which is the root of union solidarity.

The decline in direct production work resulting from automation has led to the oft-repeated assertion that unions will seek to organize white-collar workers in order to compensate for the shrinkage of their blue-collar ranks. The case studies produced little evidence of union success along these lines. Nor are there any indications nationally of significant union inroads among office employees in private industry. Although few direct attempts of unions to broaden their organizational base were uncovered in the course of this survey, it was evident that many managements were anticipating organizational campaigns among their nonbargaining-unit employees.

Interunion Strife

Because modern technology is melting away the number of production jobs, industrial unions crave to preserve all work opportunities in plants for their own members. Though there has been but little raiding of memberships among unions, the dwindling in the ranks of some large industrial unions brings them sometimes into open conflict with unions in the building trades. Jurisdictional issues arise over the assignment of maintenance and construction work at the plant site.

Many companies have traditionally hired independent contractors to handle such work, and others have begun to do so in order to cut costs. But in-plant unions are increasingly opposing this practice. Often, unions try to take advantage of court rulings that obligate an employer to bargain in advance of taking action on a decision to subcontract, even when it is for economic reasons.[3] Thus they use the arbitration clause of their contracts to curtail the contracting out of work. Employers have faced the continuing task of attempting to combat this trend by reinforcing management's rights through precise contract language. In the light of the court decisions, however, it is difficult for a management to protect itself adequately, even assuming that it can gain concessions from unions during negotiations.

An even more difficult task is to strike a workable balance between the need to effect immediate savings through contracting out some operations and the long-term advantages that stem from maintaining effective relationships with unions representing production employees. A number of the case-study companies never contracted out maintenance work, and they found that this practice held a twofold advantage when technological change was introduced. For one thing, it protected them from interunion strife and cemented more cordial relations with the union in the plant. Second, and perhaps of greater importance, it enabled the managements to use displaced production workers on incidental maintenance work and thus eased the transition to new methods for employees, union, and management.

For many companies contracting out has been an important method of stabilizing employment. For many others, the economic necessity of contracting out certain operations far outweighs labor relations considerations. The cost of continually employing a large enough workforce to conduct the periodic, but infrequent, major maintenance work involved in the "turnaround" of equipment for cleaning and repair in the continuous-process industries—petroleum refining and chemicals, for instance—would be prohibitive. The contracting out of such operations is today more essential

---

3 See the Supreme Court's 1960 decision in the case of *Steelworkers vs. Warrior and Gulf Navigation Company*, 363 U.S. 574 (1960); the Circuit Court's 1963 ruling in *East Bay Union of Machinists vs. NLRB*, USCA, Washington, D.C. (1960).

than ever for many companies in these industries, and some of them have endured strikes to affirm their right to take such action.

Bargaining Power

It is vain to speculate that reduction of a union's membership leads to a weakening of its bargaining power, for there is no necessary correlation between size and power in a test of strength. Indeed, those unions which have been most effective in thwarting management's aims with respect to new technology have usually been the craft unions or the skilled groups within industrial unions. Though they represent but a small proportion of a given workforce, they are strategically placed.

On the other hand, technological change has at times reduced the bargaining power of craft unions. Where new machinery fulfills functions which formerly employed the skills of individuals, the operation is far less dependent on the craftsmen. Union power among the crafts has been based on the monopolization of a scarce resource—the skills of union members—but when these rare skills are no longer in demand, as in the case of the cutters' union cited above, that power declines.

It is quite true that today unions are not winning easy collective bargaining victories as they did a decade ago, but this is attributable to a stiffening of management attitudes by force of realities on the economic scene. As one observer put it, industry's new "tough line" is not a matter of tactics, or philosophy, or a desire to take advantage of automation to beat the unions, but the result of management's belated recognition of the economic facts of life: slower economic growth, recurring recessions, and intensified competition, all combining to tighten profit margins.[4]

4 Herbert R. Northrup, "Management's 'New Look' in Labor Relations," *Industrial Relations*, Vol. 1, October 1961, pp. 16–20.

Accepting Chamberlain's definition of bargaining power as "the ability to secure another's agreement on one's own terms,"[5] we are led to conclude that union power vis-a-vis management power has declined, not because of automation but simply because it costs less for many companies to take a strike than to give in to union demands that would further undercut their competitive positions.

For most unions, the strike remains a formidable weapon unaffected by new technology. In the continuous-process industries, however, the strike weapon has been severely blunted. The manpower requirements for some modernized operations, such as a power plant, petroleum refinery, or chemical works, have been reduced in some instances to the point where supervisory personnel could run an operation at near peak efficiency for sustained periods. The management at one refinery reported that the union was well aware of this and, as a result, had altered its bargaining tactics. Union leaders now refrain from threatening to strike at every impasse in negotiations and engage in more mature bargaining.

One should not, however, attempt to extrapolate from the experience in certain continuous-process operations and say that as automation progresses the strike power of all unions will be destroyed. First, it must be recognized that in the capital-intensive continuous-process industries union power was never very formidable. Second, in the basic metalworking industries, no matter how many transfer or numerically-controlled machines are introduced, plants will not be able to operate without the services of their blue-collar production workers.

In fact, the strike is a greater threat than ever before in some situations. The processes of an automated operation are highly integrated, and interruption of any phase can close down the entire works. In view of the costliness of down-time, a company call ill afford disruptions and, therefore, will

5 Neil W. Chamberlain, *Labor* (New York: McGraw-Hill Book Company, Inc., 1958), p. 97.

hardly underestimate pressure from employee groups. The problem becomes particularly acute in the plant that has a number of separate bargaining units, for, as one writer has pointed out, each one has a "life and death hold" on the entire plant.[6] In the bulk of organized industry, therefore, the prospect for both unions and management in the foreseeable future is that of having to continue to find accommodations in their relationships.

COMMUNITY CONSIDERATIONS

Companies that attach obligations of corporate citizenship to the communities in which they have plant operations take into account the probable effects of their decisions on the economies of these local areas. Frequently, these decisions are affected by the attitudes and behavior of the local unions. Securing union cooperation in effecting change depends upon the attitudes of employees, not only as members of the union but also as citizens of the community. As citizens, they help to shape the attitude of the entire community. Attention will now be focused on the matter of company-community relationships.

Communications with the Community

In many situations, a particular plant is a vital mainstay of the local area, and any proposed changes that threaten the livelihood of individuals may have serious repercussions throughout the community. It is to be expected that local residents will react vehemently if they believe, rightly or wrongly, that their relatives, friends, and neighbors have lost their jobs because of what may seem to them to be arbitrary action by a company. To counter adverse reactions to layoffs resulting from technological change, a company

---

6 Dale D. McConkey, "The NLRB and Technological Change," *Labor Law Journal*, January, 1962, Vol. 13, p. 46.

can only try to get across the idea that improvement in methods of operation will strengthen the competitive position of the particular plant, thus enhancing future job security and the possibility of expanding employment later.

Many companies find it expedient to extend their communications concerning forthcoming technological change to the communities in which plants are located. Only where plants are small relative to the size of the local labor market do the managements regard such notification as unnecessary, feeling that their operations have only minute bearing on the overall economic activity of the area.

Where a management foresees that a contemplated change will have an unfavorable effect on local employment, giving advance notice of such action offers the community a period in which to formulate a program to cushion the dislocations that may be visited upon the local economy. Many companies notify community leaders directly, and inform the rest of the populace through press releases, explaining the reasons for the change and detailing the management's program to ease the impact on the community.

Community Pressure to Alter Decisions

Advance notice to the community may, however, induce severe pressure on a company to reverse its decision, particularly where it plans to abandon local facilities. But, on occasion, when unions have opposed modification of practices which have hampered plant efficiency and caused the company to consider relocation of the operation, the intercession of community leaders has helped to overcome union resistance. A company in the stone, clay, and glass industry, which had been a major employer in a Middle Atlantic community for many decades, contemplated moving elsewhere because the union involved insisted on the retention of an onerous incentive system. Under pressure from community leaders, union and management resumed bargaining on the issue, and the runaway individual incentive plan was replaced by a more sensible group incentive program. The company then undertook a large capital investment program at the location.

Similarly, a company operating an old rubber plant in an East North Central community had run into all sorts of union-placed obstacles to its attempts to modernize the works. These involved seniority-bumping procedures, manning requirements, rates for new jobs, and production standards under an incentive plan, all of which were restricting the management in its attempts to increase operating efficiency. As a result, the company was forced to consider closing down the operation unless the union conceded on the issues. At this point, community pressures induced the union to yield to reason, and the plant was saved. Relatively few companies, however, are forced to the point of considering relocation of a plant because of burdensome union contract provisions; and not all communities are successful in getting a company to change its decision to relocate.

While the cases just referred to were the only ones found in this study in which the interplay of community pressure and labor-management relations affected the continued existence of plants, communities have resorted to special inducements to companies to maintain plants that were about to be shut down. An old chemical plant in an isolated town of 18,000 population in an East North Central state could no longer manufacture its product at a competitive price. There were two aspects to the problem: (1) outmoded plant and equipment and (2) overburdensome local tax rates. The parent company announced its willingness to undertake correction of the first difficulty through large-scale capital investment, contingent upon local tax relief. When this was granted, the modernization program was undertaken.

The case of this chemical plant was also unusual among those studied, being the only one in which a company's locational or investment decisions were influenced by the ability to negotiate better terms of taxation with local communities.

More typical was the experience of another chemical company. Local government officials offered city aid in various forms in the hope of avoiding the scheduled shutdown of one of its old works. The company's decision was not altered by these inducements because it was based, not on labor relations or tax considerations, but on the following economic facts: the production processes were obsolete due to rapid technological advances; the plant facilities and site were poorly adapted to conversion to more up-to-date technology; the plant was remote from newer sources of raw material; the market centers for some of its products had shifted; and the markets for other products had dwindled. When community leaders received the management's full explanation of the reasons for its decision, they recognized the validity of the decision even though they were not happy about it.

Company Steps to Ease Economic Dislocations

Following upon decisions affecting local plants, many companies have attempted to ease the burden on local communities of any economic dislocations by offering various forms of assistance. As discussed in detail in Chapter III, one of the principal means of alleviating the impact of change on communities, as well as on affected employees, has been to offer help to the displaced in finding jobs with other companies in the area. It is noteworthy that a petroleum refinery in the Midwest found positive values in publicizing its outside placement program in periodic press releases issued to plant, union, and community newspapers. Keeping the community aware of the management's efforts to aid displaced employees quieted employee fears and strengthened public confidence in the integrity of the company, despite necessary heavy terminations in the workforce.

Effecting the closedown of an operation gradually is another way of easing the burden of job terminations on an affected community. This course was taken by a machinery manufacturer in relocating its operations from an old, obsolete, multi-storied plant in New England to a number of new, modern, one-story plants at more strategic locations. The company phased out the plant closing over a nine-year period, thus giving the town leaders sufficient time in which to deal with the problem of displaced employees. The management also cooperated with local officials, and with some success, in bringing in other businesses to occupy the abandoned premises. The community appreciated the company's concern for its welfare, particularly as it was in sharp contrast to the action of another company that had been an employer in the same town. The latter moved its entire operation in one fell swoop, without making any attempt to cushion the impact on the community.

An electrical machinery manufacturer demonstrated to a community in a Middle Atlantic state that its program of technological innovation was designed to save, not destroy, jobs. The company found that it had to lay off many employees because of competition from foreign producers, whose lower costs had enabled them to undersell the company in both domestic and export markets. The situation deteriorated so badly that most American producers discontinued manufacture of the items, but this company decided to try to save its plant by instituting improved methods of production.

Through the plant newspaper, motion pictures made available to community groups, plant bulletin boards, press releases to local newspapers, and graphic exhibits in the plant, the management pointed up its efforts to save the plant by cutting costs through investment in more efficient machinery. Despite the large cutbacks in employment that had taken place, the community relations program paid off, for the company's efforts to save the remaining jobs were deeply appreciated. It received the community's annual "Good Neighbor" award, which goes to companies that have had outstanding records of community service.

The experience of a transportation equipment manufacturer suggests that the community concerned should be the first to know of impending change. Having decided to abandon an old plant in a depressed East North Central city because of changed market conditions, the company recognized that shutdown of the operation would be particularly difficult for the people involved. Its plan was to explain the situation publicly and to take some action to cushion the impact of the shutdown. Before this program could be effectuated, however, a chance remark of a company officer at a press conference in Florida brought news of the contemplated closing. This led to much local bitterness toward the company, and the hostility engendered by the abrupt way in which community officials learned about the decision partially neutralized the success of the company's program of assistance.

On balance, when decisions about plant operations hold far-reaching consequences for a community, company experience indicates that local leaders appreciate being informed of such plans in time to assess and be prepared to deal with the situation. It is also evident that explanation of the necessities behind a decision develops an understanding of the company's position and forestalls a possible community impression that management has acted arbitrarily. When a company also lends whatever assistance it can to offset the impact of its action on the local economy, such demonstration of concern is likely to leave a lasting impression of the company as an employer with a sense of responsibility toward the community. This attentiveness to the interplay of company-community interests is important, as it helps to shape the corporate image in the eyes of the national public. Even further, it may mold constructive attitudes and break down resistance to technological change.

The capacity of a community to adjust successfully to the outcome of decisions affecting plant operations depends, of course, on the nature of the action taken by a company and on the state of the local economy. In an active industrial community, even though extensive modernization of a plant may result in heavy layoffs, those directly affected would have a good chance of finding new employment. On the other hand, in an area where the plant is the major employer, employment prospects would be slim. Yet in the latter circumstances community officials may be able to design public programs or to entice new industries into the area and thus eventually provide employment opportunities.

When, however, a plant is in a depressed area which has little promise of growth, drastic reduction of the workforce leaves the community with practically no resources for coping with the displacements, particularly if the operation was the main source of employment. Obviously, the difficulties of community adjustment are compounded upon plant relocation or shutdown. In such situations, any consideration given by a company to the community situation is valuable in alleviating problems that can be quite enduring.

GOVERNMENTAL CONSIDERATIONS

Mounting public concern about the impact of automation has led some people to conclude that the problems involved are too great for labor and management to handle, either individually or together, and that what is needed is government action. In the opinion of one writer, technological change has been a major factor in making the present system of collective bargaining obsolete and in need of replacement; as he sees it, in the future, the government, as a third force representing the public interest, will attempt to solve problems that are beyond the capabilities of management and labor alone.[7]

Tolling the death knell of collective bargaining because

[7] Paul Jacobs, *Old Before Its Time: Collective Bargaining at 28* (Santa Barbara: Center for the Study of Democratic Institutions, The Fund for the Republic, 1963), pp. 9–10.

of the advent of new forms of technology may be very premature. Based on more than a decade of experience with technological change, this study reveals that labor and management have adjusted to change without undue difficulty. This is not to say, however, that there is no role for government in helping the nation to adjust to the changed industrial environment. Many aspects of adjustment to the automation age go well beyond the confines of any single plant, company, or industry, and these are clearly in the province of governmental responsibility.

Concern with Unemployment

According to the terms of the Employment Act of 1946, the federal government is charged with the responsibility of promoting high levels of production and employment, and the relatively high unemployment rate of recent years has evoked demands for all sorts of governmental action to counter it. As pointed out in Chapter II, among the many theories explaining our recent unemployment experience, two predominate. The first and more prevalent view focuses on a shortage in aggregate demand as the basic cause of unemployment. The second blames higher unemployment upon structural transformation of the economy.

The Administration has adhered more to the aggregate demand theory. Its position has been stated quite explicitly by the President's Council of Economic Advisers:

> Higher unemployment is explained by the shortage of new job opportunities. . . . The source of the high unemployment rates in recent years, even in periods of cyclical expansion, lies not in labor market imbalance, but in the markets for goods and services.[8]

Walter Heller, Chairman of the Council of Economic Advisers, has argued that both the "accelerator" and "multi-

[8] *Economic Report of the President*, Transmitted to the Congress, January, 1963 (Washington: U.S. Government Printing Office, 1963), p. 25.

plier" effects are needed to bring about an increase in total spending of about $35 billion, in order to close the gap that lies between capacity and spending and to achieve a potential output at 4 percent unemployment.[9] In the hope of spurring a more rapid rate of economic growth, the Administration proposed an $11.5 billion tax cut for both individuals and corporations, which has been enacted.

Government concern with the problem of unemployment has been directed not only at correcting the situation but also toward relieving the impact of unemployment on the individual. Thus, during the depths of the 1958 recession, Congress enacted the Temporary Unemployment Compensation program, which enabled states desiring to do so to obtain interest-free loans from the federal government to extend the period over which state benefits were payable.

When the next recession occurred, Congress again acted and, under the Temporary Extended Unemployment Compensation Act of 1961, the federal government reimbursed the states for the extra-regular weeks of payments made to the unemployed in 1961 and 1962. Reimbursement was also made for post-exhaustion weeks of unemployment insurance benefits in all states, under certain conditions.[10] President Kennedy's request to continue the extended benefit payments beyond the recession period was refused by Congress, and the TEUC Act lapsed. A number of states, however, do provide benefits, on either a temporary or permanent basis, beyond the normal period of 26 weeks. The Kennedy Administration also favored improvements in benefits, through federal requirements for greater uniformity among the states, but proposals to accomplish this end, such as the McCarthy-King bill, have so far remained merely proposals.

9 Walter W. Heller, *Address to Conference on Fiscal and Monetary Policy*, sponsored by the President's Advisory Committee on Labor-Management Policy (Washington: U.S. Government Printing Office, 1962), pp. 7–11.
10 Harry Malisoff, *The Financing of Extended Unemployment Insurance Benefits in the United States* (Kalamazoo: The W. E. Upjohn Institute for Employment Research, 1963), pp. 4–5.

Early retirement as a means of handling technological and other displacement of workers has also been encouraged by the government through the federal social security program. The reduction in 1961 of the eligibility age for retirement benefits under the Old Age and Survivors Insurance program, from sixty-five to sixty-two for men, has enabled workers who are in this age bracket to retire on a reduced pension. Since many private pension plans tie their benefits in with social security, the effect of this legislation has been to give added impetus to include early retirement provisions in private plans.

Government is involved in relieving the burden of unemployment on individuals also through its welfare programs. When unemployment or social security benefits fall short of providing a subsistence level for families, or when they expire before the unemployed head of the family finds another job, some relief in the form of local public assistance may be available.[11]

American society today rejects the old *laissez-faire* notion that each individual is responsible for his own unemployment. Unemployment is seen as a social problem, over which most people can exercise only a minimal control. Thus the jobless are provided with some income for certain periods of time. But society is equally concerned with helping the unemployed to find productive employment again, and business, labor, and the public have suggested private and government programs to serve this end.

The structural transformation theory of unemployment attributes the problem to changes in the economy, including the rise of new forms of technology, which destroy jobs once held by workers who cannot qualify for the new jobs that are emerging. It is a fact that unskilled workers with low

11 Eligibility for general relief varies from one community to another, and it has been claimed that "in a good many parts of the country, regulations and policies are such as to effectively shut off any relief to the unemployed." Margaret S. Gordon, *The Economics of Welfare Policies* (New York: Columbia University Press, 1963), pp. 105–106.

levels of educational achievement, and those whose work experience is limited to a specific skill, are at a disadvantage in the labor market when they are displaced. With improvements in plant technology, job requirements change, and some displaced workers lack the skills and versatility to meet new job demands. Some observers view the restructuring of the labor force by recent technological change as buttressing their contention that the present unemployment problem is structural in nature.

A leading spokesman of this viewpoint, economist Charles C. Killingsworth, sees the pressure for automation as creating an insoluble unemployment bottleneck. He has scored the Council of Economic Advisers for repeatedly finding that a low rate of economic growth, rather than automation and structural unemployment, is at the root of the unemployment problem.[12] The key aspect, in his opinion, is labor market imbalance—too many unskilled workers competing for ever fewer unskilled jobs. Proponents of this view attempt to substantiate it by pointing to current data (November, 1963) on unemployment among occupational groups:

UNEMPLOYED PERSONS, BY OCCUPATION OF LAST JOB	UNEMPLOYMENT RATE
Total	5.4%
White-collar workers	2.8
Professional and technical	1.6
Managers, officials, proprietors	1.4
Clerical workers	4.4
Sales workers	3.8
Blue-collar workers	6.7
Craftsmen and foremen	3.9
Operatives	7.2
Nonfarm laborers	11.9

12 Charles C. Killingsworth, in testimony before the Subcommittee on Employment and Manpower of the Senate Committee on Labor and Public Welfare, reported in *Daily Labor Report,* September 20, 1963, No. 184, p. BB–1.

Service workers	5.6%
Private household workers	4.9
Other service workers	5.8
Farm workers	3.3
Farmers and farm managers ...	0.3
Farm laborers and foremen ...	6.2

Source: U.S. Bureau of Labor Statistics, *Employment and Earnings,* December, 1963, p. 4.

The Council of Economic Advisers, on the other hand, continues to challenge the theory that automation is eliminating jobs at a dangerously high rate, basing its argument on a detailed examination of unemployment figures, which differentiated workers by occupational category and industry, for the 1948–1957 period and for the period since 1957. The Council's findings not only fail to substantiate, but are in some instances at direct odds with, the view that technological progress has hit hardest at unskilled and semi-skilled blue-collar workers in the nation at large.[13]

The Council found a regular relationship in the 1948–1957 period between the jobless rate in the worker categories mentioned and the overall national unemployment situation. Then, testing to see if the relationship was intensified in the more recent period, when automation was believed to be having its effect, the Council found that a contradiction emerged: "For a majority of these supposedly 'technologically vulnerable' workers, actual unemployment in 1962 seems to have been somewhat *lower* than one would have estimated from [the] projection" of the 1948–1957 experience.

Champions of the structural transformation theory have urged massive governmental programs to retrain workers, relocate the unemployed, and provide subsidies for distressed communities. Although the Administration believes that the

13 Statement of Walter W. Heller before the Subcommittee on Employment and Manpower of the Senate Committee on Labor and Public Welfare, October 28, 1963, p. 21 (processed).

level of unemployment is determined by aggregate economic activity, it has undertaken many programs to deal with structural transformation.

Education and Retraining

Federally supported retraining programs have been launched under the Area Redevelopment Act of 1961 and the Manpower Development and Training Act of 1962. In 1963, legislation broadening the latter act, expanding youth employment services, and spurring vocational education was enacted. Various state governments and local communities also have undertaken independent retraining programs.

Because there is less unemployment among workers in those occupations which require higher educational levels, and because there is a severe shortage of highly trained people in the scientific and engineering fields, there is an ever greater stress on educating present and future generations to assume a changing productive role in the American economy. The importance of education is well recognized, for the growth of our economy depends in strategic part on our ability continually to improve the quality of our human resources. Everyone is aware that education pays. Moreover, the fact that technological and other forms of progress are increasing the earnings accruing to educated workers has aroused popular demand for increased public expenditures on education.

Improvement of educational systems is, of course, primarily the responsibility of local government, but many local communities lack the funds necessary to modernize their educational systems. This situation has led to increased demands for federal aid to education. There are, however, facets which are other than financial in the problem of providing adequate education. As pointed out in Chapter V, there must be more collaboration between employers and local educators as a basis for devising curricula that will insure that the youth emerging from schools have acquired the necessary background to qualify for jobs.

Mobility of Labor and Capital

Unemployment is hardest on the victims when industry moves away from particular geographic centers. Though job opportunities may be dispersed throughout the economy, many of the unemployed, especially older workers, are unwilling to relocate to take new jobs, even though they may be qualified to fill them.

There are two possible approaches to solving this problem: either move jobs to where the displaced workers are, or get the workers to move to where jobs are. Interestingly enough, both approaches may require government action if they are to be effective. Through the Area Redevelopment Act, the federal government is attempting to encourage the movement of capital into depressed areas. There are also many proposals for government action to induce the unemployed who live in such areas to move to other regions in which jobs may be found.

National collection and circulation of data on job vacancies might serve to encourage moves by the unemployed, and as much attention should be given to job opportunities as to job shortages. This calls for an inventory of job opportunities which would make it possible to match job seekers more effectively with existing job vacancies. Clearly, any such program would require a great deal of cooperation between business and government.

Expanding information on job vacancies in all parts of the country would probably not achieve, by itself, a sufficient degree of labor mobility, for many workers simply cannot afford the cost of relocating their homes. Supreme Court Justice Arthur Goldberg, during his tenure as Secretary of Labor, was attracted by Sweden's relocation scheme, which provides travel, family, and other allowances. The Swedish law is enthusiastically administered and, significantly, is financed jointly by employer and employee contributions. Some see it as a model program for achieving the labor mobility that is needed in the United States.

Advance Warning of Technological Change

One currently popular idea is that it would be possible for the government to anticipate the problems and to design programs to deal with the resulting dislocations of technological change if it had advance knowledge of such contemplated changes in companies. This idea of an early warning system to deal with the adjustments to technological change has been advanced from many sources, and has been endorsed by many labor leaders and political figures.

In July, 1963, President Kennedy stated in his message to Congress on the rail dispute that it was his "intention to appoint a Presidential Commission on automation." President Johnson in January, 1964, asked Congress to establish a commission on automation. Such a commission would be charged with identifying the major technological displacements that are likely to occur during the next 10 years, and it would be asked to recommend actions that could be taken by government to assist in alleviating the problems of individual workers affected by new technology. Senator Javits (Rep., N.Y.) has made similar proposals.

A system of advance warning of technological change has surface appeal. It appears rational as an approach to alleviating the hardships attendant on change, for it carries the concept of providing time to work out solutions to problems, case by case, before the change is actually effected. The difficulty with such a system is that it is not always possible to identify when and where technological change will occur, or the dimensions of its effects. It must be remembered that not all new technology is successful, and that it usually remains experimental, even after being introduced.

The experience of a chemical plant included in this study is ready evidence of this fact.

This plant converted one of its processes to a continuous-flow operation, monitored by an electronic computer, but the new machinery turned out to be too technically difficult to operate and, hence, uneconomical. After six months, the entire continuous-flow process was ripped out and the old production method was re-established, despite the expensiveness of the modern equipment and cost of training employees to operate it.

The tentative nature of so much technological change might defy fruitful application of an elaborate early warning system. Another drawback of such a system relates to the definition of "technological change." If it were defined so broadly as to embrace all change and improvements in methods, from the installation of computers to the introduction of sharper blades on cutting tools, the system might collapse of its own weight. Also, the system could operate so restrictively as to create a burden in the very instances where change is crucial to an overall operation.

The merits and deficiencies of an early warning system and of other aspects of government action relative to technological change will be considered further in Chapter XII. The questions posed by this review point up the interrelationship between the institutional setting in which a company introduces new methods of operation and its ability to do so.

CHAPTER XII

Looking to the Future

The drama of industry is illustrated by its continuing achievements in levels of output and efficiency, always attuned to the demands of society. Growth, adjustments in the utilization of resources, relocation of operations, and new methods and processes are the expressions of an economic system geared to satisfying the wants of a consuming public. Although there is a sense of excitement about progress, the fear of human dislocations acts as a damper to this excitement and hinders acceptance of change.

It is within a framework of fear and excitement, therefore, that the great labor-management debate over technological change and automation is cast. Some maintain that employment opportunities on a national scale have been curtailed; and because of the polarization of emotions, the debate becomes especially intense when statistics on unemployment and employment opportunities are brought into the argument.

Differences at the national level notwithstanding, we

have been impressed throughout this study with the ability of management, employees, and labor unions, in the many plant locations visited, to make and reach accommodations to technological change. We have been impressed by the rationality of workers and their willingness to accept change. This has been particularly true when the new methods and techniques have been realistically discussed by management, examined dispassionately by the union, and weighed practically by the employees in terms of their own long-term interests. In considering change, it is unfortunate that it is so difficult to maintain as high a degree of rationality at the national level as is possible at the plant level. Yet it is discussion beyond the plant gate that conditions the quality of the environment at the local level and therefore directly affects the ability of management, its employees, and the unions representing them, to consider realistically how best to adapt to technological change.

Certainly much of national opinion about technological change has been fashioned by the controversies over change, modernization, and automation which have occurred in several major American industries—of which transportation is illustrative—and by the persistent unemployment—alleged to derive from automation rather than from underlying evolutionary economic changes—existing in many geographic areas of the United States. While this study did not focus on such an industry as transportation, or on structural unemployment, developments in such situations affect the overall national climate of opinion about change, and cannot be disregarded.

There appears to be a combination of reasons which could foster massive resistance to change. While it is difficult to hypothesize on which of these reasons is most determining, certainly employees' fear of job loss and the desire to preserve work opportunities are important factors. But equally important has been the unions' fear of loss of membership. Even where no layoffs of employees are involved, and reductions in labor force are accomplished through normal attrition, unions fear that a diminution in membership may mean the weakening of the union as an institution. This fear can dictate a response that is as vigorous and emotional as that of an individual fearing loss of his job. A third factor conditioning the reaction of employees, their unions, or both, is how management behaves in introducing technological change.

This research found all three factors—employee fear of loss of work, union fear of the challenge to its institutional power, and management conduct—conditioning the response to change in the work situations studied. But of overwhelming importance were management actions; it is to these that employees and unions react. Where management historically has failed to handle its employee and union relations on a businesslike basis—even though acting from sound economic reasons and in a fair and open manner—it has been hampered by the unfavorable responses of both unions and employees. In such situations, management has been unable to retain its freedom to modify operations as dictated by the current level of technology. Perhaps from this perspective can be established one of the fundamental guides in considering the entire sweep of our current technological revolution. Since the roles of individuals and institutions are disrupted with changing technology, a new equilibrium must be reached by management, unions, and workers with reference to responsibility, authority, and the desire for individuality. For management, this suggests the importance of examining and re-examining traditional industrial relations approaches and techniques to be certain that they meet the test of today's management challenge.

Adapting management action to the technological changes of today is difficult, however. In recent years, the press and government have played a significant role in establishing, in the industrial relations area, an atmosphere of crisis based on the changes in the industrial process and their presumed impact on national employment. But, dealing, at the national level, with the question of the relationship of change to employment is both difficult and frustrating. It cannot be demonstrated that unemployment in the United States today derives from the technological changes taking place at the plant level. While it is true that evidences can be found of employee layoffs in particular plants because of modernization, methods improvement, or even the introduction of automated processes, these situations are no different from those which have occurred over the years. Government, however, is in the awkward position of having to deal constructively with the unemployment problem, while recognizing that the overall economic processes, national economic growth, wage movements, and the relationships of American producers to world markets directly affect our economic and employment picture. In short, the approaches to dealing with the underlying causes of unemployment must be broadly conceived. But the political necessities may lead to "quick action programs" to deal with the effects of unemployment, and thus there arises the danger of programs which might impede the introduction of new technology.

In this final chapter we consider the encompassing question of the national impact of technological change on employment and unemployment, because this is the question which is determining of national attitudes. We examine certain proposals to deal with unemployment because these are important in the maintenance of an atmosphere conducive to change in the economic sphere. Finally, we consider the elements necessary to insure economic progress through sound labor-management approaches.

NEW TECHNOLOGY AND EMPLOYMENT: THE NATIONAL PICTURE

Even though new technology displaces a worker from one factory, it need not lead to his unemployment, as long as jobs in the total economy are growing in number. Looking at technological innovation from the union point of view, Barbash recognized that ". . . the incidence of automation unemployment is a direct function of the capacity of the economy to absorb the unemployment in other sectors."[1] A glance at American history quickly shows that the economy has displayed this capacity over the long run. Labor productivity has increased at a fairly constant rate over time, averaging about $2\frac{1}{2}$ to 3 percent per annum, including the recent period which has seen the introduction of automation. Experience following World War II shows that unemployment did not become a problem until the late 1950's. Since there is little evidence of a spurt in the national rate of productivity increase between the later and the earlier years, it would seem that "automation" cannot be held responsible for recent higher rates of unemployment.[2]

The problem, of course, is the short run. Employment in those sectors of the economy which can be categorized as "goods producing" (mining, contract construction, manufacturing, transportation and public utilities) has declined by more than 500,000 during the past six years. This means that replacements have not been hired for those leaving a plant through normal attrition, and that there have not been enough other factory, mine, or construction-site jobs available for those displaced by new technology. Even this, however, need not cause unemployment. The historical record shows that other broad sectors of the economy have also declined in numbers while total employment has expanded —the shift from agricultural to nonagricultural pursuits being the most vivid example. From colonial days up to

[1] Jack Barbash, *What's Ahead for Labor* (Ann Arbor: Bureau of Industrial Relations, The University of Michigan, 1960), p. 10.

[2] A new study, conducted by The Bureau of Applied Social Research, Columbia University, shows that there is nothing unusual about the recent pace of productivity growth. It prompted A. J. Jaffe, the Bureau's Director of Manpower and Population Research, to state that this finding should help to explode the "hysteria over automation." See "What Productivity Does to Jobs," *Business Week*, September 14, 1963, pp. 188–189.

the present, the number of persons engaged in farming has declined from eight out of ten to less than one out of ten. Improved agricultural technology, however, did not lead to economic stagnation or mass unemployment; on the contrary, it freed millions of workers to go off to the growing cities to take jobs helping to produce the goods and services that have come to comprise our high standard of living.

If, today, technological progress is putting a ceiling on the number of people employed in the production of material goods—as Alvin Hansen claims is the case[3]—in a parallel manner, the displaced personnel are being freed to work in the service industries, to which consumers are directing a larger share of their incomes. The data for the past six years indicate that this is precisely what has been occurring:

EMPLOYEES ON NONAGRICULTURAL PAYROLLS,
BY INDUSTRY DIVISION

1957 and 1963
(In thousands)

Industry	1957	1963	Change
All goods-producing			
Mining	828	634	— 194
Contract construction	2,923	3,030	+ 107
Manufacturing	17,174	17,035	— 139
Transportation and public utilities	4,241	3,913	— 328
Total	25,166	24,612	— 554
All nongoods-producing			
Wholesale and retail trade	10,886	11,864	+ 978
Finance, insurance, and real estate	2,477	2,866	+ 389
Service and miscellaneous	6,749	8,297	+1,548
Government	7,626	9,535	+1,909
Total	27,738	32,562	+4,824
Grand Total	52,904	57,175[a]	+4,271[a]

a Total does not add exactly because of rounding.

Source: U.S. Bureau of Labor Statistics, *Employment and Earnings*, February, 1964, p. 13.

3 Alvin H. Hansen, *Economic Issues of the 1960's* (New York: McGraw-Hill Book Company, 1960), pp. 71–72.

The table clearly shows that the increase in employment in the nongoods-producing sector was almost nine times greater than the decline in the goods-producing sector. The net increase in employees on nonagricultural payrolls was four and one-quarter million; yet total unemployment rose by one and one-quarter million during this six-year period.[4] The rise in unemployment is explained by two other facts: agricultural employment continued to decline—dropping another one and one-quarter million during this period— and population grew, adding five million more members to the labor force. The problem, therefore, is not that the economy has failed to expand—for, as the table shows, it has expanded—but rather that the rate of expansion has not been sufficient to absorb both those displaced by improved methods of producing and distributing goods and services, and the new entrants into the labor force. But the unemployment rate has not grown in recent years—it has hovered at about 5½ percent of the labor force—indicating that economic growth has actually been rapid enough to absorb numbers almost equivalent to those currently displaced by new technology, as well as the new entrants into the labor force. The unemployment which continues is largely the excess with which the nation was saddled following the 1958 recession.

We can view today's problem in another way—as a function of the level of aggregate demand. Technological change should not be blamed for the persistent unemployment since 1957; a more important cause has been the lack of demand. It would be more sensible, therefore, to pay attention to the formulation of programs which would effectively deal with unemployment, rather than simply bemoan the disappearance of factory jobs. The solutions which seem most feasible and appropriate lie in two directions. First and foremost, it is essential to increase consumption and invest-

4 U.S. Bureau of Labor Statistics, *Employment and Earnings*, February, 1964, p. 1.

ment, and technological improvement contributes to that end. Second, in a period of shifts in labor-force demands, there must be a spur to facilitate retraining and greater labor mobility, in order to bring available jobs and workers together more quickly.

Fiscal and Monetary Policy

While fiscal and monetary policy seems far afield from industrial relations, it cannot be overlooked as a basic factor conditioning our economy. It is the proper mechanism for increasing aggregate demand and for shifting the nation's economy into higher gear, provided excessive wage demands and inflation do not ensue. Surely, not all persons in the United States, or elsewhere in the world, have the material products they desire, and there is still ample room for an expansion of production and employment in the goods-producing sectors of the economy. Technological change is itself a spur to increased demand, via two routes. First, new methods of manufacture, by reducing costs of production, permit the pricing of products so that consumer interest in them can be converted into effective demand. Second, technological change increases the demand for capital goods, thus stimulating the demand for labor.

At the same time, however, it should be recognized that in a nation with as high a standard of living as ours, goods-producing cannot carry the whole burden, and the greatest gains in employment will continue to occur in the service sectors. Attention, therefore, should be focused on quickly directing new and displaced workers into these fast-growing areas of the economy.

Labor Mobility

Too often today labor mobility is viewed unidimensionally, as the geographic movement of workers, rather than as a change of location, industry, or occupation. All types of mobility, however, are essential in a well-functioning labor market. In a rapidly changing industrial situation, the individual most likely to find work is the one who is mobile on all three levels—location, occupation, and industry. To the extent that industry, unions, and government introduce programs to enhance mobility, it will be possible to bring available workers and jobs together most quickly. The difficulty, of course, is that individuals who are most in need of help in terms of increasing their mobility may be members of the groups that are most difficult to aid: the high-school dropouts—because they frequently have little motivation; the aged—because of possible limitations on where they wish to work, or on the effort they may be able to expend; minorities—because of the conditions in their environment which make training difficult.

We have already discussed company programs to increase mobility, upon employee termination, through offers of interplant transfer and relocation and severance payments. We have examined experience with training that was designed to provide employed persons with basic reading, writing, and numbers skills; we have also examined programs involving retraining within the plant, designed to prepare employees for specific jobs. Some reference has been made to broader programs such as the Armour program. Little has been said about other possible programs.

National Manpower Development and Training Programs. Despite the limited success of many current training programs, the fact that thousands of former blue-collar production workers may not be needed again in goods-producing industries suggests that further efforts are needed to retrain them for occupations in other industries. The Area Redevelopment Act, the Manpower Development and Training Act, and the recent expansion of youth employment services and vocational education are possible moves which can aid in the overall situation. Experience to date, however, indicates that one problem with these broad national programs is the difficulty of directing an effective retraining effort on a national scale. The abilities and interests of the individual and the available resources for training in his community must all be considered. Despite the limitations, however, there is no doubt that the existence of the national programs is a spur to other efforts. The real question is whether available funds could be used more effectively to induce the individual to pursue training on his own initiative, through informing him of available resources and potential job opportunities in the local labor market or elsewhere.

One approach which might be considered in the attempt to stimulate individual self-development would be to adopt the principle of individual choice of training and occupation. Freedom of individual selection is certainly consistent with our social and political philosophy. Further, experiments in the past with similarly oriented programs suggest a possibly greater degree of success than has thus far been evidenced by broadly conceived government retraining efforts. The constructive way in which the GI Bill for World War II veterans was used is striking evidence that an adult training program can succeed. A distinguishing feature of the GI Bill was that veterans were permitted to enroll in a wide variety of courses, including those in both the liberal arts and the vocational arts. They were also allowed to take training on the job.

The success of the GI Bill suggests that one aspect of the retraining problem is a matter of financing students and trainees individually to obtain the higher education, vocational school training, or on-the-job training that they are seeking. Under any program, the extent of financing—including allowances or wage supplements—should, of course, be limited, as it was under the GI Bill. The underlying idea would be to prevent those people not seriously seeking retraining from enrolling in the program.

One of the major groups to benefit from such a broad labor force retraining program would be the unskilled workers under thirty years of age who have not completed high school. For them, the program would offer an opportunity to take on-the-job training, without significantly cutting their living standards, and a second chance to complete high school. Many who take advantage of either or both opportunities would be able to qualify for other than common-laborer jobs.

Other beneficiaries would include (1) future high-school dropouts who would thus be able to continue their educations while gaining on-the-job training; and (2) the academically talented youngsters who could not otherwise finance advanced education. There seems no reason why an ambitious, hard-working, and talented youngster growing up in a depressed area and interested in learning a profession, or in some other course of study which would prepare him for a salaried position, should not be subsidized to the same extent as the young man interested in learning a mechanical trade.

Relocation. Even with the creation of more jobs and the retraining of workers for them, there still will remain the problem of fitting together workers and jobs. As pointed out in Chapter XI, there are two means of accomplishing this: provision of assistance to people in relocating to areas where they will be able to find employment, and encouragement of the movement of capital into depressed areas.

The federal government has long recognized the need for economic development in particular regions of the country, and it has responded through the Area Redevelopment Act and the recently announced Appalachian effort. At the local level, many communities have been attempting to attract industry through the development of industrial parks, surveys of possible plant sites, inventories of labor, tax inducements, and the like. But confusion over relocation is apparent in government thinking both at the federal level and between federal and local agencies. According to recent decisions by the National Labor Relations Board and the courts, companies may not relocate or abandon uneconomic plants without negotiations with the union involved.[5] Such a requirement is an impediment to relocation; by hampering company efforts to relocate plants as dictated by sound economic principles, it may serve to deprive unemployed workers of needed job opportunities in the areas where new plants would be located, without providing long-term aid to workers in the plants to be moved. Since a company's decision to move is probably based on the noncompetitiveness of a particular plant, failure to relocate may only postpone an eventual shutdown. Thus there is an urgent need for government to clarify its policies and, subsequently, its rules concerning the relocation and abandonment of plants.

Employment opportunities often are not located where the unemployed reside or customarily work. Means must be found to induce the unemployed to move to the jobs or to seek work in localities or industries other than those they have typically explored. It is necessary to emphasize once more that the collection and circulation of data on job vacancies might serve to encourage moves by the unemployed, and as much attention should be given to job opportunities as to job shortages. A system for more effectively matching job seekers and job vacancies must be developed.

Theoretically, the offices of the state employment service act as the focal point for bringing people and available jobs into juxtaposition. No other agency exists which can offer the same facilities for obtaining information on jobs in every labor-market area in the country or the facilities for placement at the local level.

The possibility that the employment service can make a substantial contribution to solving the problems of structural unemployment today is obvious.[6] More than any other

---

[5] Industrial Relations Counselors, Inc. (New York), *Plant Relocation—Industrial Relations Implications: A Review Based on the Glidden Case,* 1962 (Industrial Relations Memo No. 142), 51 pp.

[6] For an elaboration on this subject, see E. Wight Bakke, *A Positive Labor Market Policy* (Columbus: Charles E. Merrill Books, Inc., 1963), Chapters 1, 2, and 3.

agency in the public or private area, it can effectively utilize the facilities of an advanced computer technology in processing applications for jobs and in then comparing these with existing job vacancies anywhere in the country.

Before the service can make its contribution, however, several changes will be necessary. At its inception, the functions of the employment service were seen as being of relatively broader scope than the handling of the unemployment insurance system. This concept must be re-established if the service is ever to have an important and accepted role in handling job vacancies. To attract information on available jobs, the state employment services must capture the attention and support of businessmen at all levels of enterprise by demonstrating their ability to help employers find able and qualified employees. One way to further this end is to bring programs into line with the needs and requirements of industry, so that private employers will be more willing to utilize the service. Realistic screening and testing to determine whether job applicants are really willing and actually able to work and for what types of jobs they are qualified would be welcomed. These steps may require a redefinition of the goals of the service in terms of furthering positive labor-market policies, both through intensified job-placement efforts within the local community, and attainment of greater cooperation among the individual state services, so that they may act as a national clearinghouse on job information. To the extent that the employment service could see for itself such a broadened role, it could become a more effective means of bringing together the unemployed and the available jobs. But, at the same time, the service should make it clear that it is not attempting to dominate the filling of job vacancies.

It should be recognized that expanding information on job vacancies by itself will not achieve a sufficient degree of labor mobility. For some individuals, relocation is not even within the realm of possibility; for others, the cost of relocating their homes and households would be too great to even consider. What may be needed, therefore, are broad-based informational programs to acquaint members of the labor force with available work in other occupations and industries, as well as in other localities. Beyond this, there may be need to consider means to finance relocation—including workers' moving expenses and possibly buying out the equity in a home—for those who are willing to relocate for new job opportunities. Schemes for increasing labor mobility are worth consideration. They contribute, if only in a minor way, to the solution of the problems of structural labor adjustment; more significantly, they help the worker to move to accept a job elsewhere—a cheaper solution than bearing the continuing cost of supporting him as unemployed.

Many employers, as already discussed, have arranged for the geographic transfer of employees, and a number of collective bargaining agreements provide for forms of relocation benefits. The Swedish public relocation system, cited in the foregoing chapter, is a possible model for the United States. Its joint financing by employer and employee contributions would appear equally wise for this country. Joint financing would appear essential because of the potential costs, given the geographic size of the United States and the normally high migration rates. Further, joint financing would serve to maintain a degree of responsibility that might otherwise be lacking, with respect to the use and administration of the program.

A BALANCING OF INTERESTS

The review of the broad issues and suggestions regarding national unemployment problems highlights the roles of individuals and institutions. To the extent that the potentialities of both individuals and institutions can be realized, and ideas channeled toward constructively approaching the problems of technological change, it may be possible to achieve the productive capacities of our economy and the goals of our society.

It has been maintained throughout this study that it is manifestly impossible to separate any particular change from the overall dynamics of an on-going enterprise. True, one can say that a new machine, placed in a particular location, begins to operate on a given day and therefore affects work or the work process. And yet, the introduction of that machine into the production process is but the culmination of a series of steps; it represents the prior efforts of the many workers involved in its planning, development, and construction. The effect of the introduction of the equipment on the overall operations may be far more significant than anticipated, or it may hardly cause a ripple in the plant situation. In the course of this study, illustrations of both were found; and frequently the effects of a new piece of equipment on overall employment were negligible compared with those caused by the fluctuations in demand for the product.

Within a national perspective, it is constructive and realistic to concentrate on broad matters, such as spurring national economic growth, stimulating members of the labor force to find places for themselves in a restructured industrial environment, and re-equipping them to do so. These developments are possible if we (1) bend all possible effort to create an atmosphere conducive to the acceptance of change, and (2) recognize that there are certain responsibilities which must be accepted by management, labor, government, and individuals.

Let us now consider the responsibilities of each of these groups.

Management

In the course of our research, it became apparent that there were some work settings in which change was understood and accepted, primarily because it was an inherent part

of the operations. These were situations in
changes continually affected the products the
consequently, the methods of operations. In su
ployees had to and did learn to adapt their work ber...
to constantly changing patterns of work within the plant
organization.

In those industries in which change is a normal and
periodically occurring aspect of operations, new technology
is not as readily seen as a threat. While not every company
has periodic style changes, all have the occasion to update
plant operations in line with the technology of the day. Management needs to exercise regularly its responsibility to
introduce changes and improvements in operations, for such
changes reinforce the dynamic nature of industry in the eyes
of all employees. Moreover, by so doing it may establish the
basis for sound management and employee relationships in
a period of change.

In exercising its responsibility to innovate, management
must constantly bear in mind the importance of the job to
the individual employee. Work provides his source of income, it is his attachment to society, and is of value in and of
itself. Technological change may disturb the deep and complex attachments established between the worker and his
work. Thus it is important to provide information to employees to allay fears and provide time for individual adjustments to a forthcoming change. In a period of change,
early, effective, and straightforward communications from
management generally have been found most valuable to the
maintenance of satisfactory employee relationships. The
plants examined in this study unanimously accepted early
communications, and their experience indicates that employees are far more cooperative when they believe that
management is "leveling" and keeping them informed on an
up-to-date and realistic basis.

A third responsibility of management is to fashion a
program to cushion the shock of change for employees. As

revealed by this study, many techniques have emerged for accomplishing such programs, and others may also be feasible. Recited in this volume have been corporate and union actions, including the establishment of employment offices to ease the transition to another job, training to equip the displaced to qualify for other jobs, and various forms of special payments upon termination to tide workers over periods of unemployment. The specific programs did not embrace all techniques but were designed to assist individuals in adjusting to change and, where displacement occurred, to help them find or prepare for new employment opportunities.

In addition to introducing change, informing employees of it, and formulating adjustment programs, management has a fourth area of responsibility—the need to recognize that today's technological change is not merely another step in a familiar process of industrialization. Certainly we have seen no evidences of a great revolution in methods of operation, but we are beginning to get an idea of the significance of the cumulative changes and the qualitative nature of these changes for the long-run organization of work and responsibility within an enterprise. What effect will technology have on supervision, and on management controls, and how will changes in these areas modify relations with nonsupervisory workers? It is not too early to consider the impact of technology, with respect to such questions as these, on the organization of responsibility within the enterprise and the implications for the future.

Labor

In recent years, there have been a rash of articles and scholarly comment about the hardening of labor's arteries.[7] Today, the question is whether a union can achieve its long-term interests while working with management to achieve

---

[7] See, for example, George Strauss, "The Shifting Power Balance in the Plant," *Industrial Relations*, Vol. 1, May, 1962, pp. 65–96.

the necessary adjustments to new methods of operation. This is a particularly difficult problem because, as suggested earlier, when the organization is challenged by technological change, it responds vigorously and emotionally, particularly because of the erosion of union membership. Full cooperation with the management by a union simply may not be possible. But certainly a rational response to technological change is in keeping with the realities and challenges of our modern industrial society.

The problem for the unions is further compounded because of the issue of contracting out work, which has come to the fore as a result of technological change and declining membership in in-plant unions. Management decisions to subcontract may be related to the advancing level of technology existing within a plant and the inability of a particular workforce to deal with that level of technology. And, to some extent, subcontracting occurs as a purely economic response by a company to its current situation. The desire to stabilize employment may also lead to contracting out irregular work—particularly of the maintenance variety. These changes and adjustments in companies have led to jurisdictional and membership questions which themselves could become either the impediments to technological change or the stumbling blocks that create national crises. Unions apparently recognize the problem, for attempts are now being made to deal with it within the structure of the AFL-CIO.

The nature of new technology in effect means that the life of some small craft unions may be drawing to a close. For example, the sweep of technological change has been such in the transportation industry (rail, air and maritime) that specialized crafts, threatened with extinction, have acted to bar changes in operations, as in the case of the locomotive firemen and the airline engineers. It is imperative for unions to rethink the matter of maintaining separate bargaining units for such groups.

Government

The twentieth century has witnessed the emergence of government as a positive force in almost every aspect of our economic and social lives. There is no question in this era that government plays a very distinct, and in some cases very decisive, role in the industrial sector of the economy. Its role is asserted through its monetary, fiscal, and trade policies, all of which directly affect business. Its expenditures can stimulate an industry's production and marketing policies, and can spur its research and development efforts. Government is the single greatest consumer of industry's goods. Its labor policy affects—directly and indirectly—both business and labor in their relationships with each other.

What is it, then, that government can do to aid in the establishment of a climate where attitudes toward change will be constructive and positive? In theory, government's role should be one of setting a framework within which both management and labor can operate to the advantage of the nation. In actuality, there has been a confusing patchwork of governmental actions by the executive, legislative, and judicial branches in response to either short-term demands or political crises. The questions for government today are: How to foster economic expansion; how to speed redistribution of our labor force; and how to enable business to be competitive in world markets. It is in relatively good times that the nation as a whole, and management and labor in particular, are most able to afford the development of programs to alleviate the individual hardships of readjustment.

Frustrated, however, in attempts to reduce the level of unemployment, some in government today direct too much attention toward negative ideas: slowing down the process of technological change by developing early warning systems —as though progress in the industrial sector is today's curse —or spreading work by a shortening of work time, by higher penalties for overtime work, or by both.

Despite private efforts to ease the impact of technological change, such efforts cannot be directed toward the unemployed youth who has just entered the labor market, or toward the poorly educated adult who suffers because of changes in what we want to consume and in the ways we make and distribute goods and services. It is to the education and retraining of the labor force that government's particular attention must be directed—and both local and federal government have important contributions to make.

In the local community, much can be done to bolster the educational system, by interpreting for educators both the current and future needs of industry and the necessity of providing the essential educational exposure for children. Such exposure must prepare individuals to use leisure time in adulthood on a regular and continuing basis for further educational development. To orient education in such a direction is essential.

On the national level, government actions designed to curtail change, or which impose a greater individual burden on those companies introducing change, are not in the best interests of economic growth or alleviation of the difficulties of those who have been displaced because of change. Government's responsibility, therefore, is to eschew the politically attractive idea which can deal only with the manifestations, and not the fundamentals, of today's challenges. And government is in the unique position today of being able to shape an environment which will permit the development of a vastly improved economic and social situation for all.

The Individual

Probably the greatest and clearest responsibility for adjusting to technological change rests with the individual. Quite frequently, however, the individual affected, because of his training and background, is the least able to shoulder that responsibility. We are now entering a new but stimulating and challenging industrial era which, conceivably, could overawe many persons. Methods and techniques are changing, and these may threaten both the security of the job and the skills traditionally associated with certain work. What can be done? As an essential, the future demands an educational foundation upon which, throughout a lifetime work-career, an individual will be able to build for new employment opportunities. Such an education must equip each person with a high level of basic skills—reading comprehension, writing, and mathematics.

Calling for improvements in formal education alone may be an empty cry. In a progressive economic society, where technological change is and will be the rule, the individual himself—in order most effectively to adjust to and grow with technological change—must aggressively broaden his horizons and develop his awareness and appreciation of the world around him. The education *he* gets, the actions of *his* union, and the actions of *his* government will be the ultimate reflection of the actions he takes in satisfying his responsibilities to himself and his family.

There is an unfortunate tendency for many to assume that government should shoulder all responsibility for their welfare. Each individual has the responsibility to reach out—for new job opportunities, even if this requires relocation; for retraining, when his skills are no longer in demand; and for education, as the basis of personal progress. His government can only provide an environment that offers economic opportunity, but the individual must respond to that opportunity.

GEARING INDUSTRIAL RELATIONS TO THE AUTOMATION AGE

The need for reappraising industrial relations today is only due in part to technological changes now occurring. A more significant reason is that many of the basic corporate industrial relations policies and practices followed today were developed in response to problems that are no longer as prevalent as when the industrial relations function first emerged. The growth of mass production industry and the consequent urbanization of the workforce called for certain practices in the fields of induction, training, and placement of workers. Changes in production techniques led to, what were then, new systems of organizing work and determining pay. A changing social view in the 1920's stimulated the emergence of company-wide vacation, retirement, and pay policies; and they were in tune with the philosophy of that period. It was the development in the 1930's of strong and aggressive unions that set the stage for the evolution of the labor relations function as we know it within industry today.

Obviously, there continues to be a need to staff our organizations, to reward work and satisfactory performance with fair pay and other benefits, and to bargain effectively with labor unions. But, to an extent greater than ever before, there is a need to re-examine practices in the light of both the changes taking place within industry and the overwhelming pressure to resolve current problems, by balancing or accommodating the interests of the company with those of society at large.

It is the idea of balancing interests that gives significance to the discussion earlier in this chapter of the national employment problem and the enlarged responsibilities caused by technological change. The kind of impact which change is now having on individuals and institutions precludes the possibility of dealing with industrial relations problems solely within the framework of the individual company and its needs. Today, a company's best interests are served when it acts in a socially acceptable manner.

It is within this framework that we draw together our observations on the impact of technological change on the practice of industrial relations. The discussion is divided into three areas. The first embraces the specific industrial relations programs and practices which, on the basis of field study, require reappraisal. The second considers the reorientation of the assignment of responsibility for industrial relations matters. The third deals with the value of interpreting company responsibilities and actions to, and interrelating them with, those of the community at large.

Adjusting Industrial Relations Policies and Practices

Throughout the study, illustrations were given of specific areas in which an adjustment in thinking on industrial relations, in terms of specific policies and practices, appeared necessary. In some cases, the impact of new technology made essential a complete renovation of past practices. In other cases, modest adjustments in company approaches appeared necessary. The main areas of concern are discussed below.

Incentives. The area of company practice which raised some of the most important questions concerned those pay systems built on individual incentives. In the case-study companies using incentives, there was an obvious move away from individual toward group incentives. In some cases, this movement was recognized and taken account of in the formulation of company practices concerned with pay, the organization of work, and the establishment of precedents which might possibly affect the ability of the company to introduce further changes in operations. In other companies, however, no significance was attached to the modifications being made in incentive plans, even with respect to the implications for the control of work, the measurement of work performance, and the need for the strengthening of supervision.

Distinctions Between Blue- and White-Collar Workers. With the adaptation of new technology to industry, blue-collar and white-collar work become more alike, and the categorization of work as either one or the other becomes more difficult. A clear example of the fading distinction can be seen in comparing the work of a blue-collar worker stationed at a console board and that of a white-collar worker similarly situated as he monitors an office computer. The tendency of new technology to erase some of the significant differences between factory and office work has led many critics to question the continued legitimacy of distinctions between blue-collar employees—who are usually paid on an hourly basis—and white-collar employees—who are usually compensated on a weekly basis.[8] A long-term goal announced by some unions is the achievement of salaried status for production and maintenance workers. Indeed, the short work-week guarantees now in effect in some manufacturing industries might be construed as conferring such status on their production and maintenance employees; one nationally known company has formally placed its blue-collar employees on weekly salaries.

But the manner in which employees are compensated is hardly the most important of the factors to consider with respect to the blurring distinctions between blue- and white-collar work. Through automation, work becomes less discrete and more continuous, and the cost of down-time becomes almost prohibitive. Management can no longer afford to be shutting down and starting up operations continually; it assigns increasing importance to scheduling production work more carefully. Shift work—an entirely new phenomenon in office work—increases. Thus, the nature of automation both in the factory and in the office makes the two more similar. And the fact is that such changes have implications for both management and employee relations, because elements of tradition, status, and personal adjustment are involved.

Retirement Plans. Early retirement is another development which has come about because of recent concern with technological change. As shown in Chapters III and VII, it has proved immensely valuable as a means of dealing with the dislocations caused by technological change. Al-

8 See, for example, Daniel Bell, "The Subversion of Collective Bargaining," *Commentary*, Vol. 29, March, 1960, pp. 185–197.

though early retirement can be most helpful in specific situations of adjusting to change, there also could be drawbacks to its extensive use throughout the economy.

The use of early retirement by so many companies, with the approval of unions, to increase the attrition rate and thus prevent layoffs might be causing companies to assume a new high cost for pensions, which, in some cases, might be economically unsound. As pointed out earlier, however, actuarial advice can help obviate such difficulties. Also, widespread use of early retirement could conceivably lead to a general lowering of the normal retirement age—from age sixty-five to sixty-two, or sixty—or even less—in coming years. Indeed, Old Age and Survivors Insurance permits retirement at age sixty-two on an actuarially reduced pension, and many private plans provide pensions at even younger ages.

Although recognizing the value of early retirement in those instances where it serves a purpose as a part of the adjustment to new technology, lowering the retirement age introduces new problems. From a broad, social point of view, such action would result in a waste of manpower and operate to the disadvantage of large segments of the labor force. Many older people could, and want to be, effective workers contributing to the national economy, and it would be wrong to discourage them, and force them against their will to curtail their working careers. Early retirement of those employees who are no longer able to adjust to a new technological environment is justifiable. But forced early retirement of those who are still competent does a disservice to the national economy and to many individuals for whom a job has been a source not merely of income but of status and meaning in life. Despite some immediate advantages, younger workers would also suffer from such a development, for it would mean that a continually smaller working population would have to support not only itself, but also a relatively larger nonworking population.

Working Time. Managements, and all of society, must

also reorient their thinking with respect to working time and leisure time. Opposition to the present union proposals to cut the standard forty-hour workweek is quite understandable. To advocate such a move at this time would serve only to intensify wage pressure on prices, and this would seriously worsen the nation's already difficult problem with the balance of international payments. Yet it seems that over the long run the historic pattern of shortening the time spent at work will continue. But, before this is possible, its value to the individual must be considered.

The very possibility of increased leisure necessitates broad thinking by all groups in society. How can we use time away from the job most advantageously? Are we prepared to adjust to a situation in which—in terms of time— work plays an increasingly less important role in our lives? Can a society in which the Puritan concept of hard work is deeply rooted shift easily into an age in which leisure plays an increasingly important role in our lives?[9] There are no ready or easy answers to these questions, but in the long run they may be the most important problems involved in adjusting to technological change.

Structure of Union Relations. The nature of the challenges facing industrial relations today has tended to shape corporate policies with respect to the handling of union relations. Contacts between the parties are no longer limited to contract renewal negotiations; rather, in a growing number of industries, discussions of current problems take place during the life of the collective bargaining agreement. These discussions are viewed by management not necessarily as an extension of the bargaining process, but rather as a method of keeping unions informed of current developments and alerting them to the changes in the organization of production operations that will affect union relations. It would be

[9] For development of this concept, see David Riesman, *Individualism Reconsidered* (Glencoe: The Free Press, 1954), 529 pp., with specific reference to Chapter 13, pp. 202–218.

desirable if both labor and management exhibited a greater willingness to view the contract as a framework within which to make peaceable and intelligent adjustments to the employment relationship as these are necessitated by technological change. The danger, of course, is that the contract might lose its power and value. The labor relations practitioner must face this challenge and learn how to gain adherence to the basic principles established by the agreement, while seeking union cooperation in other areas.

Communications. The universal experience of the companies participating in this survey substantiates the theory that early communications are of inordinate value in securing employee confidence in management's actions. Of even more importance than the timing or nature of communications is the necessity to incorporate communications into the overall management process. Where communications flow easily and quickly, confusion and misunderstandings do not arise. Moreover, direct and early communications support employee, union, and community faith in the integrity of company announcements.

As yet, however, too much lip service is given to the need for communications without enough understanding of its value and the importance of its integration into the very process of managing an enterprise. Here is a challenge to industrial relations practitioners—to develop techniques of communication and stimulate an awareness, on the part of line managers, of their value.

Employment and "Disemployment." During any period of technological change there is a need for capable employees. Sometimes the skills necessary for new operations can be developed among the members of the existing workforce, but often they must be secured by going outside of the plant and hiring new employees with the necessary skills to do particular jobs. In any case, since today's skills may not be those needed tomorrow, it is essential that industry hire people who are retrainable and capable of undertaking new assignments in the future. Based on the assumption that a high school diploma is evidence of the necessary background for future training, many companies today hire only high school graduates. But this is not the sole answer, for it was not too many years ago that the eighth-grade diploma was viewed as a discriminating element in selection. What are needed, of course, are better determinants of individual ability for adaptability. But only a slight amount of experimental work has been done by industry in this area, perhaps because too many industrial relations departments are oriented toward standard testing techniques which measure only cognitive or performance factors.

As we have seen, extensive technological change may also bring to a close the working careers of some individuals within a particular company. "Disemployment," as it was referred to in one company, is an increasingly important factor in industry today. Whether selecting for employment or disemployment, the problem is to keep industrial relations programs in balance, at a particular juncture in time, with the overall staffing needs of the enterprise.

Reorienting Organizational and Staff Responsibilities

The function of a staff in any organization is to help give expression to the work of the line organization. But this job is made difficult for the industrial relations staff because of the impediments to anticipating changes in the nature of both the work and the jobs themselves. Thus, long-term planning assumes a critical role in the management of an enterprise, and here we urge the exploration of the concept of integrated management planning referred to in Chapter X, in which line management comes to recognize operational needs in terms of the impact of these on staffing. Realistic and effective planning is vital in meeting new requirements and reshaping policies and practices.

Reorienting the industrial relations function is complicated for many companies by growth in both the size and scope of their operations. These two factors have disturbed the traditional areas of responsibility within industrial relations departments. They have complicated normal communications processes and have made it difficult to exert the controls necessary in all areas of industrial relations activity. To overcome such problems, particularly in a period of major technological change, it is necessary to align and identify the staff function of industrial relations with the objectives of management. Recognition by line management of the value of this staff service will permit the industrial relations department to contribute to the development of policies designed to ease the impact of technological change on employees.

Asserting a Leadership Role in the Community

An interesting shift has taken place in many of the companies visited in the course of this study; they are no longer operating in isolation from the community. Government action has an impact on the decision-making processes within the company, and this, in turn, requires that companies participate more actively in community activities. Industry has the obligation to help shape the views held by the community by accepting representation on boards, commissions, and other groups and by being prepared to present information and analyses concerning community problems.

One way the company can recognize its responsibilities in a community is to work closely with the local educational system—by participating in and contributing to the development of curriculum—not only because the company must assume a role as a corporate citizen, but because the very individuals being educated will one day be its employees. Another way in which the company can make a contribution to the community is to explore activities which are not only body-building—the bowling team or the soft ball team—but also mind-strengthening. Some companies already engage in such activities, where their workforces are comprised of large groups of engineers or scientists. For the future, a broad field exists for corporate contribution on behalf of all employees in the area of leisure-time cultural activities.

Finally, the company has the responsibility to itself, as well as to the community, to communicate its story and to explain its problems and possible ways of solving them. Without such communications, the company cannot expect people within a community to be aware of, or alert to, either the difficulties faced by the company or the periodic necessity to redirect company plans and activities in both the product and labor markets. The alternative to assuming the role of community leader is to be defensive when, without the facts, the community moves to restrict the company's means of adjusting to changed circumstances through the introduction of new technology.

*   *   *

The paradox of the emerging automation age is that it has so far induced defensive reactions, although its benefits are manifold. Among workers and unions the reaction often takes the form of fear of change and resistance to it. Government—responding to the short-term problems created—sometimes seeks to impede or slow down the process. Even within management, there are those who react with fear because of the deep changes necessitated in their accustomed way of managing the enterprise.

That technological change and automation bring problems is obvious, but careful study indicates that management and labor are adjusting without undue difficulty. Even though not all problems have been overcome, of course, solutions are being worked out. But not all problems emerging from a changing social, political, economic and technological environment can be solved entirely within the framework of

APPENDIX

Areas of Company Experience Explored in Interviews

1. Background Information
   a. General
   b. Nature of operations affected by technological change
   c. Nature of past management practices with regard to technological change—the anticipation factor
   d. Types of products manufactured and history of product improvement
   e. Structure of company's industrial relations department
2. The Major Technological Change
   a. Motivation for undertaking the change—cut labor costs, improve quality, etc.
   b. The nature of the change

    c. Operations affected by change—plant, department, location

    d. Date of introduction of change

3. Role of the Industrial Relations Staff in Planning for Change

    a. Ways in which industrial relations personnel were involved

    b. The stage of planning at which industrial relations staff was included

    c. Evaluation of industrial relations role in change

4. Steps Taken to Allay Worker Fear and Resistance

    a. Communications—when and how

    b. Consultation

    c. Other

    d. Preparing the community

5. Specific Industrial Relations Problems Encountered in Effecting Change

    a. Turnover and job-hopping

    b. Grievances

    c. Strikes and slowdowns

    d. Procedures for resolving conflict

6. Impact of the Change on Labor-Management Relations

    a. Extent and character of unionism—industrial or craft

    b. Collective bargaining demands

    c. Conflicts with management goals—need to change labor contract

    d. Pay issues—wage rates, job evaluation, wage incentives, etc.

    e. Other issues—union jurisdiction, manning requirements, seniority

    f. Management rights

7. Impact on the Nature of Work and Jobs and its Effect on Policies

    a. Methods of compensation

    b. Benefits

   c. Training
   d. Organization of work
8. Effect of the Change on Employment
   a. Size and composition of the labor force
   b. Recruitment, selection and placement policies
   c. Promotions and transfers
   d. Separations
   e. Aids to displaced employees
9. Impact on Supervision and Technical Employees
   a. New technical groups resulting from change
   b. Training and recruitment of such groups
   c. New approaches to supervisory and technical employees
10. Impact on Industrial Relations Function
   a. Structure of industrial relations department and its ability to cope with change
   b. Structure of industrial relations and opportunity to be involved in change
   c. Manpower planning
11. General Evaluation
   a. Problems encountered in instituting and adjusting to major technological change
   b. Degree to which company objectives achieved
   c. Lessons learned from experience
   d. Basic changes advisable in industrial relations policies
   e. Change in role of industrial relations within the company

Fact Sheet–Impact of Technological Change on Employee Relations

NAME OF COMPANY _____

PLANT LOCATION _____UNIT COVERED _____

1. Average number of workers employed at various skill levels and ages in periods before and after the change:

Skill Level and Age	Before Change	After Change
PRODUCTION WORKERS (NONSUPERVISORY)		
Skill level		
Skilled		
Semiskilled		
Unskilled		
Total		
Age		
Under 25 years		
25-54 years		
55 years and over		
Total		

1. Average number of workers employed at various skill levels and ages in periods before and after the change: (Continued)

Skill Level and Age	Before Change	After Change
TECHNICAL WORKERS (NONSUPERVISORY)		
Skill level		
Skilled		
Semiskilled		
Unskilled		
Total		
Age		
Under 25 years		
25-54 years		
55 years and over		
Total		
MAINTENANCE WORKERS (NONSUPERVISORY)		
Skill level		
Skilled		
Semiskilled		
Unskilled		
Total		
Age		
Under 25 years		
25-54 years		
55 years and over		
Total		
SUPERVISORY EMPLOYEES (PRODUCTION, MAINTENANCE, TECHNICAL)		
Skill level		
Skilled		
Semiskilled		
Unskilled		
Total		
Age		
Under 25 years		
25-54 years		
55 years and over		
Total		

2. *Number of nonsupervisory jobs in categories below which require the worker to be a college or university graduate:*

Production   Maintenance   Technical
—————————   —————————   —————————

3. *Average number of workers employed before and after the change, by shift:*

Shift	Before Change	After Change
Main	————————	————————
Second	————————	————————
Third	————————	————————
Total	————————	————————

4. *Changes in the job status of all employees (including supervisors) in the units in which the change was introduced, for the 12-month period following such change:*

Type of Job Change	Number of Employees in Affected Units			
	Total	Less Than 5 Years' Service	5–15 Years' Service	Over 15 Years' Service
No change in position				
Reassignment in same work unit				
Transfers to Other— Departments ..... Plants				
Separations— Discharges .... Layoffs .... Leaves of absence . Quits .... Retirements, deaths				
All employees				

5a. Composition of employee group displaced by technological change, by type of employment and skill level:

Type of Employment	Number of Employees
Production	————
Maintenance	————
Technical	————
Supervisory	————
Total	————

Skill Level	
Skilled	————
Semiskilled	————
Unskilled	————
Total	————

5b. Company aid to displaced employees:

Type of Aid	Number of Employees
Referred to other companies for jobs	————
Retrained for other employment	
Outside the company	————
Within the company........	————
Paid relocation allowances	————
Given severance pay	————
Early retirement	————
Other (specify)	————

6. *Comparison of wage rates of workers reassigned or transferred to other jobs or plants within the company.*

New Wage Rate Compared to Old	Number of Employees
Higher	_____
Same	_____
Lower	_____
Total	_____

7. *Manpower needs resulting from change:*
   a. Please list the new key jobs resulting from the change.
   b. Please list those occupations which were in short supply for the first year after the change.
   c. Please indicate the means used to alleviate the shortage of workers in these occupations.

8. *Production*
   Output*:

   Monthly average for 12 months before change _____
   Monthly average for first 12 months after change _____
   Monthly average for second 12 months after change _____

9. *Number of work stoppages before and after change:*

Work Stoppages	Before Change	After Change
Number		
Man-hours lost		
Group participating .		
Grievances alleged . .		

* Please use either standard measure of output used for purposes of internal company reports or an index showing output ratios.

Example of a Company Promotion and Transfer Policy

POLICY NO. 1—PROMOTION AND PLACEMENT

Practice over many years testifies to the convictions of the Company's management—

(1) That individual employees have the right to seek to better themselves by making application through their supervisor for promotion or transfer,

(2) That, wherever feasible and practicable, job openings should be filled by promotion or transfer from within a department in a geographical area, or, dependent upon the level of the job, from within the department as a whole, and

(3) That, with respect to job openings which cannot be filled from within a department by promotion or transfer, every consideration should be given to the qualifications of employees in other departments who are available for any reason and are recommended by their departments for transfer consideration.

The Employee Relations Department is responsible for coordinating interdepartmental placement activities to help achieve these aims. Its function in this respect is to bring to the attention of departments with existing job openings which cannot be filled from within that department, those qualified employees in other departments who are available for transfer. The general procedures and rules concerning such placement activities are as follows:

1. *Job Openings.* Each job opening should be carefully analyzed to determine that it is necessary for the duties to be continued. If possible, the work of the vacated job or proposed new job should be distributed among the other jobs in the unit involved. Should it be determined that the job must be continued, that the duties cannot be assumed by other jobs and that the position cannot be filled by promotion or transfer within the department, the job opening is to be reported to the Employee Relations Department on Form_____, Request for Employee. When such openings may be filled by personnel within the Company, the Employee Relations Department (with due regard to procedures in effect from time to time regarding the types and levels of jobs to be posted) will prepare bulletins describing the duties of the job, its salary grade or rate of pay, and minimum qualifications. These bulletins will be posted at locations where employees having the necessary qualifications may be located. The decision as to the selection of the employee to fill the job opening is the responsibility of the requesting department. If the opening is not filled by transfer, the department head, with approval of management, may then proceed to fill the job by outside employment.

2. *Employees Available for Transfer.* In any case where (1) it occurs or is anticipated that one or more employees are or will no longer be required on a job, and no suitable openings are available within that department or (2) an employee desires a transfer and the department is agreeable to making him available, the department shall make a report to the Employee Relations Department on Form_____, Employee Available for Transfer. Where a department unqualifiedly recommends a surplus

employee for transfer, it shall mean that that department, on the basis of its knowledge of the employee's performance and ability, would be willing to either retain him, if possible, or unhesitatingly accept him by transfer if it had an appropriate job opening. The Employee Relations Department will inform the originating department of any known vacancies for which its surplus employees may be qualified, inform other departments of the availability of such personnel, or render such other assistance as may be advisable in attempting to place the employee or employees. The same procedure will be followed with respect to an employee who desires different work, a different location, or better opportunity, if the department in which he is employed believes he merits consideration and recommends him for interdepartmental transfer.

POLICY NO. 2—TRANSFERS

Because of unavoidable shifts and fluctations in operations, it frequently is necessary to transfer employees from one area to another. In all such cases, the selection of the employees to be transferred, together with their transferring destinations, must be at the discretion of the appropriate supervisor.

Where possible, individual preference of employees will be regarded, due consideration being given to the entire group or groups of employees involved.

POLICY NO. 3—EXPENSES IN CASE OF TRANSFER

To assist an eligible employee in defraying expenses resulting from a transfer requiring a change in domicile, the Company will pay certain expenses as outlined in this Policy.

A. *Eligible Employee*—An employee transferred at the direct request of the Company, providing:

1. The request is directed to the specific employee involved and the job opening has not been posted, or
2. The Company's right to select the one to be transferred is not limited and such employee is expressly needed because—
   a. Of his qualifications and Company experience, and

  b. No one else is available, by transfer or new hire, at the location of the job to be filled, who fulfills the job's requirements.

It should be noted that an offer of a transfer which results from a job posting shall not, by itself, be construed as a direct request by the Company.

Reimbursement of Expenses—For eligible employees defined above, the Company will pay Essential Moving Expenses and will reimburse the employee for reasonable costs for the following:

 1. Incidental expenses:
  a. Disconnecting appliances at the former location,
  b. Preparing appliances for move,
  c. Installing appliances at the new location,
  d. Taking down and installing TV antenna,
  e. Refitting rugs, draperies and curtains.
 2. Costs of cancelling lease at the former location.
 3. Expenses, as follows, connected with the disposal of the employee-owned residence at the former location:
  a. Commission of a licensed real estate broker, limited to the amount customarily charged in the community and not to exceed 6 percent of the sale price of the house. This will apply only to those cases in which the house is placed in the hands of a realtor within a reasonable period of time,
  b. Appraisal fee,
  c. Abstract *updating* or title insurance,
  d. Revenue stamps for deed,
  e. Miscellaneous legal fees,
  f. Fee for prepayment of mortgage at former location.
 4. As a part of Essential Moving Expenses, the employee will be reimbursed personal car mileage to the new location at the rate of 8 cents per mile for the first 800 miles and 5 cents per mile for all miles thereafter. If the employee owns two cars, the miles driven to the new location in both cars will be totaled and the mileage rate applied to that total.

An exception to the above is when an employee regularly used a personal car on company business at his former location and will continue to use it on company business at his new location. In this case, the transferee may be continued on his established mileage rate for the miles driven to the new location. For additional cars not used on company business, the employee will be reimbursed at the rate of 8 cents per mile for the first 800 miles and 5 cents per mile for all miles thereafter for one additional car only.

Excluding Essential Moving Expenses and the commission of a licensed real estate broker, the maximum reimbursement is limited to one month's pay.

B. *Eligible Employees*—An employee with one or more years of service, who—

1. Is displaced from his job through no fault of his own, or
2. Is scheduled for layoff because of lack of work, or
3. Has been laid off for lack of work for less than 90 days, and who is qualified for and accepted by the Company to fill a job in some other geographical area, which requires a change in domicile.

Reimbursement of Expenses—For eligible employees defined above, the Company will pay Essential Moving Expenses in accordance with the following schedule:

Full Years of Recognized Continuous Service		Percent of Essential Moving Expenses Paid by Company	Maximum Company Expenditure
At Least	Less Than		
1	5	50	½ employee's monthly earnings
5	10	75	¾ "
10	15	100	1 "
15 or more		100	No maximum

C. *Definitions*

Essential Moving Expenses—The transportation of the employee, his immediate family and his household goods, exclusive of any insurance.

Recognized Continuous Service—Service in accordance with

"Rules for Determination of Service." For purposes of this Policy the length of service is computed as of the effective date of the transfer or re-employment.

Monthly Earnings

1. The monthly salary in effect prior to the date of the transfer, displacement or layoff, or
2. The regular hourly rate multiplied by the number of hours regularly scheduled to be worked in the month prior to the transfer, displacement, or layoff. All non-scheduled overtime, scheduled shift premium pay for holidays, and other such premium pay are eliminated.

D. *Arrangements for Transportation of Household Goods*

This portion of Essential Moving Expenses may be separated into two parts—in either one, the payment or reimbursement is subject to certain stipulations.

1. *When the Company Assumes the Full Cost.* Transportation arrangements must be made or approved by the Traffic Division. The Company will be responsible for any loss or damage to the household goods resulting from the move, to the extent set forth in the Employee Moving Guide. This guide will be furnished to the employee by his department at the time of the move.
2. *When the Company and Employee Share the Cost.*
   a. The employee may elect to make his own arrangements. He may rent a truck or trailer and make the move himself. He may hire someone else to perform this service for him; however, if that person is not an authorized carrier, the employee may be subject to penalty and fine for law violation. The employee must pay the carrier he elects, in full; then, the Company will reimburse the employee for its proportionate share of this expense. The Company will not be responsible for any loss or damage to the household goods as a result of the move.
   b. The employee may choose to have the Company arrange for the move. The services of an authorized carrier shall be arranged for or approved by the Traffic Division. The Company will pay the carrier it selects, in full. The employee will then reimburse the Company

for his proportionate share of the expense. Reimbursement will be made according to terms agreed upon prior to the move. The Company will be responsible for any loss or damage to the household goods resulting from the move, to the extent set forth in the Employee Moving Guide. This guide will be furnished to the employee by his department at the time of the move.

E. *The Company reserves the right to administer, interpret, revise or revoke any or all of the provisions and incidents of this Policy.*

REQUEST FOR EMPLOYEE   Job Bulletin No. _____ Will Expire _____

DEPARTMENT _____ Sex: Male _____ Female _____

An opening for _____ employee(s) exists in the above department as follows:

Job Title _____ Job Grade _____ or Fixed Rate _____

Location(s) _____

SUMMARY OF JOB DUTIES

MINIMUM QUALIFICATIONS

If qualified and interested, please obtain Form _____ from your supervisor. Complete required portion of _____ and return to your Supervisor before expiration date of this bulletin.

Form _____ will then be submitted by your personnel group to the location where opening exists.

SUBMIT ORIGINAL AND 2 COPIES TO EMPLOYEE RELATIONS DEPARTMENT

If this vacancy can not be filled by transfer, do you want this to serve as a request to Management for authority to employ from the outside?   Yes ☐   No ☐

Date Wanted _____   Job is Permanent ☐   Temporary ☐

New Job ☐   Additional Employee in Existing Job ☐   Direct Replacement ☐   Indirect Replacement ☐

Classification Code or Job Specification No. _____

Name and Disposition of Predecessor

IMPORTANT: How many employees are doing this same type of work in this particular unit? _____

Justification for Request (Use reverse side if necessary):

Approved, Dept. Head	Requested By	Date

PLACEMENT DIVISION REMARKS

Status of available personnel
☐ Should attempt to fill by transfer.
☐ Vacancy cannot be filled by transfer.

☐ Expiration of bulletin — no response.
☐ _____ Files reviewed — none acceptable
   Did files reviewed include
   any excess or surplus employee? Yes ☐   No ☐

Date _____   By _____

DISPOSITION OF REQUEST

☐ Approved for transfer only
☐ Approved for hiring after exhausting all transfer possibilities

☐ Approved for hiring
☐ Disapproved

Date _____   Approval No. _____   By _____

EMPLOYEE AVAILABLE FOR TRANSFER
ENTER X IN ALL APPROPRIATE SQUARES

QUESTIONS TO THE FIRST DOUBLE LINES WILL BE COMPLETED BY EMPLOYEE IF THIS IS A REQUEST BY EMPLOYEE

FIRST NAME (PLEASE PRINT)	MIDDLE	LAST NAME	LOCATION	DEPARTMENT

SINGLE	MARRIED	MALE	FEMALE	AGE	YEAR EMPLOYED	NO. OF DEPENDENT CHILDREN	EMPLOYEE NO.	EDUCATION	STATE DEGREE AND FIELD
								H.S. ☐ COLLEGE ☐	

IS THIS A JOB BULLETIN BID? ☐   IF SO, GIVE BULLETIN NO.

OR IS THIS A REQUEST FOR PERSONAL REASON? ☐   IF SO, PLEASE GIVE REASON

WOULD YOU TRANSFER AT YOUR OWN EXPENSE? YES ☐ NO ☐   TYPE OF WORK PREFERRED   LOCATION PREFERENCE

WOULD YOU CONSIDER TRANSFERRING WITH PAY REDUCTION? YES ☐ NO ☐

WHY DO YOU FEEL THAT YOU ARE QUALIFIED FOR WORK PREFERRED OR OPENING REQUESTED?   DO YOU HAVE PHYSICAL LIMITATIONS? IF SO, EXPLAIN   HEIGHT   WEIGHT

SUMMARY OF WORK EXPERIENCE

DATE   SIGNATURE OF EMPLOYEE REQUESTING TRANSFER

THIS PORTION TO BE COMPLETED BY EMPLOYEE'S DEPARTMENT

IS THIS EMPLOYEE SURPLUS? YES ☐ NO ☐   SCHEDULED FOR LAYOFF? YES ☐ NO ☐   APPROXIMATE DATE AVAILABLE

WILL TRANFER RESULT IN NET PERSONNEL REDUCTION? YES ☐ NO ☐   PRESENT JOB TITLE   GRADE   RATE OF PAY   WONDERLIE TEST SCORE

CAN YOU UNQUALIFIEDLY RECOMMEND THIS EMPLOYEE AND, BASED ON HIS PERFORMANCE AND ABILITY, WOULD YOU UNHESITATINGLY RETAIN HIM IF POSSIBLE? YES ☐ NO ☐

IF ANSWER ABOVE IS NO, PLEASE EXPLAIN

OTHER REMARKS (SPECIFY MEDICAL RESTRICTIONS):

FOR FURTHER INFORMATION CONTACT: APPROVAL

NAME   PHONE

ADDRESS

THIS PORTION TO BE COMPLETED BY RECEIVING DEPARTMENT

ABOVE EMPLOYEE CONSIDERED BY_____ DEPARTMENT FOR:

1 JOB BULLETIN NO._____ OR EXISTING VACANCY_____
                                                      JOB TITLE AND LOCATION

     ☐ TRANSFER OFFER MADE: EMPLOYEE ACCEPTED ☐   REJECTED ☐
     ☐ NO TRANSFER OFFER WILL BE MADE
     REASON: ☐ FILLED BY ANOTHER EMPLOYEE ☐ NOT FULLY QUALIFIED FOR THIS OPENING

         ☐ OTHER_____
                         STATE OTHER REASON

2. NO SUITABLE OPENING AVAILABLE AS OF_____
                                        DATE

Index

INDEX

DATE DUE